Secret Selves

OLIVER S. BUCKTON

Secret Selves

*Confession and Same-Sex Desire
in Victorian Autobiography*

The University of North Carolina Press

Chapel Hill and London

Designed by Richard Hendel

Set in Minion types by Tseng Information Systems

Manufactured in the United States of America

The paper in this book meets the guidelines for permanence
and durability of the Committee on Production Guidelines for
Book Longevity of the Council on Library Resources.

Library of Congress Cataloging-in-Publication Data

Buckton, Oliver S.

Secret selves: confession and same-sex desire in Victorian
autobiography / Oliver S. Buckton.

p.   cm.

Includes bibliographical references and index.

ISBN 0-8078-2435-6 (cloth : alk. paper). —
ISBN 0-8078-4702-x (pbk. : alk. paper)

1. English prose literature — 19th century — History and criticism. 2. Autobiography.
3. Men authors, English — 19th century — Biography — History and criticism.
4. Homosexuality and literature — Great Britain — History — 19th century. 5. Gay
men — Great Britain — Biography — History and criticism. 6. Gay men's writings,
English — History and criticism. 7. Great Britain — History — Victoria, 1837–1901 —
Historiography. 8. Confession in literature. 9. Desire in literature. I. Title.

PR788.A95B83   1998

828'.80809492 — dc21   97-30007

CIP

Chapter 1 appeared earlier, in somewhat different form, as
" 'An Unnatural State': Gender, 'Perversion,' and
Newman's *Apologia pro Vita Sua,*" *Victorian Studies* 35, no. 4
(Summer 1992): 359–83, and is reprinted here with permission
of the journal.

02 01 00 99 98   5 4 3 2 1

FOR LAURICE

CONTENTS

ACKNOWLEDGMENTS

In working on this project over a number of years, I have benefited from the friendship, generosity, and insights of numerous individuals and institutions. It is a pleasure to be able to thank them here. I offer my apologies to those whom I may have omitted.

In the early stages this project, I was fortunate to work with Paul Sawyer and Dorothy Mermin, who served as my dissertation advisers at Cornell. Their profound knowledge of Victorian literature and culture, together with their extraordinary intellectual generosity toward a struggling graduate student, contributed substantially to the process of constructing a clear argument. Walter Cohen read my dissertation with care and attention, and I offer him thanks for sharing his insights into contemporary critical theory. Others at Cornell who offered welcome encouragement and support include Lynda Bogel, Patty Chu, Susan Duhig, Heather Findlay, Mary Jacobus, Paul McClure, Lisa Moore, Terry Rowden, Talia Schaffer, and Mark Scroggins.

My work on the manuscript has benefited from the suggestions and comments of other critics and scholars in the fields of Victorian literature and gender studies. In particular, Richard Dellamora has been an invaluable source of advice and information as I have been working toward producing the final form of a book I am happy with. Lee Edelman's work has been a model of incisive thinking and critical insight to me since I first encountered him in the classroom at Tufts. I can only hope that his influence as a teacher and thinker may be detected in these pages. Joseph Bristow provided some helpful guidance while I was working on Edward Carpenter in Sheffield. Mary Poovey offered most constructive suggestions for revision at a later stage of the project. My editors at the UNC Press, Sian Hunter White and Ron Maner, have been models of energy, efficiency, and courtesy.

The completion of the work at the dissertation stage was made possible by a Mellon Dissertation Fellowship provided by the Cornell University Graduate School. The international travel and research for several chapters of this book was funded by grants from the Mario Einaudi Center for International Studies and the Institute for European Studies at Cornell University. The archival research for the epilogue was made possible by a Summer Research Fellowship granted by the Schmidt Foundation, under the auspices of the Schmidt College of Arts and Humanities at Florida Atlantic University.

I would like to thank the members of the staff at the following libraries for their prompt and professional assistance during my research at these institutions: the Olin Library at Cornell University, the British Library in London, the London Library, and the Sheffield City Library. I am grateful to Jacqueline Cox of the Modern Archive Center at King's College, Cambridge, for her assistance with my efforts to locate manuscript drafts of E. M. Forster's novels and journals.

I would like to thank the Provost and Scholars of King's College, Cambridge, for permission to reproduce manuscript material by E. M. Forster, and the Sheffield City Library for permission to publish extracts from the papers of Edward Carpenter.

An earlier version of Chapter 1 appeared in *Victorian Studies* 35, no. 4 (Summer 1992). I gratefully acknowledge the journal's permission to reprint the essay in the current volume.

My colleagues at Florida Atlantic University have helped to provide a supportive and stimulating environment in which I was able to complete this project. For their helpful suggestions and encouraging words, I would like to thank David Anderson, Mike Budd, Mary Faraci, Krishna Lewis, Carol McGuirk, Priscilla Paton, Howard Pearce, and Mark Scroggins. Thanks also to my good friend Nick Anikitou in London, with whom I have enjoyed numerous conversations about this project.

There are two special debts that I cannot adequately put into words. To my parents, my first and best teachers, I offer thanks for their wisdom, love, and support for as long as I can remember. Finally, I dedicate this book to my wife and best friend, Laurice Campbell Buckton.

Secret Selves

INTRODUCTION

The Self and Its Secrets

The study that follows takes as its subject the intersection between secrecy as a narrative strategy deployed in Victorian autobiographical writing, and the emergence of same-sex desire as a particular site, or "subject," of secrecy in nineteenth- and early-twentieth-century British culture. As a genre exploring the possibility of representing forms of subjective experience, autobiography offers rich opportunities for apprehending the ways in which the "self" is conceived of and constituted in specific historical periods and social contexts. At the same time, it is precisely this "subjective" mode of autobiographical discourse—often in the form of "personal" revelations and reminiscences, directed toward the evolution of a particular identity or self— that makes its status suspect, with respect to both historical analysis and literary value. If, as Paul de Man suggests, "autobiography always looks slightly disreputable and self-indulgent in a way that may be symptomatic of its incompatibility with the monumental dignity of aesthetic values," then this is because the subjectivity of the genre always threatens to undermine its historical authority.[1] In this book I focus on autobiography as a discourse of the self in which the significant product is not a referential "truth" but a cultural effect: what we conceive of as the self may, in fact, be derived from autobiography rather than being its prediscursive "referent."

1

Hence, secrecy is used here not to denote information that is withheld utterly from discourse or knowledge but to illuminate a central and productive component of autobiographical discourse itself. "Secrecy" is used to indicate a dynamic oscillation between self-disclosure and concealment, a technique for arousing the reader's interest and establishing a relation based on shared knowledge, while preventing the disclosure of traits that might be incriminating, scandalous, or simply incompatible with the version of the self being represented. Michel Foucault's formulation on the discursive function of "silence" might, with some appropriate modifications, be usefully applied to secrecy as I employ it in this book: silence is "less the absolute limit of discourse, the other side from which it is separated by a strict boundary, than an element that functions alongside the things said, with them and in relation to them within over-all strategies. There is no binary division to be made between what one says and what one does not say."[2]

The period during which the autobiographical narratives that I discuss were written (though not in some cases during which they were published) coincides with the emergence of autobiography as one of the most influential and popular of literary genres. As several important critics have demonstrated, there was an explosion of autobiographical writing and publishing in the nineteenth century, in terms of both the volume of autobiographies written and published and the diversity of social groups achieving representation in this literary form. As the genre became more inclusive, the issue of the relationship between author and readership became increasingly urgent and significant. The question of an individual author's allegiance to a social group might become particularly vexed, for, as Julia Swindells observes, "the individual neither constitutes nor is constituted by the social group, but is in tension with it, and autobiography . . . displays and produces meaning from and through this tension."[3]

Victorian autobiographical writing is characterized by a deep preoccupation with the unique value and significance of the individual self, a perspective that perhaps takes on its fullest cultural embodiment in the middle-class liberal ideology of individualism in the Victorian period. In this context, the autobiography is a manifestation of the nineteenth-century culture of individualism as well as the literary form that most directly influences the Victorian novel in its exploration of individual origins, identity, experience, and development. Without the literary and philosophical investment in the individual as the fundamental unit of society and as an autonomous free agent, capable of self-determination, self-consciousness, and self-development, neither the Victorian novel nor the autobiography as we know it would have come into being. In both the novel of development, or bildungsroman, and the nonfictional autobiography, the constitution of the self by the representation and analysis of individual experience is a paramount feature.[4] To dispense with—or at least to question the validity of—the rigid categories of "novel" and "autobiography" is merely to acknowledge, as Paul John Eakin has expressed it, that "autobiographical truth is not a fixed but an evolving content, what we call fact and fiction being rather slippery variables in an intricate process of self-discovery."[5]

The problem of the relation between autobiographer and reader has produced some of the most interesting work in the field of contemporary narrative theory. Philippe Lejeune, for example, has sought to differentiate the autobiography from other forms of narrative by focusing on the specific "contract" or "pact" formed between author and reader. In an important passage with direct bearing on the question of autobiographical fiction, Lejeune seeks to include in the definition of the autobiographical novel "all fictional texts in which the reader has reason to suspect, from the resemblances that he thinks he sees, that there is identity of author and *protagonist*, whereas the author has chosen to deny this identity, or at least not to affirm it."[6]

Lejeune's important insight raises the intriguing question of why an author would choose to deny his or her identity with the protagonist of the novel. In the case of perhaps the most famous secret of Victorian autobiographical novels, Dickens sought at once to conceal and to reveal his own "shameful" childhood experience as a menial laborer in Warren's Blacking Warehouse, by writing of this experience under the guise of the fictional protagonist in *David Copperfield*. Dickens's compulsion to confess this "secret" to the public who knew him only as a successful author is matched by a desire to prevent the secret from being identified with the author himself.[7]

For Lejeune, *David Copperfield* would not qualify as an autobiography, because "what defines autobiography for the one who is reading is above all a contract of identity that is sealed by the proper name." Lejeune argues that "this is true also for the one who is writing the text. If I write the story of my life without mentioning my name in it, how will my reader know that it was *I*? It is impossible for the auto-biographical vocation and the passion for anonymity to coexist in the same person."[8] Lejeune's definition does not account for the produc-tive tension between secrecy and disclosure, while his disavowal of the coexistence of impulses of revelation and self-concealment is un-helpfully rigid. Each of the autobiographies discussed in this book was produced under conflicting pressures and impulses of secrecy and disclosure, and each narrative reveals ambivalence about the risks and exposure encountered by the self that seeks to "confess."

Though the thematic context for this autobiographical tension between secrecy and disclosure is that of homosexuality, central to my argument is that no essential, innate relationship exists between secrecy and homosexual narrative. Rather, the desire for certain kinds of secrecy that appears in these autobiographies is relative to a specific historical context in which homosexuality is associated with a range of perverse, antisocial, and subversive practices and characteristics. To "confess" to homosexuality, therefore, is inevitably to go beyond the statement of sexual preference for other men. It is, inescapably, to receive the label of the "homosexual" or "invert" as ideologically and prejudicially defined by official Victorian discourse. It is in their confrontation with this powerful sexual ideology, as much as through their literary exploration of personal sexual desires and practices, that these autobiographers find their subject matter and strive to achieve their aesthetic form.

With this book I seek to participate in and hope to contrib-ute to the exciting critical project of exploring the various *forms* of autobiography in terms of their social, aesthetic, and cultural signifi-cations. I do not want to define the genre in an abstract, theoretical fashion that aims to limit it to particular, formal paradigms or ideals. Hence, the chapters are based on readings of individual works that are formally and thematically heterogeneous, aside from thematic co-incidence of same-sex desire. In the chapter on John Henry Newman's *Apologia pro Vita Sua*, the narrative account of the author's conver-sion from Anglicanism to Roman Catholicism in 1845, I endeavor to restore the work to its original context of the religious controversy with the Anglican writer Charles Kingsley. The immediate, polemi-cal purpose of Newman's work is disguised by its almost exclusive focus on Newman's religious history. Yet, as a response to Kingsley's accusations of treachery and duplicity, Newman's narrative inevitably addresses issues of personal and sexual identity. In particular, Newman's defense against Kingsley's claims that Newman was a betrayer of worldly, heterosexual values and national, political interests required him to articulate his own version of "manliness" that would counter and refute Kingsley's ideal of the "muscular Christian."

The publication histories of the other narratives that I discuss here are considerably more complex than that of the *Apologia*, and my readings take account of these complexities in their exploration of autobiographical meanings that are culturally produced and historically determined. For example, John Addington Symonds's memoirs, written during the four years before his death in 1893, were not published until nearly a century later, chiefly because they represented the author's "secret" life as a homosexual in Victorian England. Written in response to the public ignorance of Symonds's own homosexuality and general prejudice against sexual "inversion," the memoirs largely ignore his public persona as a respectable, bourgeois (and, as a married man, presumptively heterosexual) man of letters, developing instead the representation of a "double" existence based on a transgressive sexuality that is lived out in secret. Knowing that his autobiography would not be published during his lifetime, Symonds addresses himself to a future reader of whose identity and sympathy he cannot be sure. Symonds moreover seeks to combat the popular stereotype of same-sex desire as effeminate and degenerate by emphasizing its roots in ancient Greek culture and by insisting on the ennobling effect of masculine love on his own character. The conflicts and tensions in Symonds's writing position surface in the patterns of displacement and disavowal, whereby negative sexual characteristics are transferred to other characters in the narrative, inevitably repudiated as sexual predators and manipulators.

By contrast, Oscar Wilde's letter to his lover, Lord Alfred Douglas —written in 1897 while Wilde was incarcerated in Reading Gaol— was written by the most notorious invert of the Victorian age. *De Profundis*—the title given to the letter, only on its posthumous publication, in expurgated form, in 1905 —is similar to Symonds's narrative in its assertion of the possibility of a life defined by the promptings of same-sex desire; yet the notion of an individual sexual "identity," which Symonds found so attractive and empowering, was dismissed by Wilde as limiting, indeed as symptomatic of the very system of classifications that had condemned him on the basis of his sexuality.

In his letter—addressed to "Bosie," the nickname used for Douglas by his family and close friends—Wilde rejects the rigidity of sexual typologies and instead constructs a dual confession in which author and reader are linked by a shared responsibility for the tragic downfall of Wilde. However, this duality is impeded by Wilde's determination to portray Bosie as the guilty party, whose greedy and destructive personality is in sharp contrast to Wilde's saintly generosity. Bosie comes to function as a figure for Wilde's own disavowed past, which he must repudiate to arrive at what he terms his "new life."

Finally, Edward Carpenter's autobiography, *My Days and Dreams*, though begun in the nineteenth century, was completed only during World War I. Hence, I treat it as a post-Victorian autobiographical narrative characterized by a new willingness to disclose the author's homosexuality to the reading public. But Carpenter's narrative—written over a much longer period of time than were the other autobiographies discussed here—disavows an identity based *exclusively* on desire for men, choosing to subordinate same-sex desire to a more broadly defined Socialist agenda. The very "openness" of Carpenter's autobiographical persona—a reaction against Victorian restraint and prudery—is in fact enabled by a countervailing secrecy, in which the narrative presents a selective and incomplete portrait of Carpenter's sexual history. Though Carpenter's courage in revealing his homosexuality in a published autobiography was unprecedented, it is balanced by his caution in constructing a narrative of the self that would emphasize his political idealism and downplay his sexual transgression.

The autobiographical narration of a "secret self" might seem a paradoxical act—to reveal the self in published form is apparently to render it no longer a "secret." One important common feature of the works discussed is the narration of a self that is not simply revealed but also produced or mediated by the pressure of secrecy. Each narrative was either undertaken as a response to charges of secrecy, duplicity, or corruption or initiated in an attempt to disburden the author of secrets by means of a purifying confessional act. Because the secrecy that shapes these narratives is closely related to the representation of same-sex desire—whether or not such desire is acknowledged as the author's own—another important discourse informing this book is the emergence of homosexuality as a specific category for the classification and representation of individuals and the gradual crystallization (or configuration) of a range of "perverse" sexual acts into the identity formation of "the homosexual."

Readers will recall Foucault's famous account in the *History of Sexuality* of how "homosexuality appeared as one of the forms of sexuality when it was transposed from the practice of sodomy onto a kind of interior androgyny, a hermaphrodism of the soul."[9] Foucault's characterization indicates not only the classification of new sexual categories but also the modern conception of sexuality itself in terms of an identity. The relationship between sexuality and discourse is central, for Foucault, to the way in which sexuality itself has come to signify the "truth" of the self in modern Western culture. The modern imperative, he argues, is an "incitement to speech," whereby the individual "will seek to transform desire . . . into discourse." For modern subjects, therefore, the "fundamental duty" becomes "the task of passing everything having to do with sex through the endless mill of speech."[10]

Yet others have challenged or sought to modify the historical basis of Foucault's thesis, instead emphasizing the central role of the 1895 trials of Oscar Wilde in forming the modern definition of the homosexual according to the specific stereotype of the sexual "corrupter." Alan Sinfield, for example, argues that "the trials helped to produce a major shift in perceptions of the scope of same-sex passion" and suggests that "there is no reason to suppose that Wilde either envisaged, or would have wanted, a distinctively queer identity."[11] For Sinfield, Foucault's reliance on medical and legal discourses leads to a distorting emphasis on the pathological construction of the "homosexual" in terms of a specific sexual crime, sodomy. In Sinfield's account, the modern homosexual emerges when "the entire, vaguely disconcerting nexus of effeminacy, leisure, idleness, immorality, luxury, insouciance, decadence and aestheticism, which Wilde was perceived, variously, as instantiating, was transformed into a brilliantly precise image."[12]

The question at stake here is nothing less than the timing and circumstances of the emergence of modern sexual identities. Though the Wilde trials undoubtedly offered the most spectacular public drama of sexual crime and punishment of the nineteenth century, I aim to uncover a more gradual—and less visible—autobiographical formation of a self predicated on same-sex desire. The key to this phenomenon is the private discourse of "confession," precisely because it establishes the origin of the narrative in an individual's "secret" and foregrounds the irreducible complicity of individual desire and textuality, sexuality and self-representation. With respect to the relation between confession, desire, and subjectivity, Foucault argues that "the truthful confession was inscribed at the heart of the procedures of individualization by power."[13] This formulation, more than any other, links the confession to what he elsewhere describes as "a new *specification of individuals*," among which Foucault includes the "nineteenth-century homosexual."[14] Hence, confession plays a unique role in the representation of new, transgressive forms of sexuality *and* subjectivity. As Jeremy Tambling writes, "The subject is fully constituted when aspects of behaviour (subjective, free) are read by others as characteristic of a personality-type: as happened, of course, with the 'homosexual,' that new descriptive term born of nineteenth-century sexology."[15]

The role attributed by Foucault and his followers to confession in the formation of new categories of sexual identity is a pivotal one, for it is only with its *textual* inscription that same-sex desire becomes legible as a basis of subjectivity that transcends a range of same-sex practices. Autobiography, in particular, has been centrally involved in the discursive construction of modern sexual subjectivities, establishing a confessional practice whereby a "reverse discourse" might alternately appropriate, reinscribe, decode, and subvert dominant discourses of power, desire, and gender. It is by using such discursive strategies, according to Jonathan Dollimore, that "deviant desire reacts against, disrupts, and displaces from within . . . and relentlessly inverts the binaries upon which that ordering [of sexuality] depends."[16] Confession capitulates to power by telling it what it wants to hear: hence, confession, rather than being founded in the authentic disclosure of a deep, subjective "truth," functions as the ideological reflection of the fantasies of the dominant class about its transgressive "others," whether that "otherness" be determined by class, religion, sexuality, politics, or some other factor. By employing and *manipulating* the discourse of the dominant order, however, the confessing subject constitutes itself in the act of self-disclosure in such a way as to disturb or alter the power-knowledge relations of a culture. For the injunction of telling power what it wants to hear may also serve as a ruse by which the confessing subject evades recognition, scrutiny, or surveillance precisely by dint of revealing its inessential secrets.

{ *Introduction* }

The confession as a subgenre may be differentiated from "auto-biography" in two chief respects, according to de Man's observation that "the concept of genre designates an aesthetic as well as a historical function."[17] The first would identify "confession" as the historically prior and religiously sanctioned form of oral discourse, to be later supplanted by the secular, written autobiography. Hence, as James Olney writes, the early stage of the genre occurred "when autobiography as a literary mode was emerging out of autobiography as a confessional act."[18] More relevant to my argument, however, is the second, "aesthetic" definition of the confession as a particular mode of self-referential writing, with a specific ideological function of self-disclosure by means of a self-scarifying discourse. If the aim of the autobiography is to delineate the growth of the self, from childhood to adulthood, and to arrive at the representation of a mature and unique identity, the purpose of the confession is at once narrower and more punitive. The confession takes as its starting point the admission of sin, guilt, or some other form of error, the purpose of the narrative being to strip the self of its protective secrets, ostensibly to satisfy the demands of an external listener or reader. In this sense, the confession is structured around an oppressive relationship with a reader or auditor, without whose presence the confession would not achieve legitimacy or resolution. It is, above all, the pivotal dynamic of secrecy and disclosure in the narratives here discussed that requires the term "confession" to account adequately for their rhetorical strategies and ideological import.

The pressures brought to bear on these particular autobiographical subjects might seem somewhat diffuse and abstract compared with the punishments and other forms of oppression applied in the prison cell, the torture chamber, or the religious sanctuary. Even in the case of Wilde, who produced his narrative while in prison, the impetus to provide an account of his pre-prison existence came not from explicit official authority or command but from within the dynamics of his sexual relationship with Douglas. Yet there nonetheless emerges the autobiographical impulse to reveal private information about the self, in response to demands that are to some extent externally—that is, culturally—brought to bear. Although there is no clear "confessor" figure in a literary work, several of the writers in effect construct their own confessor/auditor to whom the narrative is implicitly or explicitly addressed and from whom a subsequent response may be anticipated. Accordingly, in these narratives "confession" is to be understood less as a straightforward revelation of the self's secrets—designed to appease an external authority—than as a dialogic narrative strategy deeply invested in the negotiation of cultural and personal power. If the secrets of the self are constituted by (and, arguably, by nothing other than) the very "act" of disclosure, the particular self represented in autobiography is only one of many possible personae that might have been articulated: the choice of a particular emphasis or a specific "secret" on which to base the confession determines the course and aesthetic form of the narrative. Yet, at the same time, the specific import of the confessional secret is not individually determined but historically contingent and culturally embedded.

This approach to the confession as constitutive of the self it claims to represent is, of course, a significant departure from the traditional view of the relationship between self and autobiography, aptly summarized by Elizabeth Bruss: "First we have selfhood, a state of being with its own metaphysical necessity; and only then autobiography, a discourse that springs from that state of being and gives it voice." Following Foucault, Lacan, and Derrida—whose work Bruss characterizes as "various assaults . . . on the Cartesian 'cogito' "—much contemporary theory rejects the conceptualizing of the autobiographical narrative as the revelation of a preexisting subjectivity that merely awaits an opportunity for self-disclosure.[19] Rather, the autobiography is considered as a strategy for the delineation of a self that serves the author's individual and rhetorical purposes, even as it responds to specific historical and cultural pressures.

Thus the "self" is not simply independent of or prior to autobiographical discourse but is also to some extent produced by it. As Bruss writes, "The discourse that had seemed a mere reflection or instrument of the self becomes its foundation and sine qua non."[20] Bearing in mind that the force of "subjectivity" may be experienced as precisely that realm of knowledge which cannot be adequately expressed or fully disclosed, one finds an inevitable disjunction between the individual experience of the self and the cultural discourse of autobiography. The autobiographical subject is as inclined to resist as to collaborate with the formal constraints and demands of the genre. Hence, the discursive analysis of what I call "secret selves" often becomes a matter of exploring the interstices of literary texts— their silences, opacities, evasions, and omissions. For if the self is constituted by the very act of "confession," then the secret becomes an integral part of a given narrative rather than simply that which narrative seeks to conceal or expose. Accordingly, "confessional" writing frequently reverberates with and reproduces the secrecy it claims or appears to eschew.

Without the concept of a unique, prediscursive subjectivity motivating its composition, the confessional narrative at times approaches, rhetorically speaking, the form of the dramatic monologue in which the construction of a specific narrative persona enables the work of confession to take place. Of course, it is conventional to assume that confession differs from the dramatic monologue precisely in that the narrator, protagonist, and author share the same identity and that the sins or transgressions confessed by the narrator are the author's own. While many critics would accept the notion that Browning's "Andrea del Sarto," Tennyson's "Ulysses," and Swinburne's "Anactoria" suggest autobiographical resonances, for example, few would interpret the dramatic personae exclusively as the autobiographical surrogates of their authors. And yet the self that is represented in the text— the autobiographical protagonist—can never precisely coincide with the "I" of the speaking narrator; moreover, the "I" of the narrator is of course constructed according to literary convention and cannot give us direct access to the author's consciousness. Hence, for poststructuralist theory, "the autobiographical text becomes a narrative artifice, privileging a presence, or identity, that does not exist outside language. Given the very nature of language, embedded in the text lie alternative or deferred identities that constantly subvert any pretensions of truthfulness."[21]

Indeed, as Olney argues, summarizing the poststructuralist assault on autobiography, the authority to assert a consistent "I"—linking author, protagonist, and narrator—in a text "has been of late so thoroughly compromised philosophically and linguistically . . . that the very basis on which a traditional autobiography might be commenced has simply been worn away."[22] De Man, in his attack on this basis of "traditional autobiography," has attempted to sever the genre once and for all from its referential function, asking whether "the illusion of reference [is] not a correlation of the structure of the figure, that is to say no longer clearly and simply a referent at all but something more akin to a fiction." Along these lines, de Man takes the approach that the formal limits and rhetorical structure of autobiography take priority over the "referential" content, that "the autobiographical project may itself produce and determine the life and that whatever the writer does is in fact governed by the technical demands of self-portraiture and thus determined, in all its aspects, by the resources of his medium."[23]

To the extent that autobiographical discourse produces, rather than merely reproduces, our versions of the self, it becomes all the more urgent to scrutinize the rhetorical gestures that encode subjectivity in the text, and particularly to consider the forms of textual reticence that adumbrate the space in which a private "self" might be construed. According to Sidonie Smith, "As notions of an authoritative speaker, intentionality, truth, meaning, and generic integrity are rejected, the former preoccupations of autobiography critics — the nature of its truth, the emergence of its formal structures, the struggle with identity, even the assumption of a motivating self — are displaced by a new concern for the *graphia*."[24] The significance of writing, or textuality, in autobiography therefore increases in proportion to the dissolution of critical faith in a stable, pretextual self; to the point where, as Olney states, "it is through that act [of writing] that the self and the life, complexly intertwined and entangled, take on a certain form, assume a particular shape and image, and endlessly reflect that image back and forth."[25]

With this *textual* emphasis in mind, the secretive strategies of self-representation in these Victorian narratives concern us far more than they would if it were simply a matter of tracing the effects of legal prohibitions and scientific classifications which afflict certain subject positions and which criminalize sexual relations between men. Important as these legal and scientific factors are, they cannot fully account for the preeminence of secrecy in Victorian autobiographical narrative. Instead of focusing on an author's desire to avoid self-incriminating revelations that would result in censorship, stigma, or punishment, I explore the productive power of secrecy to constitute particular forms of subjectivity. As a group, these autobiographical works occupy a vexed relation to secrecy, both gesturing toward the possibility of a full self-revelation and retreating periodically into opacity, resistance, or concealment that hints at the unreliability and elusiveness of narrative self-representation. The "secret" in terms of which an autobiographical narrative develops need not, of course, be a sexual one. Rather, same-sex desire emerges discursively as a specific site of secrecy, in relation to which the self may be newly conceived, supplementing, or even displacing, other marginalized positions, such as religious or class "difference."

Even while one pursues the textuality of the self, it is important to recognize the crucial relation between the social and cultural situation of the author and the status of his or her literary self-representation. Of women's autobiography, for example, Sidonie Smith argues that "male writing about self . . . assumed a privileged place in the canon; female writing about self, a devalued position at the margins of the canon."[26] Smith's work is valuable for developing a theory of "marginal" autobiography, in which the writer's social embeddedness — particularly with respect to gender — determines the degree of authority with which she or he speaks as an autobiographer. Yet although what Smith calls "the intersection between ideologies of selfhood and ideologies of gender" has been explored in relation to female autobiographers, it has been largely ignored in its application to autobiographies by homosexual men.[27] The significance of "marginality" is considerable in tracing the history of Victorian homosexual confession, because the confessional subject writes from a position explicitly defined as one of cultural exclusion. Hence, I will argue that the confessional secrecy of these narratives is produced in part by an unwillingness to jeopardize the cultural privilege and textual authority of the Victorian male author.

If, as Smith argues, "theories of sexual and textual difference have an impact on theories of narrative, particularly autobiographical narrative," then the specific and historically changing forms of this relationship between sexuality and textuality need to be traced in relation to particular narratives.[28] One cannot, for instance, reduce the textual "difference" between male and female autobiography to a generalized binary opposition between public and private roles and experiences, because, as Smith writes, "examples that bely the opposition abound. Men write of private experiences; women, of their public activities."[29] To argue that the male autobiographers discussed in this book were contesting a dominant view of masculine identity that privileged heterosexual desire is not to deny that they were also culturally privileged as male authors. Rather, it is to seek out a more nuanced and satisfactory application of textual difference to autobiographical criticism: one that recognizes the multiplicity of conflicting desires and identifications — in effect, the coexistence of different "voices" — that may be resonating within a single narrative.

Though the relationship between secrecy and same-sex desire might be fruitfully explored in autobiographical narratives by women — Elizabeth Barrett Browning's *Aurora Leigh* and Charlotte Brontë's *Villette*, for example, would certainly reward such attention — I will concentrate on narratives of masculinity in the Victorian period. The critical and theoretical framework of this book is influenced by a range of theoretical texts that explore the construction of and contradictions within male roles and "identities" in the Victorian period. In particular, the pivotal role of same-sex desire in influencing — at times contesting or subverting — the hegemonic representations of masculinity has emerged as a central theme in more recent readings of the homoerotic significations of Victorian texts.[30]

As the groundbreaking work of Eve Kosofsky Sedgwick has taught us, it is precisely the male "homosocial" system of patriarchy — by which masculine friendship and bonding are used to further the interests of nation, class, and (male) gender — that requires the injunction against a transgressive same-sex desire that would destabilize such bonds by making explicit their sexual nature. This injunction surfaces in the sexual and textual crises Sedgwick designates as "homosexual panic."[31] By the same token, the role of "woman" is determined, in homosocial texts, by the displacement of prohibited same-sex desire that underwrites the male homosocial bond. The conflict between a public, culturally enforced imperative of heterosexual desire and a privately experienced and prohibited same-sex desire is in some cases apparent in misogynistic impulses toward "woman" — as the site and object of a publicly sanctioned but erotically resisted desire. Even as "woman" may be idealized by Victorian writers, therefore, it is often within the very narrow confines of domestic roles and space, with which she is frequently and somewhat ambivalently associated.

That each of these narratives renounces a rigid conformity to the Victorian masculine ideal does not mean we should read them as being apart from, still less "ahead of" their age. On the contrary, the significance of these works, read collectively, might be to broaden and modify our current understanding of Victorian gender roles and representations. The risk of occupying a "feminine" role — of being stigmatized as "effeminate" and excluded from the privileges of male bourgeois society—is inevitably encountered by the male autobiographer who explores transgressive modes of feeling, desire, and intimacy. If a certain blurring occurs between the categories of "effeminacy," "homosexuality," and other forms of sexual or gendered difference in discourses of the Victorian age, this serves only to reinforce the threat to masculine privilege posed by the various forms of sexual and cultural dissidence, especially when articulated together. Cumulatively, then, the schisms and fissures that these autobiographies reveal in the patriarchal discourse of selfhood partially deconstruct the Victorian ideal of masculinity, much as they complicate the unique "identity" of the Victorian writer.

In the broadest sense, this book is deeply influenced by the field of gender theory. The writings of Judith Butler and Eve Kosofsky Sedgwick are exemplary in this respect, less for their theoretical insistence on the culturally inscribed status of gender roles and sexual categories than for their rigorously detailed pursuit of the historically specific forms of those constructions. Moreover, by subjecting the cultural forms of "masculinity" to the same critical scrutiny that has previously been reserved for constructions of feminine roles, Butler and Sedgwick have succeeded in significantly broadening the range of gender studies. Each of the readings that follow seeks to develop the exploration of male autobiographical writing in terms that complicate—and hopefully enrich—our understanding of Victorian constructions of gender roles and the ways in which they depend on the subjective work performed by autobiography.

It would be impossible of course to cover all the significant landmarks of Victorian homosexual confession in a single book. A key figure in the transition between the Oxford movement, represented by Newman, and later Victorian constructions of same sex-desire is that of Walter Pater. Though Pater might seem to be missing from this volume—in that there is no chapter devoted exclusively to his writing—his influence should be discernible in each section. Part of the reason for devoting less exclusive attention to Pater is that the homoerotic force of his work has been so ably discussed by other critics. Richard Dellamora's notable book on the representation of masculine desire in Pater's aesthetic writing, for example, has enriched our awareness of the cultural centrality of same-sex desire in the Victorian period. Subsequent discussions of Pater by Herbert Sussman and James Eli Adams have built on Dellamora's insights into Pater's transgressions of aesthetic and sexual norms. These critics begin with a theoretical premise similar to mine — that Victorian "masculinity" or "manliness" is not only an important subject for historical analysis and academic study but is also of central significance to our current constructions of gender roles and ideologies. The work of these critics is of consequence because in it they explore the intersections between same-sex desire and other key Victorian discourses, such as aestheticism, dandyism, and male self-fashioning.

Sussman, for example, considers "early Victorian masculine poetics and technologies of the male self within the emerging poetics of the 'aesthetic' and within the construction of the homosexual in the later nineteenth century."[32] By exploring what he calls "Pater's dialectical relation to earlier discourses of masculinity,"[33] Sussman extends the analysis of same-sex desire and manliness into the regions of what has been termed Victorian "sage discourse."[34] The work of Adams has a somewhat different focus: the process by which the male "self-discipline," described by Sussman in aesthetic terms, is displaced onto the suspiciously feminized figure of the "dandy," which becomes more vulnerable to attack as forms of masculine gender transgression become conflated with homosexuality toward the end of the century. Adams investigates the seeming paradox that Victorian "programs of self-consciously masculine discipline are attacked as forms of effeminacy," going on to develop the idea of the Paterian "mask" as a defense against the various forms of hostility provoked by the sexually ambiguous "dandy." The mask, for Adams, functions as "a public withholding of private experience," thereby at once creating an aura of mystique and prohibition around the concealed experience and establishing "a peculiar authority in the author." Adams allows still more specificity to the "secret" in Pater as a "mask" for homoerotic desire, referring to a "calculated affiliation of his aestheticism with homoerotic subcultures that still remain shadowy." As Adams points out, the tendency to read Pater's secret in terms of a forbidden desire is marked by a "hermeneutics of suspicion" that informs late-Victorian practices of reading.[35]

Dellamora, in the most far-reaching analysis of Pater's aesthetic discourse to date, has revealed the carefully crafted transgression of Victorian gender roles at the very heart of Pater's critical practice. Of Pater's work on Leonardo, Dellamora observes that "Pater pushes further the suggestions of sexual perversity that occur already in nineteenth-century French accounts of the painter."[36] Pater's readings of Renaissance paintings, Dellamora shows, give the clearest possible indications of his engagement with "perverse" and transgressive sexual desires. If, for Pater, "the possibility of sexual contact with another man in an uncontrolled situation induces both apprehension and enticement," then the imaginative engagement with homoerotic art offered a safer — and more private — site for transgressive experience and fantasy. Dellamora points out that Pater's "model of masculine identity requires a metaphorical becoming-woman as part of a process whereby men who desire emotional and sexual ties with other men may dispel the fear of women . . . that masculinist culture normally produces."[37] In particular, Dellamora's argument that "the metamorphic power that [Pater] associates with artistic creativity implies openness to the varieties of sexual experience" is an apt reminder of the intimate relation of transgressive sexuality and aesthetic discourse in Victorian culture.[38]

While what Adams has called "the rhetoric of secrecy" characterizes each of the narratives I discuss, therefore, the specific dynamic between such rhetoric and forms of aestheticized self-disclosure varies in each case: the erotic-aesthetic discourses of Wilde and Symonds, for example, differ from each other far more than a monolithic definition of the Victorian "homosexual" would suggest. Indeed, the uses of secrecy by Newman, Symonds, Wilde, and Carpenter — each of whom is writing an autobiography that provides a very different account of the relation between sexual desire and social persona — are remarkably distinct, even contradictory at times. What is at stake, in other words, is not just the forbidden "content" behind the "veil" of secrecy but also the nature of the particular relationship between the rhetoric of a text and the sexual discourse of the wider culture: that is, to what aesthetic, erotic, and ideological ends the strategy of secrecy is deployed.

The central figures of Victorian aestheticism, as Dellamora has shown, produced the most elaborate and influential counterdiscourse with which to contest the increasingly dominant and negative categorizations of same-sex desire. If the cataclysmic effects of the prosecution and imprisonment of Oscar Wilde in some ways contributed toward the formation of new identities based on same-sex desire — a position taken by Sinfield, as well as by Wayne Koestenbaum, who asserts roundly "that gay identity was born from Wilde's trial"[39] —

it is important that the "birth" of new sexual possibilities was first manifested not in a scandalous and tragic court case but in representational practices seeking the articulation of same-sex desire, while being inevitably shaped by the incriminating logic of the Labouchère Amendment of 1885. Moreover, although one must never forget that secrecy had an urgent ideological function for the containment of those seeking to enact or to represent illicit sexual desires, we would be ill advised to negate the potent erotic and aesthetic pleasures of secrecy itself, perhaps best described by Basil Hallward in *The Picture of Dorian Gray*: "I have grown to love secrecy. It seems to be the one thing that can make modern life mysterious or marvellous to us." [40]

In this introductory chapter, it remains to point out that the aim of this book is not to argue that an autobiographical narrative characterized by same-sex desire will, ipso facto, be determined or even influenced by strategies of secrecy. Rather, it is to explore the historically specific emergence of the narration of an officially prohibited, yet aesthetically idealized, form of erotic experience and desire. Viewed in this light, it will be clear that in no sense do I attempt to construct a teleological model of sexual discourse in Victorian autobiography, linking the series of studies in a narrative trajectory of erotic liberation. The later narratives I discuss indeed demonstrate a greater tendency to constitute the self and narrate the life in terms of a desire for other men. Yet it is equally important to observe the increasing level of textual anxiety and reserve surrounding representations of desire in the later narratives and to acknowledge the constraints that continued to affect their production.

An important index of this intensification of cultural hostility toward same-sex desire is that the publication of the later works here examined was long delayed or indeed posthumous. The significance of these convoluted publication histories should not be underestimated in determining the meanings of the narratives themselves. Dellamora, in a 1993 position paper, has addressed this issue with the question, "When an author decides that a text will not be published until after his death, what is implied? . . . What demands do such appeals make? And what responsibilities do they entail for a historical understanding of texts?" [41] In Chapters 2–4 of this book and in my concluding discussion of E. M. Forster's posthumously published novel, *Maurice*, I attempt to provide an answer to these questions, even while calling attention to the fact — encountered frequently during the research involved in writing this volume — that the decision to delay or abandon the publication of an autobiographical work is one of the most effective strategies of textual secrecy, in effect by withholding a secret that has already been (textually) disclosed. Indeed, the delay in publishing a potentially self-incriminating autobiography may sometimes be defined less as a specific choice than as a kind of prolonged ambivalence. In this respect, an unfavorable cultural and ideological climate may take precedence over the desire or intention of the individual author when the possibility of publishing such a work arises.

The peculiar circumstances that obstructed the publication of the narratives of Wilde, Symonds, and Carpenter serve to remind us, moreover, of the historically constituted meaning of the literary text. As Jerome McGann writes, "Every text enters the world under determinate sociohistorical conditions, and while these conditions may and should be variously defined and imagined, they establish the horizon within which the life histories of different texts can play themselves out."[42] Indeed, to focus on the life history of the text rather than that of the author is to reassert the textual nature of autobiographical identity. In an effort to remind us of the importance of historical context, Dellamora attacks the popular fantasy among literary readers that "if one can specify and define the actual language of a text, one can experience unmediated access to the consciousness that produced that text" — a belief that undoubtedly has a particularly strong appeal for readers of autobiography.[43] Insisting that the context in which a work is published has a material and determining influence on the way that it is received and read — that is, on what the text "means" — Dellamora uses the test case of posthumous publication to assert the priority of historically specific meanings over the authorial consciousness or intention. A posthumously published work, "because of the materials entrusted to posterity by the writer, always differs from itself."[44]

Moreover, the removal of the posthumously published work from authorial control often results in the active, creative involvement of other individuals in capacities such as editor, biographer, or literary executor. Hence, whether by means of the selection (or deletion) of specific passages, the naming of a work, or the choice of form in which it is to be published, the posthumously published autobiography reminds us that, in the words of McGann, "literary texts and their meanings are collaborative events," a reality that "we confront . . . most forcefully when we read texts which, while 'written by' certain writers, were never 'authorized' by them. The production of this kind of text is carried out under the authority, and by the final intentions, of persons other than the writer of the texts."[45] The interpretive problems confronted in the criticism of such "collaborative" works are, of course, daunting. Dellamora's solution calls for a "double framing that exploits the possibilities of temporal difference in order to put in question both historical and contemporary truths. In this process, textual politics can never be freed from sexual politics."[46] It remains to be seen whether such "double framing" can be accomplished in practice.

In the chapters that follow, I strive for, rather than attempt to resist, such a superimposition of contemporary theoretical insights, sexual ideologies, and Victorian autobiographical texts. I aim to develop an argument that is not exclusively determined or authorized by any one of the various "framings" but produced by their hopefully productive interaction. By foregrounding the complex publishing histories that impeded public access to some of the works until after the authors' deaths, the individual chapters place the specific textual functions of secrecy within a broader, historical framework of literary reticence. The multiple and fluctuating forces — historical, textual, cultural — that mediate our readings of these texts can never be fully grasped, any more than the material forms of language can allow us direct access to an autobiographer's consciousness. Yet it is precisely this materiality — of history, of language, of desire — that proves most fascinating, instructive, and seductive, as the attempt to reconstruct and reimagine Victorian subjectivities and desires continues to unfold. The refusal, whether on the part of the author or his survivors, to publish a potentially scandalous or incriminating autobiography may arise from the most rational, self-preserving motives, but it is certainly an effective and durable method by means of which the "secret self" may be withheld from public knowledge. Yet the publication of a previously "secret" text brings the rhetoric and erotics of secrecy itself into the range of critical insight and investigation, restoring to us some of the lost or abandoned sources of sexual and literary history. It is to the critical analysis of these restored histories that I devote this book.

An Unnatural State

Secrecy and "Perversion" in John Henry Newman's
Apologia pro Vita Sua

Newman's autobiography was first published in 1864, but the event at
the center of the narrative—Newman's conversion to Roman Catholicism—had occurred twenty years earlier, at the height of the Oxford
movement. As a dramatic shift in allegiance by an immensely influential figure in the Church of England, Newman's apostasy sent shock
waves through the nation that could still be felt almost a generation
later. Indeed, the Newman-Kingsley controversy was in part a revival
of an earlier debate over the relationship between church and state.
The stakes of the conflict had changed, however, and Kingsley's invocation of masculine and sexual norms in his assertion of his own
worldly and procreative mid-Victorian creed make the controversy a
fascinating study for the exploration of Victorian discourses of gender, sexuality, and selfhood.

Long before he actually wrote the autobiography that resulted in
the transformation of his reputation in his own country, John Henry
Newman had considered the possibility of writing a narrative of
self-justification to clarify the motives for his conversion to Roman
Catholicism in 1845.[1] For twenty years following this conversion he
had been treated with suspicion and hostility by the majority of his
compatriots, and public attacks calumniating him for his "treachery"
were not uncommon. Yet as he explained to Alexander Macmil-

lan, Newman felt that such anonymous hostilities were not generally worth reciprocation:[2] "I have never been very sensitive of such attacks; rarely taken notice of them. Now, when I have long ceased from controversy, they continue: they have lasted incessantly from the year 1833 to this day. They do not ordinarily come in my way: when they do, I let them pass through indolence."[3] Realizing that the extent of public distrust of his religious career meant that any attempt to clear his name would be deemed inappropriate and almost certainly prove unsuccessful, he kept his peace for twenty years, remaining in relative obscurity near Birmingham at the Oratory of St. Philip Neri that he had founded in 1848.

Toward the end of 1863, however, Newman received a copy of the January 1864 issue of *Macmillan's Magazine* from an anonymous source; it contained a favorable review of J. A. Froude's ultra-Protestant *History of England*, parts of which had been underlined by the unidentified sender (later discovered to be William Pope, an admirer of Newman's). The review, signed merely "C. K.," included an attack on Newman's honesty as part of a wider attempt to discredit the Catholic priesthood. Newman immediately wrote to the publishers of the magazine to ask for an explanation of the unprovoked attack and discovered the author of the review to be Charles Kingsley, the prominent Anglican clergyman and novelist. Kingsley was at this time riding high in public and royal favor — he had just published *The Water Babies*, now one of the most popular children's novels of all time; was Regius professor of modern history at Cambridge University (having been appointed to the position by the prince consort); and served as private tutor to the Prince of Wales at Cambridge. His name was widely associated with the cult of "muscular Christianity" — a type of Anglicanism emphasizing physical health and exertion, connubial felicity, and other worldly, purportedly "masculine," values.[4]

Declaring his "extreme astonishment"[5] at this discovery of Kingsley's authorship of the review, Newman promptly wrote a letter of protest to Kingsley himself, who eventually agreed to publish an apology in the next issue of *Macmillan's Magazine*. This apology was so halfhearted, however, as to be unsatisfactory to both Newman and his lawyer-friend Edward Badeley, whom he consulted on the matter. In January 1864, therefore, he acted on his previous warning to Kingsley that he viewed their letters as "public property"[6] and published their correspondence in pamphlet form, adding some satirical "reflections" on Kingsley's part in the exchange. Fully aware that he now had an excellent opportunity to produce the self-justification that he had been contemplating for years, Newman wrote to Badeley on 8 March 1864: "By now I am expecting Kingsley's Pamphlet, on 'what does Dr Newman teach?' for which of course I have prepared myself from the first. I mean, I never have had an opening to defend myself as to various passages in my life and writings and I have always looked forward to the possibility of that opening being presented to me. I have for a long time been attempting to arrange my letters and papers with a view to it."[7]

Events began to take exactly the turn Newman had hoped for when Kingsley published an ill-considered and grotesquely exaggerated attack on Newman's career, repeating his previous slanders against him and adding numerous others for good measure. The hysterically bellicose tone of this pamphlet—entitled "What, Then, Does Dr. Newman Mean?"—alienated even the staunchest of Kingsley's supporters, such as R. H. Hutton at the *Spectator*, and gave Newman the opportunity he needed to proceed with his autobiographical self-defense. This work, originally entitled *Apologia pro Vita Sua: Being a Reply to a Pamphlet Entitled "What, Then, Does Dr. Newman Mean?,"* appeared in seven weekly pamphlets between 21 April and 2 June 1864.

In this chapter I will argue that the complex nature of Newman's autobiography can more fully be understood by examining the work in the context of the controversy that led to its production. I attempt, therefore, to resituate the *Apologia* in its historical and cultural framework and to reinstate Newman's antagonist, Charles Kingsley, in a position of some centrality to the conflict that culminated in the publication of the *Apologia*. I hope that a greater emphasis on Kingsley's contribution to the debate than has been offered by most critics of the *Apologia* will help to reestablish a balance between the competing ideologies represented by the two writers. I will examine the rhetoric deployed both by the antagonists themselves and in subsequent discussions of the Newman-Kingsley controversy in order to show that Kingsley's accusation of dishonesty was the culmination of a long period of public distrust of Newman. Moreover, this distrust stemmed not merely from widespread concern about Newman's "honesty" but also from hostility toward his "perversion"—a term that included his religious transgression as well as his perceived sexual ambiguity.

Kingsley's assault on Newman, I will posit, was one remarkably extreme manifestation of Victorian orthodoxies of gender and religion. The chief problem in exploring these issues is that Kingsley's attack was clearly overdetermined, suggesting a whole range of anxieties that are irreducible to any single causative factor. For example, Newman's Catholicism represented (among other things) the foreignness of Romanism and the unknown and frightening mysteries of Catholic ritual and belief in miracles. At the same time, Newman's celibacy (connected with, but by no means inseparable from, his Catholicism) produced another range of anxieties concerning the precariousness of marriage as an institution and the instability of gender (particularly masculine) identities and roles. These anxieties will be discussed in the following section.

Naming Newman's "Perversion"

Allegations concerning Newman's perversion formed a recurring theme of Kingsley's bombastic assault and one that was closely related to his paranoid account of Newman's corrupting influence on the young. I want to argue, in fact, that "perversion" is closer than any other term to being a catchall for the various layers of Newman's "otherness," as identified and anathematized by Kingsley—his allegedly secret Catholicism, his celibacy, his perceived gender transgression, or "effeminacy," and, relatedly, his possible homosexuality.[8] It is important to remember, of course, that "perversion" did not then invoke the specifically sexual connotations that it does for post-Victorian readers. But more recent work on the "histories of perversion" has found a striking continuity between pre- and post-Freudian definitions of the term, revealing that its religious and scriptural uses included a demonization of the feminine as being inherently "perverse" and errant:

> Although the "modern" sexual pervert does not appear in the OED, the wayward woman figures prominently as one of the two kinds of pervert who recur in the original dictionary's numerous citations for the perverse and its cognate terms. The other is the religious heretic. At the start of the Christian narrative they went together. . . . In theological discourse perversion may describe the

{ An Unnatural State }

opposite of conversion, signifying that terrible, unforgivable deviation *from* the true faith to the false. It is this use which suggests the first of two central and related paradoxes of the perverse, and another reason why it is so despised and feared—namely that perversion has its origins in, or exists in an intimate relation with, that which it subverts.

Newman's conversion to Catholicism was, of course, interpreted by Kingsley and others as just such a perverse "deviation from the true faith to the false." Moreover, the feminization of Newman by Kingsley and others would result in his being portrayed as a kind of "wayward woman," an effeminate betrayer of the "masculine" values of openness, honesty, and straightforwardness who, like Eve (or, indeed, Satan himself), had perversely forsaken his position of privilege and fallen from grace (as Kingsley apostrophized Newman, "How art thou fallen from heaven, O Lucifer, son of the Morning!").[9]

Despite the primarily religious usage of "perversion" in the rhetoric of the controversy, its attribution to Newman ought not to be entirely separated from the sexual and gender anxieties that motivated Kingsley's attack. Indeed, it appears that during this controversy we see an early instance of "perversion" being used as a sexually and erotically charged term. Whether or not Kingsley was referring to or imagining any sexual "perversion" in particular, the resonance of the word in this context is inseparable from the attacks on Newman's "celibacy" and "effeminacy," the sexual implications of which I will examine here. The usefulness of perversion as a category is precisely that it allows one to cross between the sexual and the religious components of Newman's transgressions and Kingsley's phobias.[10]

The primary reason for my emphasis on this contextual significance of the controversy is that while there is already a plethora of published work examining the literary (and, to a lesser extent, theological) facets of Newman's autobiography, work that considers the Newman-Kingsley controversy in terms of its sexual and gender politics is comparatively scarce.[11] I am interested in tracing both the personal and the cultural sources of Kingsley's antipathy for Newman and in investigating the extent to which his hostility was representative of attitudes prevalent in Victorian society. As Owen Chadwick has expressed the question: "Why was the anti-Catholicism [of Kingsley] so intense? This is not a Protestant of the reformation; not a man who thinks the Pope anti-Christ. . . . This was a broad church-man, a man with an open mind in other respects, as his attitude to Darwin or to Socialism showed; a man who looked for truth in all men even when they were wrong. And Kingsley the broad churchman loathed Roman Catholicism."[12] More to the point, Kingsley loathed Newman; and it is an analysis of the interdependencies and inter-relations between the personal and cultural sources of this deep and long-lasting antagonism toward Catholicism in general and Newman in particular that will form the basis of this chapter.

An important part of my project is to examine issues of gender and sexuality as they surfaced in the controversy between Kingsley and Newman and as they have recurred in subsequent criticism, as well as to interrogate some of the ways in which these issues informed or intersected with the religious and ethical issues that were immediately at stake. My purpose is to highlight the complexity of the *Apologia* by reading it in terms of a theoretical approach informed by an under-standing of the constructedness (that is, the cultural nature) of gen-dered identity and especially masculinity, defined in part as an intense and at times phobic resistance or hostility to the "feminine." I am especially interested in the representation of Newman's conversion to Roman Catholicism as the result of an identity crisis that has intrigu-ing parallels with the crises of sexual identity I examine in other con-texts, such as that described in John Addington Symonds's *Memoirs*.[13]

To the extent that Newman's conversion to Catholicism was car-ried out in secret, it involved a profound subjective and cultural investment in the distinctions between knowledge and ignorance, secrecy and disclosure. As Eve Sedgwick has shown in *Epistemology of the Closet*, such distinctions were pivotal to the discursive emergence of homosexuality in Victorian writing. Issues of secrecy and disclo-sure were crucially at stake in Newman's dispute with Kingsley, and his success in clearing his name hinged to a large extent on his ability to convince his readership that he had not, in fact, been secretly a Catholic while pretending to be an Anglican. Moreover, the impu-tation of homosexuality that Kingsley leveled, however obliquely, at Newman suggests that the "secret" may have had a more than reli-gious significance for his attack on Newman's character. Whether Newman's secret was "Catholic," in the sense that it concealed his Catholic faith behind his Anglican status, or whether his Catholicism (or, indeed, his Anglicanism) itself served to conceal or sublimate his

{ *An Unnatural State* }

homosexuality, the structure of secrecy and disclosure is of central importance for deciphering both the sexual politics and the confessional poetics of the *Apologia*.

Naming Newman's Secret: Confession and the Aesthetics of Disclosure

Newman's conversion to Roman Catholicism in 1845 led to his exile from Oxford and his exit from the center stage of British religious life, culture, and society for a generation. It led to his being anathematized as a traitor to his country and ostracized even by some of his closest Anglican friends. How was it, then, that the *narrative* of his conversion, written almost twenty years later, had exactly the reverse effect? It removed many of the doubts entertained against him and lifted much of the contempt that he had endured, restoring him to an eminent place in the public's esteem. Newman's career blossomed after the publication of the *Apologia*, culminating in his elevation to the status of cardinal in 1879.

What had changed between 1845 and 1864 that allowed Newman to transform his position in England by recounting the very events that had led him into disgrace and exile? Possibly, it was the maliciously ad hominem nature of Kingsley's accusations that made the public sympathetic to Newman's account and provided him the opportunity to redeem himself with a justification of his whole career. It is clear, for example, that the support of R. H. Hutton at the *Spectator*, who turned away from Kingsley after the publication of his pamphlet, did Newman's public image a great deal of good.[14] Had Newman been challenged by a less extreme and aggressive antagonist, the outcome of the conflict might have been quite different.

Newman's ultimate success, however, hinged less on the mistakes of his opponent than on his own willingness to disclose, with the appropriate tone of humility and drama, the history of his inner life. As we have seen, Newman was ready to tell his story and, equally important, the public was ready to hear it. The key to Newman's triumph was his decision to answer Kingsley's attack with an autobiographical self-defense, rather than a refutation based on abstract reasoning. It was his own particular history, a self-portrayal he referred to as "the living man," that alone was capable of destroying the "scarecrow" of Kingsley's—and the British public's—imagination; and it was this difficult but skillfully crafted self-disclosure by means of which he accounted for himself, (re)wrote his life history, and dispelled the myth of his corrupt nature.

Newman's drama of religious discovery and conversion in some ways anticipates the narratives of sexual self-disclosure by Symonds, Wilde, and Carpenter. For Newman, however, the question of his sexual identity was eclipsed by the struggle for religious self-definition, and the dynamics of his conversion unfolded through a crisis of faith, rather than a crisis of sexuality. Nonetheless, as I show, Catholicism was itself associated with behavior and relationships that might now be described as homosexual, not least because of its often "secretive" status and the intense anti-Catholic prejudices widespread in Protestant England. Newman's celibacy, for example, was cited by Kingsley as an indicator or his religious *and* his sexual "perversion"; and this was itself enough to establish a suspicious link between two deeply threatening forms of "otherness."

Even if I am correct in asserting that Catholicism and celibacy were associated, in the minds of Kingsley and others, with homosexuality, there is likely to be one important objection to a reading of Newman's autobiography that foregrounds his erotic preferences—namely, that Newman himself refers only fleetingly, in the *Apologia*, to his sexual history, and does so in the least revealing way possible, ascribing his single status to the "will of God" rather than same-sex desire: "I am obliged to mention, though I do it with great reluctance, another deep imagination, which at this time, the autumn of 1816, took possession of me,—there can be no mistake about the fact; viz. that it would be the will of God that I should lead a single life." [15]

Despite Newman's self-proclaimed celibacy, his life was in fact characterized by a series of intense and emotionally (if not physically) intimate relationships with other men. Precisely by withholding the full nature of his attachments, Newman is in effect eroticizing them. For the very resistance to disclosure implies a "secret" that, as Newman's opening quotation from *Isaiah* suggests, he is tantalizingly reluctant to reveal: "It may easily be conceived how great a trial it is to me to write the following history of myself; but I must not shrink from the task. The words, 'Secretum meum mihi [my secret is my own],' keep ringing in my ears; but as men draw towards their end, they care less for disclosures" (15).

Of the relationship between secrecy and homosexuality in the second half of the nineteenth century, Sedgwick argues "that knowledge meant sexual knowledge, and secrets sexual secrets," while "there had in fact developed one particular sexuality that was distinctively constituted *as* secrecy."[16] In other words, Newman's narrative of self-revelation, even as it attempts to refute the eroticized perception of his Catholic identity, actually reinforces it. Newman asserts a certain degree of control over the information he will disclose: his secret is "his own"; it is in his power to decide whether to tell it. Knowledge/ignorance and secrecy/disclosure here divide (or appear to divide) fairly straightforwardly between author and reader. Newman, imagining himself to be near death, feels he has little to lose in conveying the facts that we wish to know. Yet the sense remains ambiguous: Newman's claim that, as they approach death, "men care less for disclosures" can mean either that he has become less secretive or that he no longer relishes the prospect of disclosure, as he might once have done.

At a later juncture in his autobiography, however, Newman suggests that this dual structure of author and reader as the possessor and seeker of (secret) knowledge, respectively, may in fact be oversimplified. For part of the challenge of writing an autobiography, he claims, is the difficulty (indeed, the impossibility) of such "knowing" (or possessing) of oneself: "For who can know himself, and the multitude of subtle influences which act upon him? And who can recollect, at the distance of twenty-five years, all that he once knew about his thoughts and his deeds, and that, during a portion of his life, when, even at the time, his observation, whether of himself or of the external world, was less than before or after, by very reason of the perplexity and dismay which weighed upon him, — when, in spite of the light given to him according to his need amid his darkness, yet a darkness it emphatically was?" (90). At one level, this disclaimer is simply a conventional autobiographer's admission of partial amnesia. At the same time, the passage casts a more radical and far-reaching doubt over the very possibility of the "self-possession" presumably required for any self-conscious narrative of selfhood. Might not Newman's "secret," the passage seems to ask, rather than being "his own," "belong" to whomever is able to interpret it plausibly by placing it in a compelling context?

Even while using this argument to legitimate my own reading of Newman's autobiographical self-disclosure, I am inclined to invoke Michel Foucault's commentary on the complex relationship between secrecy and sexuality, as a caution against the overextension of such a reading:

> This often-stated theme, that sex is outside of discourse and that only the removing of an obstacle, the breaking of a secret, can clear the way leading to it, is precisely what needs to be examined. Does it not partake of the injunction by which discourse is provoked? Is it not with the aim of inciting people to speak of sex that it is made to mirror, at the outer limit of every actual discourse, something akin to a secret whose discovery is imperative, a thing abusively reduced to silence, and at the same time difficult and necessary, dangerous and precious to divulge? We must not forget that by making sex into that which, above all else, had to be confessed, the Christian pastoral always presented it as the disquieting enigma.[17]

In light of Foucault's argument, Newman's silence about his sexuality is as interesting and, in a sense, as revealing as Kingsley's vociferously uttered fantasies about Newman's sexual identity. We ought, of course, to be wary of repeating Kingsley's obsessive practice of eroticizing every aspect of Newman's life and faith. At the same time, it would be unwise to ignore the significance for the Newman-Kingsley controversy — and for the autobiography that resulted from it — of the multiply charged erotic valences of secrecy and disclosure.

Newman, Celibacy, and Same-Sex Desire

The passage in Kingsley's review of Froude's *History* that had been marked, Newman observed, "emphatically, not to say indignantly" by the person who anonymously sent Newman the fateful copy of *Macmillan's Magazine* asserted that "truth, for its own sake, had never been a virtue with the Roman clergy. Father Newman informs us that it need not, and on the whole ought not to be; that cunning is the weapon which Heaven has given to the saints wherewith to withstand the brute male force of the wicked world which marries and is given in marriage. Whether his notion be doctrinally correct or not, it is at least historically so."[18] A close reading reveals that this passage contains more than a straightforward challenge to Newman's honesty. Kingsley sarcastically divides the world into two categories: the "brute male force of the wicked world"—implicitly himself and his fellow "muscular Christians"—on one side, versus the implicitly feminized "saints"—celibate Catholic priests—on the other. In claiming that the institution of marriage was a key indication of "worldliness" and masculinity, moreover, Kingsley calls into question the meaning of Newman's celibacy. While the ostensible task Kingsley set himself was to upbraid Newman for his ambiguous position on truth as a virtue, one effect of his words was to take Newman—and implicitly other Catholic clergymen—to task for their ambiguous status regarding heterosexuality.

Newman's choice of celibacy has been described as "a mystery."[19] Yet it was his celibacy, as much as anything else, that led to his construction as perverse, untrustworthy, and alien in the minds and eyes of "manly" Victorian Christians such as Kingsley. Even "old-fashioned High Churchmen," it has been alleged, would have experienced "horror . . . had they known how far [Newman] took his commitment to celibacy, into emotional difficulties over the marriage of his friends."[20] Of course, celibacy had an established and respected tradition in monastic and priestly life, as well as among many fellows of the Oxbridge colleges. Nothing, however, could have been more alien to the worldly, procreative, and anti-Manichean vision of Christian life espoused by Kingsley, for whom celibacy, as a renunciation of marriage, evoked the stigma of "effeminacy."

It has fairly recently emerged that an important source of Kingsley's hostility to Newman's celibacy was his own deep attachment to his wife, Fanny, and his insecurity about his hold on her affections. Kingsley believed that Fanny's love had operated in his life as a form of quasi-religious salvation. Sheridan Gilley describes Kingsley as "an insecure and emotional young man . . . [who] had been attracted to Newman's ideal of monastic purity, but had violently reacted against it when delivered from it, as he saw it himself, by an ecstatically happy marriage."[21] In a letter of 1864, Kingsley wrote that "there is one thing more glorious and precious than the whole material universe—and that is a woman's love."[22] For Kingsley, therefore, "anything which threatened so intense and pure a bliss [as marriage], the very fulfill-ment of man's nature and therefore indisputably good, was a thing of evil."[23]

Newman, the celibate ex-Tractarian, was viewed by Kingsley as a profound threat to his marital bliss. The Tractarian tendencies of Kingsley's wife were a source of great concern to him; as Susan Chitty writes, "He was anxious to cure her of what he called her Ma-nicheanism, the doctrine that the flesh is evil," which implied "the unpalatable conclusion that the clergy should not marry."[24] Newman himself, moreover, had greatly influenced the religious experience of Fanny Kingsley, and it was his books that she gave to Kingsley when she was trying to convert him back to Christianity.[25] In fact, Newman, for a variety of reasons, was a figure of great personal significance to Kingsley, though it is important to remember that Newman "had no idea of the role he played in Kingsley's inner life. He was so used to sneers about celibacy that he probably did not realize there was any particular significance in Kingsley's linking, quite gratuitously, virility with truth and cunning with virginity."[26]

Several twentieth-century critics have commented on the sexual innuendos contained in Kingsley's words. For example, Una Pope-Hennessy notes that the charge against Newman's honesty carried "an implicit gibe at celibacy," while Robert B. Martin points out that "neither masculinity nor matrimony is mentioned by Newman; they are the invention of Kingsley's memory."[27] G. Egner, the most stal-wart modern defender of Kingsley, has remarked on the "significance in the phraseology in which [Kingsley] couched the original jibe in *Macmillan's Magazine*" and describes the relevant passage as contain-ing an "erotic image . . . entirely of Kingsley's making."[28] These claims are misleading, however, in their suggestion that the "erotic image" contained in the attack was "entirely of Kingsley's making" or "the invention of Kingsley's memory" rather than a reflection of assump-tions about masculine identity and its relation to religious faith that were deeply inscribed in Victorian culture.

Kingsley's phobic response to Newman's celibacy has been ex-plored in more detail by David Hilliard, who argues that Kingsley "abhorred" the "idea of celibacy" as "both contrary to nature and a sin against God," suggesting that the clash between the two should be viewed "as a conflict of fundamentally opposing personalities — the subtle misogamy of Newman versus the robust uxoriousness of

Kingsley."[29] Robert B. Martin justifies his decision to dwell on the "sexual differences" between Newman and Kingsley by arguing that "it is at such deep-seated, less articulate levels of the personality that one must look for an explanation of the deadly enmity which characterized their controversy, enmity which is not fully explained by the overt grounds on which they contested."[30] This account of their inherent "enmity," which at first strikes the reader as somewhat extreme, would seem to be supported by Kingsley's own rhetorical stance in an anti-Roman essay of 1848, in which he wrote that "the married layman and the celibate priest may make truce for a time, but they are foes in grain."[31]

Yet, as Kingsley's youthful admiration of Newman suggests, their conflict sheds light on their sometimes uncanny resemblances, which expose the limitations of the conventional strategy of dividing Newman and Kingsley into opposite and antagonistic camps. As we have seen, Kingsley admitted that he had once been greatly influenced by Newman, and it appears that Kingsley himself had been on the brink of converting to Roman Catholicism. Chitty comments interestingly on this aspect of Kingsley's career: "In later life Kingsley was often to repeat that he knew the attraction of Rome better than any convert, and to Fanny he confided 'There is no middle course. Either deism, or the highest and most monarchical system of Catholicism.' Further proof of his leaning towards not merely Catholicism but monasticism has recently come to light in a letter which Fanny always intended to burn. 'I once formed a strange project, I would have travelled to a monastery in France, gone barefoot into the chapel at matins (midnight) and there confessed every sin of my whole life before the monks and offered my naked body to be scourged by them.' "[32]

There is no evidence of misogamy, identified by Hilliard as a key facet of Newman's personality, in Newman's fleeting reference in the *Apologia* to his celibate state. The attribution of his single life to "the will of God" might be interpreted as a defense against Kingsley's imputations of sexual abnormality, but it is by no means a slight against marriage. One has to turn to other autobiographical sources, therefore, for a clearer sense of where Newman stood on this issue. For instance, toward the end of his account of a near fatal illness in Sicily, Newman writes in terms that suggest he would have found Kingsley's aggressive heterosexuality as offensive—indeed, shocking —as Kingsley considered Newman's resolute celibacy: "All my habits for years, my tendencies, are towards celibacy. I could not take that interest in this world which marriage requires. I am too disgusted with this world—And, above all, call it what one will, I have a repugnance to a clergyman's marrying. I do not say that it is not lawful—I cannot deny the right—but whether a prejudice or not, it shocks me."[33]

Newman's position regarding celibacy is further elaborated in his semiautobiographical novel, set during the high point of the Oxford movement. *Loss and Gain*, first published three years after Newman's own conversion, contains an interesting dialogue between the hero, Charles Reding, and his Oxford tutor, Carlton, on the subject of celibacy:

> "Sheffield fancies I have some sneaking kindness for . . . celibacy myself."
> "Kindness for whom?" said Carlton.
> "Kindness for celibacy."
> There was a pause, and Carlton's face somewhat changed.
> "Oh, my dear good fellow," he said kindly, "so you are one of them; but it will go off."

Reding's predilection for celibacy does not "go off," however, and Carlton subsequently attempts to discover the reasons for his student's perverse inclinations:

> "Tell me, Reding," said Carlton, "for really I don't understand, what are your reasons for admiring what, in truth, is simply an unnatural state?"
> "Don't let us talk more, my dear Carlton," answered Reding. "I shall go on making a fool of myself."

The dialogue continues in this vein, until Reding is eventually persuaded to offer the following defense of his position: "Surely the idea of an Apostle, unmarried, pure, in fast and nakedness, and at length a martyr, is a higher idea than that of one of the old Israelites sitting under his vine and fig-tree, full of temporal goods, and surrounded by sons and grandsons?"[34]

Kingsley, like Carlton, believed celibacy to be an "unnatural state" and cultivated the patrilineal status eschewed by Newman's fictional hero. Kingsley's commitment to the soul-saving virtues of marriage is manifest in his own novels, in which "the manly hero is redeemed and enlisted as a soldier of Christ by his love for a good woman."[35] Reding's tentative confession of his preference for celibacy suggests the extent to which this preference is understood, in the novel, to be indicative both of Catholic tendencies and of other, possibly same-sex, leanings.

Considerable attention has more recently been given to the widely perceived connection in Victorian culture between religiously motivated celibacy and homosexuality. Norman Vance points out, for example, that Kingsley "leaves it open to the reader to suspect" that the Tractarian preference for celibacy "may include this element of unspoken and unspeakable sin." W. S. F. Pickering suggests that "there exist ambiguities in Anglo-Catholicism which relate to the ideal of celibacy for the clergy. Might it not be possible that the adulation of celibacy is seen as a legitimate rationalization of actual or latent homosexuality?" It is certainly also worth bearing in mind Hilliard's point that celibacy was "a religiously sanctioned alternative to marriage" for "young men who were secretly troubled by homosexual feelings that they could not publicly acknowledge."[36] It was the Catholic Church, rather than the Anglican, that insisted on celibacy as a requirement of its priesthood. Newman's motives for gravitating toward Rome, that is, may have included a component of same-sex desire that could not find expression in his own church, outside the close ties of the Oxford movement.

The Anglo-Catholic Oxford movement was characterized by passionate friendships between men that were certainly homoerotic, if not homosexual, in nature. Among the most significant of such friendships was that between Newman and Richard Hurrell Froude, who died in 1836 but whose impact on the sensibility, imagination, and religious beliefs of Newman lasted for long afterward.[37] In the *Apologia*, Newman describes Froude as the friend who "taught me to look with admiration towards the Church of Rome" (35), writing that he "was in the closest and most affectionate friendship with him from about 1829 till his death" (33). Newman goes on to depict the remarkable qualities of his friend in terms guaranteed to affront the "manly" sensibilities of Charles Kingsley: "He was a man of the highest gifts, — so truly many-sided, that it would be presumptuous in me to attempt to describe him, except under those aspects in which he came before me . . . the gentleness and tenderness of nature, the playfulness, the free elastic force and graceful versatility of mind, and the patient winning considerateness in discussion, which endeared him to those to whom he opened his heart" (33).

Of the Newman-Froude friendship, Geoffrey Faber writes that "of all [Newman's] friends Froude filled the deepest place in his heart, and I am not the first to point out that his occasional notions of marrying definitely ceased with the beginning of his real intimacy with Froude."[38] Faber was the first critic of the Oxford movement to dwell at any length on Newman's sexuality and to take seriously the homosexual component of Newman's relationships with men. In the words of Brian Reade, "Since Geoffrey Faber wrote *Oxford Apostles* in 1933, a book in which he disclosed underlying or repressed homosexuality in Newman's make-up, it should have been plausible to see in Newman an archetype of Englishmen passing through homosexual and religious crises during the period."[39]

Other critics, however, have dissented from the attribution of homosexuality to the leaders of the Oxford Movement, particularly when discussing the relationship between Newman and Froude. Piers Brendon, for example, acknowledges that "Newman and Froude were . . . united in an intimate chivalric comradeship which was only broken by the latter's death" but disputes the "suspicions . . . that there was something 'unusual, and even indecent' about their friendship,' " arguing that "such endearments were common to the age in general and were not restricted simply to the Tractarians." Gilley, in his 1990 biography of Newman, argues that "the lack of any overt genital element in his affections makes it grossly inappropriate, despite Geoffrey Faber's suggestion to the contrary, to call them homosexual."[40]

Kingsley's hostility toward Newman was undoubtedly connected to the fact that he himself had as a young man experienced strong emotional attachments to men. One relationship in particular, with his closest undergraduate friend at Cambridge, Charles Mansfield, ranks with the friendship between Newman and Froude—or that between Tennyson and Arthur Hallam—as a poignant example of male bonding hovering on the brink of prohibited same-sex desire. Kingsley described Mansfield as "my first love" and claimed that he was the "first human being, save my mother, I ever met who knew what I meant"; he also eulogized love between men more generally in letters to his wife, on one occasion writing, "There is something awful, spiritual, in man's [*sic*] love for each other. . . . Had you been a

{ *An Unnatural State* }

man we should have been like David and Jonathan."[41] Kingsley had reviewed Tennyson's elegy to Hallam in similarly exultant terms, rejoicing "to find that hero-worship is not yet passed away; that the heart of man still beats young and fresh; that the old tales of David and Jonathan, Damon and Pythias, Socrates and Alcibiades, Shakespeare and his nameless friend, of 'love passing the love of woman' . . . can still blossom out." In this passage, as Alan Sinfield remarks, Kingsley "works hard to assimilate *In Memoriam* to his idea of Christian manliness."[42]

Kingsley, unsurprisingly, was anxious to portray his own close relationships with men as indicative of "manliness" and fought assiduously to suppress any "effeminate" qualities in himself: "Kingsley's own cult of muscular Christianity and his relentless athleticism were part of his deliberate rejection of the feminine in himself: truth and manliness were kindred virtues, and Catholicism had neither."[43] For this very reason the sexual ambiguity of the friendships between the Tractarians caused him distress, prompting him to condemn those (such as Newman) whose same-sex relationships were not, he believed, sufficiently "manly."[44] Kingsley was not unique, however, in imputing sexual abnormality to the Tractarians. Pickering has argued that "there is a positive association between certain social organizations, structures and occupations and homosexuality. Amongst these stands Anglo-Catholicism." Anglo-Catholicism was quite widely associated in the nineteenth-century popular imagination with sexual deviance and "unspeakable" practices, an association that was probably not entirely chimerical, as Hilliard points out: "Despite the traditional teaching of the Christian Church that homosexual behaviour is always sinful, there are grounds for believing that Anglo-Catholic religion . . . has offered emotional and aesthetic satisfactions that have been particularly attractive to members of a stigmatised sexual minority." It is likely that the association between religious deviance and unorthodox sexuality was already emergent at the time Kingsley made his attack on Newman and that even by the 1860s there was "an affinity in outlook between a sexual minority and a minority religious movement within the established church."[45]

This inevitably raises the question of the extent to which characteristics and behavior that would now be described unequivocally as "homosexual" can legitimately be interpreted as such when referring to the mid-Victorian age (before, that is, the specific category of "homosexual" had become available). It has been posited that there was considerably more license for the expression of affection and passion between men in the first half of the nineteenth century than in the second half. According to Jeffrey Weeks, "it was widely accepted in Victorian society that strong relationships between men were normal. . . . Such relationships were deeply ambivalent, however, and became increasingly dangerous for the respectable as awareness of homosexuality grew."[46] J. R. de S. Honey has expressed it, in the context of changing attitudes toward schoolboy friendships in Britain's public schools, "what began to die in later Victorian England were attitudes and spontaneous expressions of love between males which were characteristic of the earlier period."[47] Even by the late 1850s, writers such as Thomas Hughes had to distinguish carefully between "wholesome friendship like that between Tom [Brown] and Arthur" and "the homosexual patronage of the 'small friend system.' "[48]

It may be true, as Hilliard claims, that the close male friendships that characterized the Oxford movement were "not regarded by contemporaries as unnatural, for intimate friendships were common at the time in the exclusively male communities of public school and university." Gilley is undoubtedly correct in asserting that the early Victorian period was "an age which in its innocence was unafraid of strong expressions of love between individuals of the same sex."[49] This innocence was no longer in fashion, however, by the time of Kingsley's attack, when such close male-male bonds were coming to be viewed in a less sympathetic and increasingly sexualized light.

"A Feminine Mind": Newman's Gender Transgression

Like the adverse responses to his celibacy, the perception of Newman as effeminate has pervaded numerous accounts of the controversy with Kingsley. Several contemporary reviewers of the *Apologia* demonstrated the same combination of deep-seated distrust of male "effeminacy" and xenophobic contempt for Roman Catholicism that emerged in Kingsley's own attack on Newman. For example, an unfavorable response to Newman's autobiographical account of his conversion to Catholicism appeared in the *London Quarterly Review* for October 1864: "With Newman, as with people of a commoner sort, feelings, prepossessions, prejudices have determined the creed; his logic has ever been an afterthought and a mere instrument of defence or of persuasion. In this, as in many other respects, Newman's is eminently a feminine mind — poetic, impressible, receptive and reproductive, rather than original and commanding."[50]

The *British Quarterly* built its review of the *Apologia* on a similar set of assumptions about gender, judging that "the instances of perversion to the Romish faith which have come within our knowledge have been nearly all such as may be traced to a womanly weakness in the women, and to the want of a manly courage in the men."[51] The implication here is that a failure of masculinity on Newman's part, whether defined as "womanly weakness" or "want of a manly courage," was directly responsible for his religious "perversion." Kingsley's attribution of perversion to Newman on the basis of his Catholicism and his perceived effeminacy, was, therefore, not atypical, and here we see the various meanings of perversion — religious and sexual — conflated in an utterance worthy of Kingsley himself.

This assumption of Newman's effeminacy has persisted throughout the twentieth century. One of Kingsley's biographers, Susan Chitty, writes that "Newman stood for the things that Kingsley most disliked and feared in himself. He was a Catholic and he was effeminate"; Brenda Colloms refers to Newman as "graceful, delicate and ascetic," qualities clearly intended to evoke Newman's femininity in the context of his relationship with Hurrell Froude. Newman is described by Robert B. Martin as Kingsley's "maidenly opponent," whose "peculiarly feminine qualities" drew comment from eminent Victorians ranging from Matthew Arnold to Aubrey de Vere. Charles F. Harrold, a critic more favorable to Newman, acknowledges that "a certain feminine strain in Newman's complex character repelled [Kingsley]" and, "together with his mistrust of his opponent's argumentative subtlety, led him to say the unpardonable."[52]

Most of Newman's defenders, however, resist the attribution of "effeminacy" to their subject, but in a way that actually reinforces rather than challenges such gender stereotyping. Martin Svaglic, editor of the definitive modern edition of the *Apologia*, for example, writing in his introduction to the work that "Newman was almost as much influenced by the 'bright and beautiful' Hurrell Froude as Tennyson, say, was by Hallam," finds it necessary to add that "like Tennyson, Newman had a well-attested masculine as well as a feminine side to his character." The campaign to emphasize the "masculine" Newman is continued in Ian Ker's major biography of 1988, in which he writes: "The 'feminine' side of Newman's character has been much emphasized; without in any way denying it, I have endeavoured to stress also the other highly 'masculine' side of his temperament, which showed itself in an astonishing resilience and uncompromising toughness in the face of adversity, as well as in the kind of resourceful practicality one associates with the man of action rather than the thinker." [53]

These approaches obviously fail to consider that the more interesting problem might be to analyze the *division* itself between "masculine" and "feminine" in the Newman-Kingsley controversy, in order to question the unqualified attribution of "typical" gender qualities to each participant, rather than to fix Newman's and Kingsley's positions on one side or the other of the "great divide." More recent work in gender studies has emphasized the extent to which bodily mannerisms, styles of dress, and patterns of speech are not intrinsically masculine or feminine but have to be read as such in terms of cultural codes of gender identity and that therefore, in the words of Judith Butler, "gender is a kind of persistent impersonation that passes as the real." [54] An important assumption of Butler's approach is that gender, far from being merely an attribute or expression of a preexisting identity, is actually productive of that identity: "There is no volitional subject behind the mime who decides, as it were, which gender it will be today. On the contrary, the very possibility of becoming a viable subject requires that a certain gender mime be already underway. . . . In this sense, gender is not a performance that a prior subject elects to do, but gender is *performative* in the sense that it constitutes as an effect the very subject it appears to express." [55]

Equally important, however, the kinds of "impersonations" or "performances" that attain the status of highly valorized or, alternatively, systematically oppressed and stigmatized gender roles are both politically contested and historically and culturally variable. Several important studies have started from this premise, examining the social construction of gender in a number of different settings and periods to show how an understanding of the culturally produced status of masculinity and femininity can be used to decipher and problematize apparently "natural" identities, relations, and institutions. Julia Epstein and Kristina Straub, for example, define gender as

{ *An Unnatural State* }

what we make of sex on a daily basis, how we deploy our embodiedness and our multivalent sexualities in order to construct ourselves in relation to the classifications of male and female. This deployment does not arise from any "natural" or scientifically representable idea of the body as a physical object, nor is it individually negotiable. . . . Sex/gender systems, as we understand them, are historically and culturally specific arrogations of the human body for ideological purposes. In sex/gender systems, physiology, anatomy, and body codes (clothing, cosmetics, behaviors, miens, affective and sexual object choices) are taken over by institutions that use bodily difference to define and to coerce gender identity.[56]

This collapsing of sexuality and gender into a single "system" for analytical purposes has, unsurprisingly, tended to provoke as many questions as it resolves, and there has been much debate during the 1990s about the exact relation between such critical analyses of the construction of gender and work that focuses on the construction and organization of sexual identities.

Eve Kosofsky Sedgwick, for example, makes a powerful case for the conceptual separation of gender and sexuality as analytic categories, primarily because to assume an equivalence between these categories tends to privilege the heterosexual matrix of society that is oppressive to members of sexual minorities: "Although many gender-based forms of analysis do involve accounts, sometimes fairly rich ones, of intragender behaviors and relations, the ultimate definitional appeal in any gender-based analysis must necessarily be to the diacritical frontier between different genders. This gives heterosocial and heterosexual relations a conceptual privilege of incalculable consequence." While Sedgwick believes that "gender-based analysis can never be dispensed with in even the most purely intragender context," she nonetheless asserts the likelihood that "the analytic bite of a purely gender-based account will grow less incisive and direct as the distance of its subject from a social interface between different genders increases" and that, therefore, it is "unrealistic to expect a close, textured analysis of same-sex relations through an optic calibrated in the first place to the coarser stigmata of gender difference."[57]

Sedgwick's argument is particularly important for the controversy under scrutiny in this chapter, which featured intense antagonisms and equally intense affectional ties that occurred almost exclusively "between men." Difference, as it will be read through the "optic" of gender, can be conceived of less as a "difference between" (intergender) than as a "difference within" (intragender): precisely the kind of situation that, for Sedgwick, requires an account focusing on sexuality—specifically, same-sex relations—rather than on gender as such. Arguably, however, the explosive potential of gender-role dissidence is increased rather than diminished when confined to members of what is purportedly the "same" gender. If the "masculine" subject, in other words, is interpellated in part by means of an intense resistance and hostility toward the "feminine," then the violence of its self-regulating mechanisms is likely to be all the more visible when the very "femininity" that is constructed as its "perverse" opposite appears in men.

It is extremely difficult, of course, to separate the strands of gender and sexual anxieties invoked by the attacks on Newman for his effeminacy. It has been argued, for example, that "for Kingsley 'effeminate,' which he so frequently used in describing Roman Catholicism, had an old-fashioned meaning which included self-indulgence and lack of public spirit, as well as the modern significance of the word"; but "when he applied it to Newman . . . the term may have had a more specifically sexual connotation."[58] Richard Dellamora discusses this "sexual connotation" of effeminacy in his groundbreaking study of Victorian aestheticism and male homosexuality, pointing out that "'effeminacy' as a term of personal abuse often connotes male-male desire, a threat of deviance that seems to haunt gentlemen should they become too gentle, refined, or glamorous."[59] It is important to note that Kingsley's charge of effeminacy against Newman might have contained this imputation of homosexuality. Indeed, the same conclusion is reached by Hilliard in the specific context of the Oxford movement, in which Newman first attained prominence: "The charge of effeminacy—the usual nineteenth-century caricature of male homosexuality—stuck to the successors of the Tractarians."[60]

Alan Sinfield and Linda Dowling, however, suggest a greater complexity to Victorian uses and perceptions of "effeminacy." For Sinfield, the charge of "effeminacy" was not, before the trials of Oscar Wilde, usually taken as an indication of sexual deviance or perversion. Only when Wilde's conviction for "acts of gross indecency" established an indelible link between the effeminate, decadent "aes-

{ *An Unnatural State* }

thete" and the perverse sexual actor or "sodomite," Sinfield claims, did effeminacy and homosexuality become inseparable in the cultural imagination. Hence, "the function of effeminacy, as a concept, is to police sexual categories, keeping them pure." For Dowling, the roots of "effeminacy" go back to the classical republican discourse of ancient Greece, where it was used to denote a failure to live up to the strict requirements of the masculine code in civic society. Interestingly, Dowling cites Kingsley's anti-Catholic phobia as a case in point, arguing that "when Kingsley protests that the age is 'an effeminate one' . . . we instantly recognize the old language of classical republicanism. . . . In the same way, we understand that Kingsley's indignation at the 'sleek passionless men' brought forth from Anglo- and Roman Catholicism is nothing other than the ancient voice of civic alarm as it confronts the approach of dangers threatening the nation at its most fundamental level as a polity." [61]

For both these critics, therefore, the association of effeminacy and homosexuality before the fin de siècle is improbable. And yet one cannot ignore the evidence that Kingsley, in his accusations of effeminacy against Newman and the Tractarians, was invoking a specifically sexual anxiety and responding to a threat to his own status as a married clergyman. In 1851, Kingsley had written a letter in which he gave furious vent to his prejudices against the "effeminacy" he found in the leaders of the Oxford movement, Newman being uppermost in his mind: "In . . . all that school, there is an element of foppery—even in dress and manner; a fastidious, maundering die-away effeminacy, which is mistaken for purity and refinement; and I confess myself unable to cope with it, so alluring is it to the minds of an effeminate and luxurious aristocracy." [62] Interestingly, it is the "dress and manner" of Newman and his colleagues—crucial indicators of gendered identity—that Kingsley here declares himself "unable to cope with." Just as significantly, Kingsley associates effeminacy with the "aristocracy," revealing the extent to which his own notion of "manliness" was a middle-class one defined against the image of upper-class idleness. Newman and the other Tractarians were decried because they failed to enact the norms of middle-class, masculine behavior. It is their perceived "effeminacy," even more than the nature of their religious beliefs, that here threatens the stability of Kingsley's masculine ideal and provokes an outburst which in some ways rehearses the terms of his later and more public diatribe against Newman.

For instance, in his pamphlet of 1864, Kingsley evoked the scene of Newman's preaching in terms suggesting a malevolent, emasculating influence: "I found him, by a strange perversion of Scripture, insinuating that St. Paul's conduct and manner were such as naturally to bring down on him the reputation of being a crafty deceiver. . . . I found him telling Christians that they will always seem 'artificial,' and 'wanting in openness and manliness'; that they will always be 'a mystery' to the world, and that the world will always think them rogues." Kingsley here establishes a link between Newman's "perversion of Scripture" and the implication that he is "wanting in . . . manliness" and is likely to contaminate his listeners with the same deplorable condition. This begins to shed some light on the nature of the "perversion" that Kingsley imagined Newman to be inflicting on his audience of "fanatic and hot-headed young men, who hung over his every word."[63]

⁂

"In the Service of the Enemy": Newman's "Polluting" Influence

Newman's magnetic influence in the pulpit was legendary in the Victorian age. The most famous account of his spellbinding gifts as a preacher is perhaps that by Matthew Arnold: "Oxford has more criticism now, more knowledge, more light; but such voices as those of our youth it has no longer. . . . Newman . . . was preaching in St Mary's pulpit every Sunday. . . . Who could resist the charm of that spiritual apparition, gliding in the dim afternoon light through the aisles of St Mary's, rising into the pulpit, and then, in the most entrancing of voices, breaking the silence with words and thoughts which were a religious music — subtle, sweet, mournful?"[64] One interesting fact that emerged from the conflict was that Kingsley himself, as a young man, had come under Newman's "entrancing" influence. Claiming privately to have "a score of more than twenty years to pay" and that his pamphlet was "an instalment of it,"[65] Kingsley singled out one particular sermon of Newman's — "Wisdom and Innocence," preached in 1844 shortly before his conversion to Catholicism — as the source of his impression of Newman's dishonesty, remarking that "it was in consequence of that Sermon, that I finally shook off the strong influence which your writings exerted on me; and for much of which I still owe you a deep debt of gratitude." [66]

That Kingsley's recollections of Newman's influence were in his mind at the time of the controversy indicates the importance of the role Newman had played as a teacher—or, as Kingsley saw it, corrupter—of young men. Although Kingsley claimed to find many of Newman's writings objectionable, had Newman never preached the sermon "Wisdom and Innocence," it is extremely unlikely that Kingsley would have attacked him as virulently as he did. Indeed, the conflict soon became a question of "Whether Dr. Newman Teaches That Truth Is No Virtue," [67] so that attention to Newman's damaging (in the eyes of Kingsley) influence as a teacher and preacher is no less important than an analysis of sexual and gender identities for an understanding of the cultural significance of the controversy.

Mary Douglas, the English social anthropologist, has developed a theory of human "pollution" that has interesting implications for this aspect of the Newman-Kingsley controversy. According to Douglas, "a polluting person is always in the wrong. He has developed some wrong condition or simply crossed some line which should not have been crossed and this displacement unleashes danger for someone." [68] Like the representatives of the sacred, then, the polluting person is contagious, and it is clear that at the time of the debate with Kingsley, Newman had long been identified as a polluting person—one likely to contaminate the minds of others (especially the young) with his own dangerous and "perverted" ideas, beliefs, and indeterminacies. Douglas points out that "our pollution behaviour is the reaction which condemns any object or idea likely to confuse or contradict cherished classifications," and Newman's perceived sexual ambiguity, no less than his conversion to Catholicism, was a source of just such distress and confusion to Kingsley.[69]

Newman himself acknowledged the widespread alarm over his polluting influence in the *Apologia*, in which he wrote with sarcastic resentment of the "calumny" spread against him that "I was actually in the service of the enemy. I had forsooth been already received into the Catholic Church, and was rearing at Littlemore a nest of Papists, who, like me, were to take the Anglican oaths which they disbelieved, by virtue of a dispensation from Rome, and thus in due time were to bring over to that unprincipled Church great numbers of the Anglican Clergy and Laity" (162). Nobody knew better than Newman the great sensitivity of his position of trust at Oxford and Littlemore. He had run afoul of the provost of Oriel College, Edward Hawkins, when, as a tutor, he had insisted that he should have primary responsibility for and influence over his own select group of pupils.[70] The result of the conflict was that Newman and his fellow tutors, Hurrell Froude and Robert Wilberforce, were banned from receiving students, and Newman sought an alternative outlet for his energies by producing the tracts. Kingsley, of course, went far beyond Hawkins's objections to Newman's influence, implying that Newman had egregiously abused his position of trust in a variety of largely unspecified ways, all, however, characterized by papist "duplicity" and "secrecy."

A crucial part of his self-defense, as Newman quickly came to realize, was to respond to the belief spread by Kingsley "that I was secretly a Catholic when I was openly professing to be a clergyman of the Established Church" (387). As he went on to explain at greater length, "There has been a general feeling that I was for years where I had no right to be; that I was a 'Romanist' in Protestant livery and service; that I was doing the work of a hostile Church in the bosom of the English Establishment, and knew it, or ought to have known it" (403). In a letter to W. J. Copeland, dated 31 March 1864, Newman expressed his sense of the force that this accusation would have on the public: "The whole strength of what [Kingsley] says, as directed rhetorically to the popular mind, lies in the antecedent prejudice that I was a Papist while I was an Anglican."[71] Newman's alleged secretiveness, therefore, was an important source of Kingsley's and the public's distrust of him.[72]

It was also the seductiveness of Newman's preaching that made him dangerous, according to Kingsley, allowing him to operate clandestinely as a perverter of Anglican youth. The scene of Newman's sermonizing is vividly evoked by Kingsley in terms of quasi-sexual seduction and penetration: "I know that men used to suspect Dr. Newman—I have been inclined to do so myself—of writing a whole sermon, not for the sake of the text or of the matter, but for the sake of one single passing hint—one phrase, one epithet, one little barbed arrow which, as he swept magnificently past on the stream of his calm eloquence, seemingly unconscious of all presences, save those unseen, he delivered unheeded, as with his finger-tip, to the very heart of an initiated hearer, never to be withdrawn again."[73] How, Kingsley went on to ask, could anyone be expected to believe that Newman "did not foresee that the natural result of the sermon on the minds of his disciples would be, to make them suspect that truth was not a virtue for its own sake, but only for the sake of the spread of 'catholic opinions' "?: "All England stood round in those days, and saw that this would be the outcome of Dr. Newman's teaching. . . . And, as a fact, his teaching had this outcome. Whatever else it did, it did this. In proportion as young men absorbed it into themselves, it injured their straightforwardness and truthfulness. The fact is notorious to all England. It spread misery and shame into many an English home."[74]

What did Kingsley mean, exactly, by the "misery and shame" for which Newman was allegedly responsible? Beneath the panicky aggressiveness of his tone lurks the message that Newman was to blame not only for the "spread of 'catholic opinions'" that had resulted in numerous conversions to Rome in England since the days of the Oxford movement but also for a range of other, unspecified evils. Kingsley was apparently scapegoating Newman both for conversions to Catholicism, such as that of Kingsley's sister-in-law Charlotte, who had remained a Catholic until her marriage to J. A. Froude,[75] as well as for the seductive allure of another, related "perversion," homosexuality, for which Kingsley's younger brother Henry was apparently sent down from Oxford.[76] Kingsley, whose vivid imagination conflated these "twin evils" to which members of his own family had fallen prey and by both of which he himself had been tempted, responded by constructing Newman as a malevolent and treacherous despoiler of youth — a teacher of quasi-Socratic seductiveness and influence. Kingsley was indeed, as Newman claimed, "furiously carried away by his feelings" (394). Yet these feelings, far from being Kingsley's alone, represented a widespread cultural anxiety about the shifting valences of religious faith and sexual identity. The two types of "perversion," religious and sexual, were inseparable — indeed, mutually reinforcing — for others besides Kingsley, who "had . . . fused into an imaginatively coherent whole a range of classic Victorian attitudes, against which Newman stood for a false sacerdotal authority in its most insidiously attractive form."[77]

To understand fully the nature of Newman's transgression, therefore, we have to recall the extent to which his religious history was interpreted through the lens of a complex web of anxieties that found its most vociferous, but by no means its only, spokesperson in Charles Kingsley. It was a combination of Kingsley's own personal phobias and a more broadly defined, *cultural* (though no less paranoid) conflation of marginalized social categories and stigmatized identities that constructed the grotesque caricature aptly described by one writer as the "great pervert"[78] and no less astutely characterized by Newman himself as a "phantom . . . which gibbers instead of me" (406). It remains to consider the extent to which this "phantom" was "extinguished," as was clearly Newman's purpose, by the publication and reception of the *Apologia*.

"An Extreme Trial": Victorian Manliness and Newman's Self-Defense

From the earliest stages of his controversy with Kingsley, Newman had sought to appropriate some of the powerful terminology of his aggressor to refute the charge of secrecy and establish his own credibility, a task that involved a substantial reversal of fortune for each writer. For, in the words of Wilfrid Ward, "Kingsley had taken up the position of the manly Englishman, of the advocate of chivalrous generosity, against the shifty Papist, the 'serpentine' dealer in 'cunning and sleight-of-hand logic.'" Newman's goal, therefore, must be to drive "his opponent from the vantage ground . . . transferring to Kingsley the reproach of a disingenuousness which sought to poison the minds of the public and divest their gaze from the actual issue."[79] In particular, the cherished concept of manliness would be deployed and indeed redefined in Newman's autobiography.

In his first letter of protest to Alexander Macmillan, therefore, Newman issued a challenge that appropriately countered the insinuations of Kingsley's attack on him by suggesting that Kingsley's masculinity, rather than his own, was in question: "I look on mainly as a spectator, and shall praise or blame, according to my best judgment, as I see what they do. Not that, in so acting, I am implying a doubt of all that you tell me of them; but 'handsome is, that handsome does.' If they set about proving their point, or, should they find that impossible, if they say so, in either case I shall call them *men*."[80]

Kingsley was not slow to respond to the challenge contained in Newman's letter, agreeing that "the course which you demand of me,

is the only course fit for a gentleman." Yet, within a week, he was refusing to strengthen his public apology to Newman, having recourse
to the same quasi-chivalric language: "I do not think it probable that
the good sense and honesty of the British Public will misinterpret my
apology, in the way in which you expect. . . . I have done as much
as one English gentleman can expect from another." Kingsley's rather
strained public pose of generosity to Newman was a recurring feature
of the debate and was clearly intended to make Kingsley himself appear at once superior and noble. He began his pamphlet by observing
that "I have declared Dr. Newman to have been an honest man up to
the 1st of February, 1864. It was, as I shall show, only Dr. Newman's
fault that I ever thought him to be anything else. It depends entirely
on Dr. Newman whether he shall sustain the reputation which he has
so recently acquired."[81]

If Kingsley thought that he would succeed in intimidating Newman with this attempted posture of magnanimity, however, he was
very much mistaken. In fact, it provoked Newman's most withering blast of sarcasm: "What a princely mind! How loyal to his rash
promise, how delicate towards the subject of it, how conscientious
in his interpretation of it!" (392). Kingsley's self-appointed role as
"gentleman" was under attack, and Newman reinforced his effort to
undermine it by again appropriating the gendered terminology, protesting against "this unmanly attempt of his, in his concluding pages,
to cut the ground from under my feet; — to poison by anticipation
the public mind against me, John Henry Newman, and to infuse into
the imaginations of my readers, suspicion and mistrust of every thing
that I may say in reply to him" (395). Newman here accused Kingsley
of precisely the kind of "unmanly" behavior and polluting influence
with which he himself was charged — once more turning the tables
on his antagonist. Not only did Newman insist on his own manly
"openness," but he also took Kingsley to task for being underhanded
himself. He did so, moreover, in terms evocative of the eroticized
nature of Kingsley's attack: "Now I ask, Why could not Mr Kingsley
be open? . . . Why must he insinuate, question, imply, and use sneering and irony, as if longing to touch a forbidden fruit, which still he
was afraid would burn his fingers, if he did so?" (392).

This struggle to implicate each other in "unmanly" conduct might
have continued indefinitely, had not Newman realized that the ex-

tent of the public prejudice against him meant that he would have to go beyond defending himself against an incriminating interpretation of one sermon. Consequently, Newman soon decided to channel his sense of outrage into a complete narrative in which he would offer a confessional self-defense: "I recognized what I had to do, though I shrank from both the task and the exposure which it would entail. I must, I said, give the true key to my whole life: I must show what I am that it may be seen what I am not. . . . I wish to be known as a living man, and not as a scarecrow which is dressed up in my clothes" (406).

Newman's "living man" serves as the counter to the "phantom" and the "scarecrow" of Kingsley's representation of him, as well as an antidote to the effeminate, "shifty" papist of the popular imagination—a caricature fed by commonly held English prejudices against everything connected with the Roman church. The qualities of this "living man," vividly dramatized in the *Apologia*, are precisely the opposite of the characteristics attributed to him by Kingsley. In his autobiography, Newman sought to be open, frank, honest, and "English."

In fact, one of Newman's key strategies in writing the *Apologia* was to convince his readers of his essential "Englishness." This was an especially important task because, as we have seen, Kingsley had suggested that Newman had in effect betrayed his country by converting to Rome. Kingsley was not alone in detecting a serious act of treason in Newman's change of religious faith. As one contemporary critic of the *Apologia* expressed it, "Converts, or perverts, to use an ugly if not offensive neologism, have always something to account for; and accusations of treason, insincerity, and double dealing in all great changes of opinion, whether political or religious, are so easily made, and with such difficulty met, that it requires something more than the surface improbability of interested motives in any given case to account for, and still more to justify, what vulgar minds will always brand as an act of desertion." [82] The particular resonance of this assertion can be more clearly understood when one remembers that Newman had begun his career within the Anglican Church, had then tried (in *Tract 90*) to prove that the Thirty-Nine Articles of the Church of England (to which all members of both universities had to subscribe) were compatible with Roman theology, and finally came to believe (and argue) that Anglicanism was an illegitimate offshoot (or corruption) of Roman Catholicism. Newman, that is, had apparently attempted to subvert the Anglican Church—which Kingsley reminded his audience was historically inseparable from the English nation—from within. In his second pamphlet, entitled "True Mode of Meeting Mr Kingsley," Newman responded by attempting to win over his readers with a carefully worded evocation of shared national identity: "Still more confident am I of such eventual acquittal, seeing that my judges are my own countrymen. I think, indeed, Englishmen the most suspicious and touchy of mankind; I think them unreasonable and unjust in their seasons of excitement; but I had rather be an Englishman (as in fact I am) than belong to any other race under heaven. They are as generous, as they are hasty and burly; and their repentance for their injustice is greater than their sin" (397). Newman here gives his audience an opportunity to forgive him for having abandoned the national church. He is able to upbraid the English for their weaknesses without being susceptible to accusations of treason, for he is careful to include himself in the category under criticism. In fact, this painstaking construction of a "common ground" between himself and his reader is an essential component of Newman's project of becoming "known as a living man" rather than as "a phantom."

The abstract logic of Newman's arguments and the specific points against which he defended himself were far less important, for his success in the controversy, than the tone and style in which he wrote. Newman frequently foregrounded the struggle of self-disclosure and the pain of recollection, in terms emphasizing his "manly" qualities of courage and resilience. Yet, equally important, he stressed his vulnerability, the human capacity for suffering, bringing into view the actual situation of writing and the difficulty of his externally induced act of self-defense:

Who can suddenly gird himself to a new and anxious undertaking, which he might be able indeed to perform well, were full and calm leisure allowed him to look through every thing that he had written, whether in published works or private letters? yet again, granting that calm contemplation of the past, in itself so desirable, who could afford to be leisurely and deliberate, while he practices on himself a cruel operation, the ripping up of old griefs, and the venturing again upon the "infandum dolorem" of years, in which the stars of this lower heaven were one by one going out? I could not in cool blood, nor except upon the imperious call of duty, attempt what I have set myself to do. It is both to head and heart an extreme trial. [90–91]

Without forsaking humility, Newman seeks to portray himself as a kind of hero in his autobiographical undertaking. Indeed, there is a clear comparison being established with Virgil's Aeneas, whose words Newman quotes in his own text. Newman's identification with the Trojan hero emphasizes both the valor and the tragedy of his own situation. Aeneas's heroism derives, particularly in this context, from the courage of the storyteller who must endure not only the doing of great deeds but also the (re)telling of them:

> The room fell silent, and all eyes were on him,
> As Father Aeneas from his high couch began:
> "Sorrow too deep to tell, your majesty,
> You order me to feel and tell once more:
> How the Danaans leveled in the dust
> The splendor of our mourned-forever kingdom —
> Heartbreaking things I saw with my own eyes
> And was myself a part of. Who could tell them,
> Even a Myrmidon or Dolopian
> Or ruffian of Ulysses, without tears?
>
> .   .   .   .
>
> But if so great desire
> Moves you to hear the tale of our disasters,
> Briefly recalled, the final throes of Troy,
> However I may shudder at the memory
> And shrink again in grief, let me begin." [83]

According to Gilley, "Newman had made himself both the Virgil and the Aeneas of the drama [of the Oxford movement], its epic poet and its hero." [84] The act of narration for Newman, as for Aeneas whose words he borrows, was indeed a "cruel operation," involving the pain of recollecting distressing events. Yet, in both cases, the painful task of the narrator is exploited to gain the sympathy and interest of the audience. The comparison thereby functions to "masculinize" Newman as a heroic figure who is not ashamed to reveal his wounds but who by no means wishes to boast of them.

Newman goes on to describe the numerous sacrifices he had made as a result of his conversion. It may seem extraordinary, in retrospect, that Newman had to demonstrate that his loss was greater than his gain, in terms of worldly success and influence, as a result of converting to Rome. Yet, it is reported that his successor at Littlemore attributed Newman's departure to an "intense unconscious desire for power," and there were many others who "were so sure that Catholicism was a system of secret power that it did not occur to them that in becoming a Catholic in 1845, Newman was giving up power rather than gaining it."[85] Newman therefore quotes in the *Apologia* from correspondence written shortly before his conversion to assure his readers of the real state of affairs: "And then, how much I am giving up in so many ways! and to me sacrifices irreparable, not only from my age, when people hate changing, but from my especial love of old associations and the pleasures of memory. Nor am I conscious of any feeling, enthusiastic or heroic, of pleasure in the sacrifice; I have nothing to support me here" (206).

In confirmation that Newman had suffered in a "worldly" sense from his conversion, there was the loss of his beloved Oxford, which he finally left a few months after his conversion to Catholicism. The description of his departure is beautifully crafted, and the pathos of its depiction of a tragic exile must surely have moved all but the most skeptical of Anglican hearts to pity: "Trinity had never been unkind to me. There used to be much snap-dragon growing on the walls opposite my freshman's rooms there, and I had for years taken it as the emblem of my own perpetual residence even unto death in my University. On the morning of the 23rd [February 1846] I left the Observatory. I have never seen Oxford since, excepting its spires, as they are seen from the railway" (213). Newman presents his departure from Oxford as one of the turning points of his life. Yet his emphasis is on the past he had renounced, rather than on the future he was embracing. The somber end of Newman's Oxford career, then, signaled the real beginning of his marginalized life as a Catholic. Yet this marginality to the stage of public life that Newman had occupied in the 1840s was itself brought to an end by the confessional account of those years.

"Having Two Minds": Contemporary
Reactions to the *Apologia*

Despite the sacrifices that it entailed, joining the Catholic church was later described by Newman as an experience "like coming into port after a rough sea" (214). The phrase might be applied equally to Newman's victory in the contest with Kingsley. From the start it was obvious to most of the contemporary followers of the dispute that, as far as combative skills of rhetoric were concerned, the Anglican clergyman was entirely out of his depth. As *Blackwood's Magazine* expressed it: "Mr Kingsley's attack upon Dr Newman was not only cruel, it was injudicious. He could scarcely expect that it would fail to provoke retort; and self-conceit must be in him even stronger than we take it to be, if he ever for a moment anticipated other issue than defeat from a controversy entered into so rashly and on such grounds." [86]

Most of Newman's contemporaries, in fact, believed that he had decisively cleared his name against Kingsley's specific accusations with the publication of his autobiography. R. H. Hutton, for example, who had previously been forthcoming as a supporter of Kingsley's, wrote in the *Spectator* that "we can scarcely conceive that Mr Kingsley himself can read this apology without the profoundest personal conviction of the stedfast [*sic*] uprightness and true simplicity of Dr Newman's theological career. . . . [I]t would be mere dulness of nature not to recognize freely the noble truthfulness and almost childlike candour of the autobiographic sketch now before us." [87]

Addressing the problem of Newman's long delay in converting from Anglicanism to Catholicism, which had been interpreted by Kingsley as evidence of his "secret" Catholicism, the *Times* wrote in Newman's support, "It is a situation which involves many tender considerations, and nice estimates, and intricate comparisons of conflicting duties; but it is a situation which a person may be in without dishonesty, and which he may carry out without dishonesty; and Dr Newman can claim with perfect right a decisive verdict in his favour on this question." [88] This "decisive verdict" has been echoed by Newman's twentieth-century supporters: "The acclaim of the Press . . . testified to a public opinion completely conquered," wrote Ward, the first major biographer of Newman, concluding that "it was a victory." [89] Svaglic states confidently that "rarely has any prophecy been more quickly fulfilled than Newman's assurance that he would vanquish, not his accuser, but his judges."[90]

Yet the decision in Newman's favor was actually far from unanimous. Several reviewers, particularly from the ecclesiastic press, remained skeptical about Newman's honesty and insistent about his "perversion." The *American Quarterly Church Review*, for example, alleged that Newman "exhibits . . . one of the most remarkable instances of the perversity of intellectual vision, which is recorded in the annals of mind" and went on to find "a vicious and stifling atmosphere of bad faith, or perverse moral and intellectual perception, which oppresses us, as we make our way through these avowals of Dr N."[91] The *Theological Review*, in an effort to distinguish its partial vindication of Newman's life from its utter condemnation of Roman Catholicism as a religion, argued that Newman's self-defense had "produce[d] a general impression prejudicial if not to Dr Newman's personal veracity, yet to the truthfulness and honesty of the theological and ecclesiastical system of which he now professes himself the servant."[92]

Unsurprisingly, the more critical responses invoked once again the ambiguity of Newman's gender identity and sought to reinforce its connection with his religious indeterminacy. The *Christian Remembrancer*, for example, portraying Newman's complex religious history in terms suggestive of the case history of a split personality, wrote that "Dr Newman . . . throws a light upon a quality of which every experience knows something, and which ordinarily meets with little indulgence, the quality — so to call it — of having two minds. . . . We can only understand such people by *believing* them; but, honest as we may know them to be, there are things we see in them which they do not. They can only express themselves in contradictions: their words contradict their actions — one time contradicts another; all in perfect good faith, because they have two selves; but one self may be the dominant one, without their knowing it."[93] In his autobiography, Newman had sought to establish the unity of his life and the basic continuity of his religious opinions, despite the evidence to the contrary provided by his conversion to Rome. Yet some, as this review attests, continued to perceive Newman in terms of Kingsley's accusations of duplicity and inconsistency — qualities stereotypically associated in Victorian culture with the feminine.

Newman's delayed conversion was characterized more explicitly as a failure of masculinity by *Macmillan's Magazine*, which evoked a scenario in which the Catholic Church wooed the feminized Newman: "If we are to express our own feeling about Dr Newman's demeanour at the final crisis . . . we cannot for a moment associate it with an idea of artifice or imposture. It seems to us to resemble nothing so much as the self-contradictions sometimes exhibited by persons of the gentler sex (and Dr Newman is, in some respects, very feminine), when they really can't, for the life of them, make up their minds whether their 'heart' tells them to marry."[94] Curiously, the stereotyped analogy was reversed in *Fraser's Magazine*, which compared Newman, in his "perverse" espousal of Catholicism, with "a man who, having been infatuated by a woman neither young, lovely, nor virtuous, marries her at the expense of destroying all his prospects in life, and of throwing up all his connexions, and who then exhausts every resource of his mind in proving that she combines, in ideal perfection, eternal youth, perfect beauty, and every moral and mental grace which could adorn such a person."[95] The irony of comparing the celibate, misogamous Newman with an uxorious husband appears to have escaped the reviewer. Although most readers of the *Apologia* were ready to decide in favor of Newman in his specific conflict with Kingsley and many felt that his honesty had been vindicated by his self-defense, some remained distrustful and uneasy concerning his "long continued waverings between England and Rome"; and these "waverings" were themselves variously interpreted as signs of his "perversity" and "effeminacy."[96]

As far as the literary status of Newman's autobiography is concerned, however, the verdict has indeed been decisive in its favor. Immediately following its serial publication in 1864, the *Apologia* was judged to be a classic work of autobiographical writing and has, since then, been republished in numerous editions and become firmly established as one of the major works of Victorian prose. That it continues to maintain the high status accorded to it in the nineteenth century is amply attested by the extensive body of criticism that has grown in response to its textual challenges and rhetorical complexity. One result of this elevated canonical status, unfortunately, is that many of the ideological—as distinct from exclusively literary—aspects of the autobiography have in effect been ignored in criticism of the work.

This is especially the case with respect to the controversy's implications for our understanding of Victorian gender and sexual identities. These meanings are fully dependent on the thorough contextualization of the *Apologia* in the controversy that led to its initial publication and cannot be deciphered by means of a purely formalist or "literary" critique. Although it is commonplace for critics of the *Apologia* to make passing reference to the fact that Newman's autobiography was written in response to an attack on the author's honesty by Charles Kingsley, few have examined the sexualized language employed by Kingsley in his attack or explored the ways in which that language bespoke larger concerns and preoccupations in Victorian society. The summary of the background to the conflict is, in most critical accounts, all too evidently a preamble to the task of examining the autobiography as a self-contained narrative and "classic" of autobiographical writing.

One's skepticism about this critical emphasis on the autonomy of the text and the individual brilliance of its author, to the exclusion of a detailed analysis of the cultural context, is not lessened by the fact that it so closely replicates Newman's own peremptory gesture of erasing Kingsley from the narrative as far as possible: "And now I am in a train of thought higher and more serene than any which slanders can disturb. Away with you, Mr Kingsley, and fly into space. Your name shall occur again as little as I can help, in the course of these pages. I shall henceforth occupy myself not with you, but with your charges" (396).[97] In the second edition of 1865—which did not contain the polemical pamphlets that formed the first two installments of the *Apologia* of 1864—even Kingsley's "charges" had been reduced to a few prefatory lines, while Newman revealed his reluctance to acknowledge the controversy as a source of his autobiography: "Did I consult indeed my own impulses, I should do my best simply to wipe out of my Volume, and consign to oblivion, every trace of the circumstances to which it is to be ascribed" (1). Yet even Newman had to concede that some knowledge of the origins of his autobiographical statement was essential for its understanding: "Its original title of 'Apologia' is too exactly borne out by its matter and structure, and these again are too suggestive of correlative circumstances, and those circumstances are of too grave a character, to allow of my indulging so natural a wish" (1).

What has been lost by the exclusion of Charles Kingsley from the history of the *Apologia* is an adequate sense of how dramatically

Newman came into conflict with cultural assumptions and prejudices about religious faith, gender, and sexuality of which Kingsley, if not the most subtle or politic, was certainly among the most zealous and influential of exponents. This is not to suggest that Kingsley should be viewed (however convenient this might be) as a "typical" Victorian, an approach condemned by Owen Chadwick, who claims, with some justification, that "anyone [who] thinks that the ordinary run of Victorian middle-class Englishmen were like Kingsley . . . has not begun to understand the Victorian age." [98] One is, however, justified in taking Kingsley's views on religious faith, sexual behavior, and gender roles (and the "manliness" that, for him, required the enactment of religious, gender, *and* sexual norms) as more broadly *representative* of mainstream British society, at the time of their conflict, than were Newman's.

In *Masculine Desire*, Dellamora draws attention to "the public contest over the meaning of masculinity that takes place in the press and courts" during the homosexual scandals in England during the 1890s. [99] An implication of my argument in this chapter is that the public conflict between Newman and Kingsley—a controversy that culminated in but is by no means reducible to the *Apologia* itself—can and should be viewed as an earlier stage of this contest, with no less significant implications for the construction of masculine identities in the Victorian age. At the beginning of the conflict, Kingsley represented one version—probably the culturally dominant one—of what it meant to be a "manly" Christian in Victorian England. Yet he could promote his ideal of masculinity only negatively, anathematizing Newman as the incarnation of its "perverse" opposites: "celibacy," "effeminacy," and "Romanism." Newman himself, meanwhile, recognized that "manliness" was among the most highly charged and cherished values in Victorian culture and, therefore, sought to appropriate it for his own agenda.

As George L. Mosse has written: "The ideal of manliness was basic both to the self-definition of bourgeois society and to the national ideology. Manliness was invoked to safeguard the existing order against . . . perils . . . which threatened the clear distinction between what was considered normal and abnormality." [100] Kingsley sought to exploit the cultural anxieties surrounding national identity and religious faith in his attack on Newman as a treacherous "pervert." Yet definitions of masculinity were undergoing considerable

{ *An Unnatural State* }

change throughout the period, and the Newman-Kingsley controversy dramatized these shifting definitions with a vigor that has not until now been fully explored: "During the course of the century . . . there was a marked shift in the meaning of 'manliness': a shift from the ideals of moral strenuousness, a Christian manliness, to a cult of the emphatically physical (what later generations would call 'machismo'), a shift from serious earnestness to robust virility, from integrity to hardness, from the ideals of godliness and good learning to those of clean manliness and good form."[101]

If the "late nineteenth century cult of manliness became a powerful and pervasive middle-class moral code," then Kingsley was clearly one of the first key figures in the inculcation of this code into mainstream British public life and discourse.[102] Yet, if the "manliness" appealed to by Newman was that of an earlier generation, his victory over Kingsley confirmed its lingering authority. It is not necessary, however, to align Newman and Kingsley with displaced and emergent definitions of manliness in order to see their conflict as of crucial significance for Victorian discourses of gender and sexuality. For those interested in tracing the cultural and historical shift from the idealized status of "manly" friendship to the stigmatized, marginalized role of "perversion" and "homosexuality," the critical project is less to identify the precise ideological agenda of each figure—useful as this is—than to decipher the discourses available at the time for addressing questions of religious, gender, and sexual transgression. Whether or not Newman's celibacy, his "effeminacy," his intense and emotional intimacy with Hurrell Froude, and his influential pedagogical role in the Oxford movement had been "suspect"—full of dubious sexual import and suggestive of a variety of "perversions"—in the 1830s, it is clear that they were so, or were rapidly becoming so, in the 1860s.

CHAPTER 2

The Secret Which I Carried

Desire and Displacement in
John Addington Symonds's *Memoirs*

"Against Nature": Symonds and Greek Love

In March 1889, John Addington Symonds, the Victorian literary critic, poet, and art historian, having just completed two translations of major autobiographies from the Italian,[1] wrote excitedly to his friend Henry Graham Dakyns about his latest literary project:

> My occupation with Cellini and Gozzi has infected me with their *Lues Autobiographica*; & I have begun scribbling my own reminiscences. This is a foolish thing to do, because I do not think they will ever be fit to publish. I have nothing to relate except the evolution of a character somewhat strangely constituted in its moral and aesthetic qualities. . . . You see I have "never spoken out." And it is a great temptation to speak out, when I have been living for two whole years in lonely intimacy with men who spoke out so magnificently as Cellini and Gozzi did.[2]

Symonds's description of his autobiographical project as "scribbling" conveys a tentative and modest literary ambition.[3] Likewise, his dismissal of the possibility of publication seems to reduce the autobiography to a merely private venture, lacking in any public significance. What is striking, in fact, is the extreme caution with which the writer hints at the mysterious motive for an autobiography that would offer a detailed account of his sexual development. The confidential tone of the letter to Dakyns invokes the autobiography itself as a scene of "lonely intimacy" in which self-revelation might take place in comparative safety.

Although the nuanced modern vocabulary of same-sex desire was not available to Symonds, he had access to the classical discourse of the Greeks and in 1883 had already printed his own treatise on pederastic culture and practices in ancient Greece, entitled *A Problem in Greek Ethics*. He was currently composing a study of homosexuality in modern culture, called *A Problem in Modern Ethics*, which would be privately printed in 1891, the same year in which Symonds would approach the young medical doctor Havelock Ellis with a view to collaborating on a work about sexual inversion. The texts stretching from *A Problem in Greek Ethics* to *Sexual Inversion* (though the latter was not published until 1897, four years after his death) represent Symonds's efforts to "speak out" on the subject of homosexuality in the voice of historical, anthropological, or scientific "objectivity."[4] An important question emerges, therefore: Why did Symonds feel it necessary to "speak out" in autobiographical form?

Symonds suggests that the motivation was provided by his interest in the genre of autobiography itself rather than any particular urgency to tell the story of his life. As he wrote to Dakyns: "I feel it a pity, after acquiring the art of the autobiographer through translation of two masterpieces, not to employ my skill upon such a rich mine of psychological curiosities as I am conscious of possessing. This may appear rather conceited. But it is not so. I speak as an artist, who sees 'a subject' of which he is confident."[5] As early as 1864 when a young fellow of Magdalen College, Oxford, he had written to his close friend A. O. Rutson: "I have often thought that if I lived to do nothing else, I should write confessions which would be better for the world to read than Rousseau's and not less interesting. I sometimes think that I am being trained for this."[6] In these letters, we see Symonds cautiously moving toward the resolution to write an autobiography of which his own homosexuality would be the central theme.

The risks of undertaking such a piece of writing would have been clear to Symonds, as would the difficulty of publishing it. The Labouchère Amendment of 1885 had not only criminalized homosexual *acts* between men, whether private or public, but also made risky literary professions and defenses of same-sex desire, whether published or unpublished. One of the most important functions of the Oscar Wilde trials in 1895 would be to demonstrate that ostensibly "private" texts, such as letters, along with published writings, could be used to incriminate the writer no less effectively than his sexual acts. Hence, the sole justification for writing on the subject of homosexuality was that the approach would be as impersonal as possible, concealing any private interest in same-sex desire under a cloak of appropriately "objective" language. In his *A Problem in Greek Ethics* and *A Problem in Modern Ethics*, Symonds self-consciously presented homosexual desire in a detached historical or anthropological light: by discussing his own desire as a "problem," Symonds acknowledged the power of homophobic culture to shape and inform the debate of greatest importance to him. In the case of his collaboration with Ellis for *Sexual Inversion*, as Wayne Koestenbaum points out, "Symonds depends on other men to make his interest in homosexuality seem respectable and professional." His memoirs, by contrast, were envisaged from the outset as a private project, one that would allow him to establish greater intimacy with his circle of close friends but would not, in all probability, attain a larger public during his life.[7]

Symonds had already experienced persecution following a too-obvious expression of interest in masculine desire, when his *Studies of the Greek Poets* came under attack in the essay "The Greek Spirit in Modern Literature," which appeared in the March 1877 issue of *Contemporary Review*. Authored by the Reverend Richard St. John Tyrwhitt, rector of St. Mary Magdalene in Oxford, the essay was in fact a review of several contemporary works identified by the reviewer as being "Hellenistic" in character, including Matthew Arnold's *Culture and Anarchy*.[8] Tyrwhitt claimed of Symonds's book, "These pages are a rebellion against nature as she is here, in the name of nature as described in Athens." Describing Symonds as "probably the most innocent of men," he nonetheless attacked his book for the "expressions put in [Socrates'] mouth" that "are not natural: and it is well known that Greek love of nature and beauty went frequently against nature."[9]

Tyrwhitt's review is significant because he was one of the first to detect in Symonds's work a predilection for sexual practices that were, for Victorian readers, "unspeakable." Tyrwhitt's inability to say what he means any more clearly than references to "unnatural" and "amoral" practices is indicative of a lack of signifying vocabulary to describe what was nonetheless perceived to be an emergent and dangerous cultural threat to sexual norms, associated in particular with the "decadent" school of criticism. Indeed, both the opponents and the apologists of same-sex desire, such as Symonds himself, were constrained by the same limitations of language. Despite his vagueness, there can have been little doubt in the minds of Tyrwhitt's readers that he objected to Symonds's idealization of Greek Hellenism because it condoned homosexual love, especially when he contrasted modern society favorably with the Greeks because "we contend for purity of sexual relation."[10]

The most dangerous passages of his book, however, were those in which Symonds identified himself as a kind of cultural refugee, a lost child of ancient Greece, in a tone that clearly rejected the objective and scientific pretensions of much aesthetic and historical criticism of Greek art and mythology, such as the work of Max Müller. Following Arnold's distinction in *Culture and Anarchy* (1869) between the Hellenistic and Hebraistic forces of British society, Symonds expressed his conviction that "some will always be found, under the conditions of this double culture, to whom Greece is a lost fatherland and who, passing through youth with the *mal du pays* of that irrecoverable land upon them, may be compared to visionaries, spending the nights in golden dreams and the days in common duties. Has then the modern man no method for making the Hellenic tradition vital instead of dream-like—invigorating instead of enervating? There is indeed this one way only—to be natural."[11] Symonds's expression of the Arnoldian dichotomy as a "double culture" prefigures the "double life" that would be the central subject of his autobiography. If his family life and voluminous critical writings demonstrated the Hebraic virtues of public duty and patriarchal productivity, the *Memoirs* would chart his secret, Hellenic existence as a poet, comrade, and lover of men. For those such as Tyrwhitt to whom the problem with Greek society was precisely that it was "unnatural" in its institutions and sexual practices, this recommendation from Symonds and his implicit self-identification as a "visionary" would scarcely have been reassuring. Such cryptic references to the "golden dreams" of the night and advocacy of the values propagated by Greek literature may not have been enough to prove that the author of the *Studies of the Greek Poets* was homosexual. Yet they could certainly make Symonds's work appear less than respectable in the eyes of many of the literary class in Victorian England.

With such a background of public persecution and embarrassing retrenchment on the subject of same-sex desire, it is small wonder that, in the preface to the *Memoirs*, written in May 1889, Symonds is circumspect about revealing his motives for writing what he describes (following Gozzi) as his "useless" memoirs: "That I have a definite object in the sacrifice of so much time and trouble upon a task so useless and so thankless, will not be doubted," he writes, adding mysteriously that "my object is known to myself" and that "it is not one I care to disclose in set phrases." [12] And yet, after this evasive reference to his "object," Symonds supposes that "someone, peradventure, will discover it" and invokes a series of imaginary readers who, in various ways, might recognize the "secret" of his autobiography. Symonds in effect defers the disclosure of his secret purpose by placing it in the hands of a future reader to discover: it was for this reader, as Symonds did not envisage publication during his lifetime, that the memoirs were written.

⁂

"The Mystery of Sex": Symonds's *Memoirs* and the Limits of Confession

The aim of much theory and criticism of autobiography since the 1980s has been to expose as a fiction the unified, unique self that supposedly authorizes autobiography as a genre. What seems to be the very premise of autobiography—that an individual life is a unique, self-conscious process of development, capable of attaining literary expression and narrative representation—is shown to be formally untenable and ideologically duplicitous. In his seminal essay, "Autobiography as De-Facement," Paul de Man attacks the notion of a generic specificity of autobiography, arguing that it is "not a genre or a mode, but a figure of reading or of understanding that occurs, to some degree, in all texts." For de Man, attempts to differentiate autobiography from fiction or other genres are bound to fail, because the "specular structure," or "alignment between the two subjects involved in the process of reading," is not exclusive to texts identified as autobiographies. The claim to referential "authority" made by the auto-biographical text is in fact a kind of displaced recognition between author and reader or between author and subject that is determined by the text itself. Hence, de Man asks the disturbing question, "Is the illusion of reference not a correlation of the structure of the figure, that is to say no longer clearly and simply a referent at all but something more akin to a fiction?"[13]

By identifying the written text with an actual, historical referent-subject, the reader of autobiography identifies with a fictional pleni-tude that he or she cannot possess; thus the "specular moment" occurs when the reader "recognizes" the fullness of self-knowledge that the autobiographer—by the very act of writing—claims to pos-sess. In many cases, the language of autobiography may also seem to transcend death itself, for when the text is published or even read posthumously, the autobiography seems to restore or reincarnate the "lost" identity of the writer. Yet this identification through textual misrecognition cannot be sustained. The imagined link between text, voice, and body of the author breaks down, for de Man, where it is revealed to be a tropological system, a linguistic structure, rather than a historical reality. Having served as the means of restoring the self to itself—by referring to and thereby invoking the presence of a physically absent or deceased person—the language of self-reference becomes associated with the death of that self, indeed now appears as the very cause of its deprivation, rather than the reversal of its demise. Hence, as de Man expresses it, "Autobiography veils a de-facement of the mind of which it is itself the cause."[14]

Initially following a de Manian thesis, Koestenbaum describes Symonds's account of his sexual history as depicting "isolated instants of sexual awakening that never coalesce into the continuous story of a life." The lack of narrative cohesion in these "instants" might be taken to demonstrate the endless deferral of autobiographical meaning, an obsessive yet futile quest after self-knowledge. For Koestenbaum, however, the lack of narrative continuity is produced not by the im-possibility of a determinate autobiographical subject or the duplici-tous nature of language itself but by an external threat in the form of Havelock Ellis's "fragmenting scissors." Symonds, Koestenbaum be-lieves, required the scientific reputation of Ellis to legitimize his work on sexual inversion but eventually fell victim to the very authority with which he had sought to collaborate. In the case of Symonds's own "case history" written for *Sexual Inversion*, which related key sexual incidents also described in the memoirs, Koestenbaum laments the violence done to the integrity of Symonds's speech, stating that "there is no connection between this anecdote [in the case history] and what Barthes would call the grain of Symonds's voice."[15]

Koestenbaum here subscribes to the idealized linking of voice, text, and body, with Ellis as the patriarchal (and sexually insecure) villain who helps to dismember that unity. Koestenbaum's questions about the possible joint authorship of the case history has crucial implications for any interpretation of the *Memoirs*: "Is there a unified Symonds beneath the case history, or is 'Symonds the homosexual' constructed by the pull between the case's two authors? Struggling with the knotty question of the case's authorship involves deciding whether the homosexual creates his identity in a moment of free self-inscription, or whether the designation 'homosexual' sprouts from the battle between a subject and a society."[16] These questions lead the reader toward engagement with some of the most interesting questions about identity formation and literary self-representation. Yet, rather than answer them, Koestenbaum proposes to resolve the apparent contradictions by invoking autobiography as a genre that is uncontaminated by the conflicts embedded in the "scientific" treatise known as *Sexual Inversion*.

In the first place, by aligning "society" with the second of "the case's two authors"—that is, Ellis—Koestenbaum furthers the marginalization of Symonds as one who indulges in various practices (such as homosexuality, aestheticism, autobiography) in some way distinct from, or opposed to, "society." Moreover, such an alignment reinforces the social power of the scientist, Ellis, who, despite being "an early and unrepentant belletrist,"[17] chose at a crucial point of his career to identify himself with a newly emergent scientific discourse of sexology, not the "decadent" aestheticism represented by Symonds. But rather than "struggling with the knotty question of the case's authorship," Koestenbaum moves on to validate a related text whose authorship is undisputed: the memoirs.

Whereas Symonds, according to Koestenbaum, is symbolically castrated by his unequal collaboration with Ellis, in the autobiography "the penis remains in place because Symonds, in his own unpublished text, is safe from Ellis's fragmenting scissors, and can speak of

{ *The Secret Which I Carried* }

his desire in the first person."[18] Koestenbaum here idealizes both the "first person" as a guarantor of authentic knowledge and sexual self-presence and the penis as a source of textual authority, as though they were free from the limits and self-disintegrating powers of what he depicts as "society" (represented, in the previous equation, by the scientist Ellis). By speaking as "I," according to Koestenbaum, Symonds not only defends himself against castration but also implicitly restores the integrity of his autobiographical voice that had been silenced in the "isolated instants" of the case history. Central to this restorative vision of the memoirs is the term "unpublished": having previously described the publication difficulties that beset *Sexual Inversion*, Koestenbaum leaves the reader to imagine the likely response to the publication of a confessional text speaking of same-sex desire in the first person. Hence, the first-person autobiography, although silenced by the impossibility of publication, is portrayed as being free from the dismembering tactics of Ellis and the punitive public reaction of the kind Symonds had suffered following his *Studies of the Greek Poets*.

Yet some peculiarities exist in the composition and publication history of the memoirs that reveal the limitations on which such a model relies. In the first place, the memoirs were begun *before* the collaborative project with Ellis had been initiated; apparently, Symonds was not satisfied with writing in the first person, perhaps for the very reason that his text could not be published and would therefore be without widespread influence. During the same period that he was working on his autobiography, therefore, Symonds actively sought out the authority of a collaborator for a scientific treatise and embraced the third-person voice used to write the case history. One can account for this by observing the "double-voiced" quality of the memoirs themselves, in which Symonds speaks alternately in the voice of the dispassionate scientist inquiring into the "problem" of inversion and in the voice of the self-proclaimed invert, troubled and tormented by forbidden desires. The deployment of the scientific voice is not evidence of a split personality, so much as a kind of "mask"—in the Wildean sense—that he might use publicly to utter his desires.[19] Rather than being what Koestenbaum negatively terms "a self-sabotage—that protected him from the larger violence of silence," the doubling with Ellis should be seen as at once a self-empowerment and a self-liberation for Symonds.[20] According to

Wilde, the mask is simply a way of multiplying one's personalities, and I believe Symonds's "double voice" is most productively viewed in this light.

Indeed, Koestenbaum suggests this very possibility, though somewhat against the grain of his central argument. For despite the claim that "Ellis was part of the reality that Symonds had to combat in order to speak out," Koestenbaum goes on to suggest that it was precisely the collaboration with Ellis that allowed Symonds to disclose his own sexual desires. Citing an episode from Symonds's childhood that is narrated, with significant differences, in both the scientific case history and the memoirs, Koestenbaum observes that the former version in the case history is "more sexually explicit. Symonds's Autobiography [sic] removed the prurience; the case history restores it." [21] Koestenbaum assumes that there is some essential (and "prurient"?) truth to the episode underlying its various narrative versions. There is, however, no textual evidence that Symonds deleted a more explicit rendition of the event in the manuscript of the memoirs. [22] Yet Koestenbaum requires this imaginary act of literary censorship on Symonds's part in order to present the case history as a "recovery" of the previously inadmissible sexual details: "In its recovery of sexual facts too often muddled by Symonds and the Uranians, the deadpan yet graphic case history succeeds where the memoirs fail." [23]

Koestenbaum's reluctance to explain Symonds's initiation of the collaborative project of *Sexual Inversion*, which he simultaneously portrays as a kind of literary suicide, is not surprising. [24] After all, the fundamental flaw with his portrayal of Ellis as a castrating, violently hierarchical representative of "society" who persecutes the unwilling Symonds into textual compliance and submission is that the proposal for the collaboration issued from Symonds himself. Koestenbaum accounts for this apparent anomaly by portraying Symonds as an irrational masochist who "enjoyed offering his own textual body as a sacrifice to be torn, voluptuously, limb by limb." [25] Though Koestenbaum does not absolutely reject more plausible motives for Symonds's collaboration, he must conclude by emphasizing "Symonds's failure to speak out through collaboration" so as to validate the greater authenticity of the solitary and private autobiographical text. [26] This becomes Symonds's "own unpublished text," his own, implicitly, *because* unpublished.

For Koestenbaum's argument, the memoirs function primarily to

{ *The Secret Which I Carried* }

establish an idealized state of expressive liberty, in contrast to the violence and constraint attributed to the collaboration with the scientist Ellis. *Sexual Inversion* is finally condemned by Koestenbaum as "duplicitous double talk," a conspiratorial and unsound attempt to feign engagement with the experience of same-sex desire, which ultimately disclaims and pathologizes it. The memoirs are thereby reclaimed as candid "single talk": the unity and immediacy of the first-person voice being equated, by Koestenbaum, with a special kind of sexual truth and authenticity. The sexual vagueness of the memoirs—which might be viewed by some readers as itself a form of "duplicity"—is, on the contrary, portrayed by Koestenbaum as a kind of innocence, the corollary of the narrative's freedom both from Ellis's "fragmenting scissors" and from the "prurience" and "obsessively punitive" sexual detail associated with the text of *Sexual Inversion*.

As should by now be clear, I will move beyond the idealizing approach to the *Memoirs* by presenting Symonds's autobiography as itself a duplicitous text. But "duplicitous" is to be understood not in a pejorative sense but with reference to the doublings, displacements, and deferrals which occur, to some extent, in any autobiography but which appear most persistently where the self is disclosed under the pressure of secrecy. A central part of the work of the *Memoirs*, I will argue, is the displacement of transgressive desires onto other characters in the narrative, figures that are constructed for its own rhetorical project of sexual self-definition. Through such displacements and fictional strategies, the *Memoirs* attempts to purge Symonds's self of the contradictions and conflicting impulses that prevent it from achieving the status of a sexual "identity," in the sense of a coherent and consistent pattern of subjective meaning. While the purpose of my critique is to draw attention to the fissures between acknowledged and transferred desires in Symonds's text, I try not to lose sight of the political function of the autobiography: namely, to construct and authorize, by means of the individual life story, a specific model of same-sex desire, derived from the texts of ancient Greece and the ideals of Whitman-esque poetics, and to discredit less aesthetically derived models. It is to this end that the "duplicity" of Symonds's text, along with its (to some) perplexing lack of explicit sexual detail, is directed.

Symonds defines the "plan of the *Memoirs*" in quasi-scientific terms as "the evolution of a somewhat abnormally constituted individual" (61) but then immediately moves into more subjective terrain, providing autobiographical details of "the first stirrings of the sexual instinct." From an early stage, therefore, the double purpose of the autobiography is made apparent. If Symonds here invokes "the voice of this imagined collaborator, the scientist with a clear plan," he also indicates the limits of such a "plan" when unaccompanied by the elaboration of personal experience.[27] Describing his early erotic experiences and fantasies, Symonds insists that his individual desires, rather than a scientific paradigm, will validate his autobiography as being unique and worthy of attention: "When I wrote these recollections of my earliest sexual impressions, I was not aware how important they were for the proper understanding of *vita sexualis*, and how impossible it would have been to omit them from a truthful autobiography" (63–64).

In effect, the writer's own sexual history has become the necessary and required "truth" of the autobiography, and Symonds's earliest sexual recollections move him toward the ultimate disclosure of his true purpose, or "object": that of defining his identity in terms of masculine desire. It was the work of P. Moreau, B. Tarnowski, R. von Krafft-Ebing, and K. H. Ulrichs, he writes, that introduced him to the existence of "sexual inversion" and made him realize that he himself was an example of "a somewhat rare aberration of sexual proclivities," elsewhere described as "abnormal sexual feelings." Yet although the work of these sexologists first awoke Symonds to the existence of his own sexual type, he nonetheless expresses his dissatisfaction with their theories and suggests that his own autobiography might help to modify them: "It appears to me that the abnormality in question is not to be explained either by Ulrichs' theory, or by presumptions of the pathological psychologists. Its solution must be sought far deeper in the mystery of sex, *and in the variety of type exhibited by nature*. For this reason, a detailed study of one subject, such as I mean to attempt, may be valuable" (65; emphasis added).

Symonds here clearly rejects the scientific conclusions of the sexologists, wishing to substitute his own individual contribution to the "solution" of "the mystery of sex." If "sex" has become essential to a life story, it is the liberal-humanist ideal of "variety of type" that will confound the "presumptions" (the word is tellingly critical) of those scientists who attempt to categorize and classify human sexuality along rigid and pathologizing lines. Symonds, by referring to Darwin's theory of evolutionary progress according to which "variety of

{ *The Secret Which I Carried* }

type" was essential for the improving mechanism of natural selection to succeed, challenges one scientific model by invoking another, more powerful one. Without natural variety, Darwin had shown, there could be no evolutionary progress of a species. When Symonds sets out to describe "the evolution of a somewhat abnormally constituted individual," therefore, he is referring not only to his own development but also to the evolutionary process that includes, as part of its natural variety, the "abnormality" of sexual inversion.

The individual "confession" is here offered as a counterdiscourse with which to challenge those presumptuously generalizing theories, in an attempt to restore personal experience to a central place in the field of sexuality and to provide a "detailed study" that would complicate, if not entirely refute, the dehumanizing theories of the sexologists. Symonds believed that his account would have more authority than he here claims for it: rather than merely "a detailed study of one subject," the memoirs would draw on another source of cultural authority by presenting a version of same-sex desire based firmly on the foundation of Greek society. As critics such as Richard Dellamora and Linda Dowling have shown, Hellenism was of central significance to the Victorian cultural establishment and became a powerful weapon for the late-Victorian apologists for same-sex desire. Only by invoking the Greeks, Symonds believed, could an alternative to the pathologizing discourse of the sexologists be asserted.

Despite the cultural prestige of Hellenism, the act of writing a "confessional" account of his homosexual history was, for Symonds, a dramatic, not to say reckless, gesture and was as close as he would ever get to speaking out on the subject of his own sexual history. He knew it was the "unspeakable" nature of the topic that would prevent his memoirs from reaching the general public during his lifetime. Although the increasing scientific interest in homosexuality in the late nineteenth century may have inspired him to write an autobiography in which he effectively declared—and narrated his life story in terms of—his "abnormal" sexual orientation, it did not provide an atmosphere conducive to its publication.

What is remarkable about the *Memoirs*, however, is that literature has a dual function in Symonds's account of his life, as both a "mirror" in which he can recognize and affirm his sexual feelings and characteristics and a "safety valve" that induces him to divert dangerous (that is, potentially self-incriminating) sexual desires into creative (and respectable) cultural activity. Yet, despite the centrality of texts in the scenes of sexual "conversion," writing soon comes to play a more sinister role in the obstruction of the very desires that such texts had helped bring into being. To a large extent, therefore, Symonds's development as a writer is represented as corresponding to a stagnation in his sexual progress, with the *Memoirs* reflecting, ultimately, a deep disillusionment with such textual displacements of desire. Various episodes in the narrative testify to the role of a self-protective dynamic that allowed Symonds to explore his sexual desires in literary form while avoiding public self-identification with the scandalous role of "the sodomite." [28]

In the *Memoirs*, this powerful opposition surfaces in the paradox that while an aesthetic, Platonic model of same-sex desire is validated by Symonds in terms of a classical duality of body and soul, unacceptable physical desire is identified with a series of figures whose scarcely representable urges are characterized in ways that Symonds demonizes and repudiates. The most important and recurring example of such a dark figure of sexual exploitation is C. F. Vaughan, headmaster of Harrow School during Symonds's residence there in the 1850s. Symonds's chapters describing his time at Harrow are among the most memorable and thematically significant in the autobiography. Vaughan's shadow extends well beyond the chapters in which he is mentioned by name, for he returns to haunt Symonds's later affairs, which uncannily reproduce the dynamic of desire and repulsion that characterized his relationship with Vaughan. I will suggest that Vaughan functions in the narrative as the first in a series of "doubles" for Symonds himself, acting out explicitly pederastic desires which Symonds could not, for various reasons, acknowledge himself and which become an obsessively recurring theme of the autobiography.

The Strange Case of Mr. Symonds and Dr. Vaughan

I begin my detailed analysis of the *Memoirs* with what seems to me and has struck other readers as the most vivid and powerful series of episodes: those in which Symonds describes his years at Harrow.[29] Throughout the early chapters of his autobiography, Symonds's tone swings dramatically from the outraged and appalled voice of a re-

{ *The Secret Which I Carried* }

spectable Victorian paterfamilias at the moral corruption of society, to a personal plea for more tolerance and understanding for homosexuals. This dual tone is explicable in the light of Symonds's "double life" as a married man and member of the respectable literary establishment, who simultaneously desired and pursued sexual relations with men. Yet this double voice also creates certain contradictions in the narrative, which it is my purpose to explore.

In the Harrow chapters of the *Memoirs*, it is the voice of moral outrage that dominates, representing the repugnance of a sheltered, middle-class English boy at the discovery of "vice" in a prestigious public school:

> One thing at Harrow very soon arrested my attention. It was the moral state of the school. Every boy of good looks had a female name, and was recognized either as a public prostitute or as some bigger fellow's "bitch." Bitch was the word in common usage to indicate a boy who yielded his person to a lover. The talk in the dormitories and the studies was incredibly obscene. Here and there one could not avoid seeing acts of onanism, mutual masturbation, the sports of naked boys in bed together. There was no refinement, no sentiment, no passion; nothing but animal lust in these occurrences. They filled me with disgust and loathing. [94]

If the intensity of his reaction shows that the blatant and aesthetically offensive nature of the sexual acts on display shocks and offends Symonds, it also reveals the erotic potential they might have for him. Symonds's assertion that "one could not avoid seeing" explicit sexual acts between boys releases him from the admission of perhaps wanting to see or even to participate in such practices. Symonds's language of abhorrence is strong in these passages, yet as he admits, "I detested in practice *what had once attracted me in fancy*" (96; emphasis added). The spectacular visibility of the sexuality on offer at Harrow fascinated as well as repelled Symonds, leading to a perplexed self-awareness of his own desires. Recent studies of the nineteenth-century British public school have shown that it was masturbation, the "secret" and "solitary vice," that caused most anxiety for the educational authorities of the Victorian age, being the cause, as was testified by numerous medical "experts," of most damage to the youthful body and soul.[30] Whatever the sexual activities witnessed by Symonds might have been, they were not secret ones. Alongside the tone of outrage, one detects a note of excitement at the very indiscretion of the schoolboy sex at Harrow, in contrast with Symonds's own secretive desire, which could hardly have been more constrained.

An important effect of Symonds's exposure to these blatant sexual scenes was to produce a divided self, which he describes as "the distinction in my character between an inner and real self and an outer and artificial self" that "emphasized itself during this period." According to Symonds, "So separate were the two selves . . . that my most intimate friends . . . have each and all emphatically told me that they thought I had passed through school without being affected by, almost without being aware of, its peculiar vices" (95–96). Despite his insistence that "while I was at school, I remained free in fact and act from this contamination" (95), he describes himself as being fascinated as well as repelled by the more overtly sexual boys at the school, writing of one that the "fierce and cruel lust of this magnificent animal excited my imagination" (95).

By learning to conceal his growing interest in schoolboy sex, Symonds constructs a defense for his inner desires, preventing others from having access to them; but this process results in "two selves" that become "separate." The outer self, unsurprisingly, is viewed as artificial, suggesting that the concealment is unsatisfactory as a way of resolving his sexual dilemma: "I allowed an outer self of commonplace cheerfulness and easy-going pliability to settle like a crust upon my inner and real character" (82). The early emergence of a self-division described here prefigures the situation of Symonds as autobiographer, struggling to represent sexual desires that he still finds, at some level, unspeakable. Moreover, it indicates that the dynamic of the double self is central to the structure of the autobiography. If Symonds *seemed* unaffected and unaware of the "peculiar vices" of the school, this was the case only for his artificial self. The *Memoirs*, Symonds suggests, will restore the balance by telling the story of his "inner and real self."

Symonds's preoccupation with the dangers and the attractions of a "double life" was connected to his uneasy sense that he himself, by pursuing his desire for men in secret, was in effect developing a split personality. This awareness is revealed in an important letter to Robert Louis Stevenson, written shortly before he began work on his memoirs. Stevenson, who had just published his *Strange Case of Dr Jekyll and Mr Hyde*, had spent several winters in Symonds's town of

Davos in the Swiss Alps, seeking to recover from the tuberculosis that had afflicted him since childhood.[31] Symonds and Stevenson became quite close friends during their time together in Davos, and Symonds was very eager to read his friend's novella when it was published in 1886. In Stevenson's famous story, the self-protective duality of an alter ego is developed to an extreme degree, resulting in the violent creation of a new identity, with a new name. Yet Jekyll was "already committed to a profound duplicity of life" before the creation of Mr. Hyde, who, rather than being the distinct incarnation of evil, is best understood as the embodiment of the split between "inner" and "outer" selves that has already taken control of Jekyll's life.[32] It was this resemblance to the self-division addressed by Symonds in the *Memoirs* that explains his intensely distressed and personal reaction to the story:

At last I have read Dr Jekyll. It makes me wonder whether a man has the right so to scrutinize "the abysmal deeps of personality." . . . As a piece of literary work, this seems to me the finest you have done—in all that regards style, invention, psychological analysis, exquisite fitting of parts, and admirable employment of motives to realize the abnormal. But it has left such a deeply painful impression on my heart that I do not know how I am ever to turn to it again. The fact is that, viewed as an allegory, it touches one too closely. Most of us at some epoch of our lives have been upon the verge of developing a Mr Hyde. . . . Your Dr Jekyll seems to me capable of loosening the last threads of self-control in one who should read it while wavering between his better and worse self.[33]

Knowing what we do of Symonds's sexual struggle, it is inevitable that we should read this letter as revelatory of his own self-conflict. In particular, his fear of "loosening the last threads of self-control" and the concern that his "worse self" would gain mastery are suggestive of Symonds's battle to manage sexual desires that were growing beyond his control. Of course, Symonds is evasive in the letter about the specific nature of his reluctant identification with Henry Jekyll. Its effect, however, is to suggest a recognition of resemblance between Stevenson's hero and Symonds's life. Symonds's fear of being adversely affected by the story suggests the fragility of his persona at this point of his history. More important, it demonstrates his conviction that an uncontrolled expression of sexuality would dissolve the boundaries of the self, as Jekyll's indulgence in the pleasures of Mr. Hyde "shook the very fortress of identity."[34]

Whether Symonds was in whole or in part the model for the character of Jekyll — a possibility, given the period of the novel's composition — a comparison of the story with the narrative of his early years at Harrow helps to show how the "division" in Symonds grew up in a context that was explicitly and traumatically one of sexual deviance. Stevenson's story depicts a homosocial world in which all sexual attraction is displaced into professional bonds and clubbish pseudo-intimacy. Indeed, one might argue that the creation of Mr. Hyde erupts as a symptom at once of the unacknowledged desire and the unexpressed hostility between the male characters. But the inner struggle implied by Symonds in his letter to Stevenson is dramatized in the *Memoirs* as a series of controversial or scandalous acts performed by other men. In particular, there is a striking similarity between Jekyll's unsuccessful attempt to control and then destroy the dark self that he himself had brought into being and the efforts of Symonds and his father to exorcise the homosexual in their midst, Charles Vaughan, headmaster of Harrow School. For all these men, it seems, the "double" represented something that they must seek to contain in themselves by means of removing it from the visible public realm.

Symonds writes in the *Memoirs* that he at first looked up to Vaughan, who had been a pupil of Dr. Thomas Arnold at Rugby School and who became headmaster of Harrow at the early age of twenty-six. At Harrow, Vaughan attempted to put Arnold's educational vision into practice by reforming an institution already notorious for its "vice." Vaughan's mission at Harrow was to improve the moral condition of the school, and his efforts to curb the sexual activities of the boys at first drew Symonds's approval: "In my own mind I felt sure that these vices were pernicious to our society; and I regarded them as sins which ought to have been harshly dealt with" (96–97). His initial admiration for the puritanical campaign of Vaughan was dramatically disrupted, however, by the discovery that the patriarch of the school, for all his condemnation of such practices, was himself involved in an amorous relationship with a fellow pupil of Symonds, Alfred Pretor: "In the month of January 1858 Alfred Pretor wrote me a note in which he informed me that Vaughan had begun

{ *The Secret Which I Carried* }

a love affair with him. I soon found that the boy was not lying, because he showed me a series of passionate letters written to him by our headmaster" (97).

Symonds found this irrefutable evidence of Vaughan's secret pederasty far more disturbing than the naked lust of his schoolfellows. The strength of Symonds's distaste is attributable to the fact that Vaughan was a grown man, supposed to be setting an example of purity to his young charges. In an appalled tone, Symonds recollects his own physical intimacy with Vaughan during his confirmation, and the religious context of this intimacy is itself an important factor in his disgust. An ostensibly sacred and pious act of physical contact between headmaster and pupil is transformed, in the light of Symonds's discovery, into a disturbing and sexually-charged incident of abuse: "It proved convincingly that I was wrong in imagining that this species of vice formed only a phase of boyish immaturity. I was disgusted to find it in a man holding the highest position of responsibility, consecrated by the Church, entrusted with the welfare of six hundred youths—a man who had recently prepared me for confirmation, from whose hands, kneeling by the side of Alfred Pretor, I received the sacrament" (97). Symonds had apparently come to acknowledge same-sex desire as an immature phase of development, without by any means recognizing it as a permanent condition of adult life. The limits of homosexuality imaginable for Symonds at this time were "a phase of boyish immaturity," on the one hand, and a pederastic corrupter of youth, on the other.[35]

This discovery of Vaughan's pederasty proved damaging for Symonds's sexual self, plunging him into a conflict between his sense of duty and his own covert identification with Vaughan's desires. Symonds "vaguely wondered whether I ought not to tell my father" (97) of what he had learned about Vaughan's practices but was prevented from doing so by what he mysteriously describes as "a dumb persistent sympathy" for one whom he "had been accustomed to regard as the pattern of conduct" (97). This sympathy becomes more explicable when one considers the high moral reputation of Vaughan and that Symonds had come to share the sexual preference of his "perverse" former headmaster for young men and boys. Moreover, by the time he wrote the *Memoirs*, Symonds had even replicated some of Vaughan's sexual behavior toward his own pupils. His unwilling complicity with Vaughan's prohibited lust for male youth is manifested in the narrative with the insistence of what he terms in the letter to Stevenson "an allegory."

The contradictions in Symonds's narrative begin to appear as he shifts erratically from the position of a judge morally condemning Vaughan for his illicit passions, to that of a sexual sympathizer rebuking him for his choice of an "inferior" object: admitting that "my own inclinations, the form which my erotic idealism had assumed, prevented me from utterly condemning Vaughan," Symonds adds that "I did indeed condemn Vaughan's taste; for I regarded Pretor as a physically and emotionally inferior being" (97). Symonds's tone of disillusionment suggests, however paradoxically, that Vaughan's "taste" would have been superior had he singled out for attention the young Symonds. And in fact Vaughan does, shortly afterward in the narrative, make advances toward him:

> I used to take essays and verses at intervals to Vaughan in the study which was the scene of his clandestine pleasures. It was a fairly sized square room, dark, on the ground floor, looking upon the street. On those occasions my young brains underwent an indescribable fermentation. I remember once that, while we sat together reading Greek iambics, he began softly to stroke my right leg from the knee to the thigh. This insignificant caress, of which I should have thought nothing two months earlier, and which probably meant nothing, seemed then disagreeably suggestive. [97–98]

Whether the "indescribable fermentation" described by Symonds is caused by his struggles with Greek literature or Vaughan's advances, the effect of the passage is to underscore the transforming power of Symonds's sexual discovery on his view of the pedagogical relationship. The inappropriateness of Vaughan's gesture of desire, following the revelation of his involvement with Pretor, is stunning. Symonds is evidently still perturbed as he relates the incident, and identification in the passage shifts uneasily between the lustful schoolmaster and the confused schoolboy. The "clandestine pleasures" that Symonds attributes to Vaughan are as fully imagined as the "disagreeably suggestive" effect of the caress on the young boy.

The intimate relationship between sexuality and textuality is firmly established by the passage. Crucially, this erotic caress occurs while Symonds and his master are reading Greek iambics, which suggests that the study of Greek literature may be erotically arousing, preliminary to the more explicit forms of sexual interaction that Vaughan desires. In fact, the formative role of literature—particularly Greek literature—in the emergence of Symonds's sexual self is a central theme of the *Memoirs*. Though it was the sexual activity at Harrow that first brought the physical realities of sex to Symonds's attention, the turning point in his sexual history occurs not during the spectacle of public schoolboy sex but in the midst of a private act of reading. It is significant that this formative reading experience is represented as taking place outside the institutional confines of Harrow, because the pedagogical encounter with Greek literature has been contaminated by its association with Vaughan's pederasty.

Symonds writes that while still a pupil at Harrow, he was staying with a friend in London when, one night after returning from a play, "I went to bed and began to read my Cary's Plato. It so happened that I stumbled on the *Phaedrus*. I read on and on, till I reached the end. Then I began the *Symposium*; and the sun was shining on the shrubs outside the ground-floor room in which I slept, before I shut the book up" (99). The apparently accidental (but implicitly fated) "stumbling" on Plato's texts, combined with the vividly detailed description of locale (also a feature of his recollection of Vaughan's caress) and the rapid passage of time, establishes this episode as a decisive "crisis" in the narrative of conversion. In the classical spiritual autobiography, a revelation of religious faith would be expected to occur at this juncture. In the case of Symonds's narrative, the religious turning point is displaced by a discovery of new sexual possibilities; but the rhetoric used to describe the "conversion" is strikingly similar to that of spiritual autobiographies.[36]

St. Augustine, for example, describes how, in the midst of his crisis of faith, he arrived at a garden in Milan, "when all at once I heard the sing-song voice of a child in a nearby house. Whether it was the voice of a boy or a girl I cannot say, but again and again it repeated the refrain 'Take it and read, take it and read.'"[37] Augustine's response is immediate and leads, with the mediation of a divine text, to the completion of his conversion: "I had put down the book containing Paul's Epistles. I seized it and opened it, and in silence I read the first passage on which my eyes fell. . . . I had no wish to read more and no need to do so. For in an instant, as I came to the end of the sentence, it was as though the light of confidence flooded into my heart and all the darkness of doubt was dispelled."[38]

A much later spiritual autobiography, Newman's *Apologia*, would refer to Augustine's account of his conversion to dramatize the momentous impact of Newman's own conversion to Catholicism. It was his reading of St. Augustine's phrase "Securus judicat orbis terrarum" that proved decisive for his rejection of the "Via Media" and subsequent conversion to Roman Catholicism:

> Who can account for the impressions which are made on him? For a mere sentence, the words of St. Augustine, struck me with a power which I never had felt from any words before. To take a familiar instance, they were like the "Turn again Whittington" of the chime; or, to take a more serious one, they were like the "Tolle, lege,— Tolle, lege," of the child, which converted St. Augustine himself. "Securus judicat orbis terrarum!" By those great words of the ancient Father interpreting and summing up the long and varied course of ecclesiastical history, the theory of the Via Media was absolutely pulverized.[39]

Symonds writes in a similar vein of his own reading of Plato: "That night was one of the most important nights of my life. . . . Here in the *Phaedrus* and the *Symposium* . . . I discovered the true *liber amoris* at last, the revelation I had been waiting for, the consecration of a long-cherished idealism. It was just as though the voice of my own soul spoke to me through Plato, as though in some antenatal experience I had lived the life of philosophical Greek lover [*sic*]" (99). Like Newman's reading of the ancient Church fathers, Symonds's discovery of Platonic love satiates a long-felt desire for knowledge. In Symonds's case, this knowledge is sexual in a crucial, but not yet physical, sense. His sudden access to the "hidden" meaning of ancient Greek texts is simultaneously represented as a discovery of his own "nature."

As with Augustine and Newman, moreover, Symonds's decisive revelation is neither sought for nor anticipated but occurs spontaneously and with devastating impact, establishing the significance of the moment as one of dramatic self-transformation. Plato's text functions in this passage as the "fatal book" that would have a determining influence on the future course of Symonds's life. The power of such a book to "seduce" its reader and produce a quasi-religious conversion has been explored by Dowling with reference to George Moore's *Confessions of a Young Man*, a work that also details the transforming power of literary texts on the self. According to Dowling, the fatal book's "power of linguistic autonomy becomes in a precise sense Decadent . . . when portrayed as a poisonous or seducing power, as when George Moore treats the fatal power of specific books as a sexually seductive presence. . . . Moore's antinomian inversion of conventional religious language is far less startling than his assertion that he was persuaded to this new life of sensualism by the sexual seductiveness of Gautier's literary style."[40]

Of course, in Symonds's case the inspiration provided by Plato is depicted as being in direct contrast to the "sensualism" that had characterized the sexual practices of his schoolfellows at Harrow. According to the *Memoirs*, this turning point produced by reading translates not only into Symonds's recognition of his sexual desire but also into his career as a classical scholar. In other words, Symonds's erotic desire and his aesthetic imagination become inextricably intertwined: "Here was the poetry, the philosophy of my own enthusiasm for male beauty, expressed with all the magic of unrivalled style. And, what was more, I now became aware that the Greek race—the actual historical Greeks of antiquity—treated this love seriously, invested it with moral charm, endowed it with sublimity" (99).

Symonds here reformulates in personal terms what he had described many years earlier in his controversial *Studies of the Greek Poets* as the nostalgia for Greek history experienced by those who had encountered the pleasures of classical literature. Yet the note sounded in the *Memoirs* is affirmative rather than wistful, communicating the writer's conviction that he has discovered his true self and his true spiritual home. This autobiographical scene of self-discovery, in other words, conveys a longing for the intimate relation between Symonds's sexual desires and his aesthetic tastes that had, by the time he wrote the *Memoirs*, become far more problematic. It also suggests the literary text as a site of fantasy in which sexual desire and knowledge can be negotiated, explored, and, at the same time, regulated. Of course, the exclusively Greek focus of Symonds's sexual desire was in some respects anachronistic, based on the social and sexual practices of a culture that, for all its influence on the Victorian education system and civic system, bore little resemblance to the modern bourgeois society in which Symonds actually lived. Symonds's idealization of

Greek culture, however, largely explains his later interest in Whitman's poetry and theories of democratic comradeship. In *A Problem in Greek Ethics*, for example, he writes that "Whitman does not conceive of comradeship as a merely personal possession, delightful to the friends it links in bonds of amity. He regards it essentially as a social and political virtue. This human emotion is destined to cement society and to render commonwealths inviolable."[41] This suggests the extent to which Symonds found in Whitman the closest modern equivalent to the social virtues of Greek literature.

It is significant, in this respect, that Symonds registers the outbreak of schoolboy sex at Harrow as being distasteful, disturbing, and profoundly unerotic. Symonds's desire was chiefly stimulated by subtle encodings or idealized visions of sexuality and was thrown into confusion by the flagrant display of lust. A key poem, "Angelo Fusato"—written about a Venetian gondolier who became Symonds's servant and lover—describes this tension between physical desire and aesthetic wonder that would characterize Symonds's subsequent account of his sexual life:

> Yes, he was here. Our four hands, laughing, made
> Brief havoc of his belt, shirt, trousers, shoes:
> Till, mother-naked, white as lilies, laid
> There on the counterpane, he bade me use
> Even as I willed his body. But Love forbade—
> Love cried, "Less than Love's best thou shalt refuse!" [274]

In this poem, Symonds is invited to take sexual pleasure in his lover's body but refuses on the grounds of "Love," a word that here signifies an aestheticized desire that cannot be satisfied by—and even recoils from—direct physical contact. It reminds us of the central fact that the version of same-sex desire produced and legitimated by Symonds's reading of Plato is specifically contrasted to the physical and moral brutishness he had witnessed at school. As Symonds describes the effects of his readings in Plato: "Harrow vanished into unreality. I had touched solid ground. I had obtained the sanction of the love which had been ruling me from childhood. . . . For the first time I saw the possibility of resolving in a practical harmony the discords of my instincts. I perceived that masculine love had its virtue as well as its vice, and stood in this respect upon the same ground as normal sexual appetite. I understood, or thought I understood, the relation which those dreams of childhood and the brutalities of vulgar lust at Harrow bore to my higher aspiration after noble passion" (99). Curiously, it is the textual realm of ancient Greek literature that Symonds describes as "solid ground," whereas the all too solid flesh to which he had been exposed at Harrow "vanished into unreality." The personal "conversion" inspired by his reading of Plato and the discovery of Greek homosexuality gives Symonds a moral and philosophical framework for his subsequent sexual explorations and fantasies. Yet this textual self-discovery leads him to formulate his homosexuality, in opposition to the public "vice" of Harrow, as something essentially interior and private: namely, "the secret which I carried" (102).

"Clandestine Ways": The Cultural Inscription of Secrecy

The act of autobiographical writing provides Symonds the opportunity to disburden himself of this "secret" and thereby to heal the prolonged rift between his "two selves." The *Memoirs* offers the story of his inner, "secret" self, which he claims to have concealed and repressed throughout his life because of its dangerous and sexually subversive desires. His outer self—the "crust" that has settled on his desire—might, he hoped, be broken through by the confessional disclosures of the autobiography. This cultural distinction between inner and outer selves has been explored in terms of the special difficulties confronting female autobiographers in the nineteenth century—particularly those engaged in public careers—as they sought to bridge a gulf between their public roles and private selves. According to Valerie Sanders: "The notion of a 'double life' lacks this special resonance for male Victorian autobiographers. They may have belonged to more than one circle of family and friends, but there was no conflict, induced by society's expectations, between their public work and their private lives." [42]

This critical generalization is shattered by the case of Symonds. For Symonds, in fact, the urge to write an autobiography grew out of just such an unresolved conflict between the private self and the public persona. As one who occupied a socially respectable and in many ways privileged position of man of letters and family patriarch, Symonds was at the same time exploring and eventually acting out desires that he knew could destroy his life and reputation. A cursory review of Symonds's career might lead one to suppose that his public and private lives were in harmony: he was, after all, writing on the subject of "inversion" from the 1870s until the time of his death. And yet Symonds's public utterances conveyed not his own sexual struggles but the confident voice of the historian and literary scholar.

Victorian codes of literary decorum required a stringent distinction between public and private roles in all those who hoped to publish their autobiographies. Although women were certainly more likely to be castigated for prurient self-disclosures, men were also encouraged by literary convention to be circumspect in discussing their private lives, if they did so at all. Two central examples of male reticence in autobiography can be found in John Stuart Mill and Anthony Trollope, both of whom, in different ways, refused to satisfy their readers' curiosity about their private lives when they wrote their autobiographies. Sexual candor was, unsurprisingly, among the first casualties of self-censorship on the part of Victorian autobiographers. Phyllis Grosskurth argues that the "confessional" model of autobiography was generally renounced in nineteenth-century British autobiography, largely as a result of the low esteem in which Rousseau's *Confessions* was held in Victorian England. Symonds's *Memoirs* is again one of the chief exceptions to this rule.[43]

Because Symonds did not comply with autobiographical self-censorship in a way that satisfied the requirements of Victorian society, the task was eventually undertaken by his literary executor, Horatio Forbes Brown, whose 1895 "biography" of Symonds was in fact an expurgated version of the *Memoirs*. Brown would later summarize the criticisms of his work made by Symonds's other friends: "The chief objection taken by those who had met Symonds was that the portrait [in the biography] was too uniformly gloomy; that the brightness, the sparkle, the play of fancy, so characteristic of Symonds's conversation in genial company, found no place in this record of himself drawn from his autobiography, his diaries and his letters." Yet, Brown defended his account of Symonds's life, writing that "after going through the material at my disposal I came to the conclusion that I at least could present no other portrait."[44]

The central part of the "material at [Brown's] disposal" was the *Memoirs*. By excluding all references to his subject's complex sexual history, Brown (who was also homosexual) in effect made a cipher of his friend's autobiographical project. As would be the case with Robert Ross's expurgation of Wilde's prison letter a decade later, the publication of an expurgated autobiography transformed an explicitly sexual crisis into an obscurely religious or spiritual one. Both Brown's *Life* and Ross's *De Profundis* were designed to shift public attention away from the controversial sexual histories of the subjects and toward their supposed spiritual and religious transformation. The actions of these men, however well-intentioned, brings to the term "literary executor" a more sinister nuance: one who executes (ends the life of) the subject, rather than one who executes (acts out) his literary will.

If even Symonds's "most intimate friends" lacked access to his "inner self" during his lifetime, then the publication of Brown's *Life* did nothing to extend the public knowledge of Symonds's sexual history: on the contrary, it served to obstruct and confuse such knowledge. Only more recently have we, as readers of his "secret" autobiography, been privileged to enjoy a greater insight into his life than any of his living companions.[45] And yet the "inner self" that Symonds claims had always been invisible or inaccessible even to his closest friends is not straightforwardly "revealed" in his autobiography but at least partially constituted by it. Symonds's secret self is in a crucial sense achieved only in the act of writing the autobiography, even though the narrative presents it as having been discovered in the past. Put more broadly, the discourse of "inner" experience—fantasies, feelings, desires, dreams, and so forth—and the related construction of an "inner self," as distinct from the public persona, are central functions of the autobiographical process and arguably its unique domain. In the *Memoirs*, Symonds achieves a match between the secret history he has to relate and the confessional genre best fitted to narrate such a story.

As Philippe Lejeune argues, "The autobiographical form is undoubtedly not the instrument of expression of a subject that preexists it, nor even a 'role,' but rather that which determines the very existence of 'subjects.'"[46] This radical claim for the power of autobiography to construct subjects has appeared in other criticism of the genre. Linda H. Peterson, for example, argues that "autobiography, apparently the most personal and individual of literary genres, is in fact a highly conventional, even prescriptive form, and . . . its generic conventions shape our ways of thinking about the most private aspects of our lives."[47] In the view of both these critics — though to different degrees — autobiographical discourse is instrumental in shaping subjectivity and self-consciousness, rather than being merely the expression of a preexisting identity. This is not to deny that Symonds felt pressure to "speak out" about his sexuality before writing the *Memoirs*; but, as we have seen, his early sense of being "trained" to write his confessions predated any specified content for a confessional narrative. Symonds's experiences of illicit sexual passion therefore gave him the ideal subject for the confessional work he had long felt he was destined to write.

It was Symonds's cultural and literary experiences that provided the material for his subsequent sexual fantasies, which are particularly derived from the textual discovery of "Platonic" love.[48] Of Willie Dyer, a Bristol schoolboy, for example, Symonds writes that "my present mood of feeling squared with the philosophy of love I had imbibed from Plato" (103). In a moving passage, he describes how, after weeks of clandestine communication, the two young men finally meet face to face: "I took Willie's slender hand into my own and gazed into his large brown eyes fringed with heavy lashes. A quite indescribable effluence of peace and satisfaction, blent with yearning, flowed from his physical presence and inundated my whole being with some healing and refreshing influence. From that morning I date the birth of my real self" (104).

The language of this passage indicates another turning point in Symonds's life — "the birth of my real self" — that might seem to resolve the self-division described in the earlier chapters. Symonds here suggests that the physical realization of his erotic ideal necessary for his full "birth" complements the influence of Plato on his self-formation. Without the powerful and enabling influences of Plato and Willie Dyer to support him, Symonds would never have reached a position from which to synthesize the various elements of his own sexuality. The key episode of Symonds "speaking out" as an undergraduate at Oxford, however, dramatizes the impossibility of "coming out" as a homosexual in the late nineteenth century and suggests that the only form of sexual disclosure available to him and to others was denunciation. The importance of the phrase "speaking out," used by Symonds frequently in his memoirs, inheres in the ambiguous subject of the utterance: the act of "speaking out" discloses the "secret" of homosexuality (a secret Symonds describes himself as having

{ *The Secret Which I Carried* }

"carried") that is never exclusively his own. Just as no individual's act of disclosure is devoid of social implications, each incident of homosexual denunciation creates repercussions for the person who makes known the sexual preferences or practices of another.

Symonds's chief accomplice in his exposure of Vaughan was his Latin tutor at Oxford, John Conington, who "sympathized with romantic attachments for boys" (109).[49] Conington had given Symonds a copy of *Jonica*, urging him to read it, and Symonds was suitably impressed with the poetry, which, he writes, "inflamed my imagination" (109). First published in 1858, *Jonica* was a book of homoerotic verse by William Johnson (later Cory), a teacher at Eton dismissed from the school in 1872, apparently as a result of a homosexual scandal involving some of his pupils: "The circumstances of William Johnson Cory's peremptory dismissal from Eton in 1872, though never explained, leave no doubt in the mind of one modern writer of the 'gross character' of his activities, but at the time the causes of his departure were veiled in discretion."[50] Symonds subsequently wrote to Johnson, "exposing the state of my feelings and asking his advice" (109), and the correspondence culminated in the younger man receiving, to his great excitement, "a long epistle on paiderastia in modern times, defending it and laying down the principle that affection between people of the same sex is not less natural and rational than the ordinary passionate relations" (109).[51]

An invitation such as Conington's to read a "special" book could easily be construed as a discreet revelation of one's sexual proclivities, and Symonds, after his experiences with Vaughan, could hardly have been unaware of the significance of this initial gift from his tutor.[52] In fact, *Jonica* functions in the narrative, following the textual impact of Plato, as another instance of the "fatal book," described by Dowling as "fatal . . . not because of its power to kill outright, but because of its power decisively to change an individual life."[53] Yet the "fatal" consequences of *Jonica* do not befall Symonds himself but his former headmaster, as the exchange of the book leads to the disclosure of Vaughan's secret while on a reading trip to the Lake District in the summer of 1859:

I was talking one hot afternoon with Conington about *Jonica* and what I then called Arcadian love. Heaven forgive the innocent euphemism! . . . Well: some turn in the argument . . . forced me to blurt out what I had so long concealed about Vaughan's story. Conington was deeply moved. He shrank into himself, and told me that such things ought not to be lightly spoken of. I replied that I could support what I had said by evidence, and that I was certain of my facts. . . . I convinced Conington that I had spoken the truth. He recommended me to go at once with Pretor's letter and my Harrow diaries to Clifton. My father ought to know the fact, whatever happened. [110–11]

The intimate teacher-pupil relationship with his companion is crucial in prompting Symonds to think of Vaughan and to substitute the revelation of his former headmaster's pederasty for the confession of his own desire. Significantly, Symonds disclaims responsibility for the disclosure by stating that he was "forced . . . to blurt out what I had so long concealed." The details of the conversation are left vague, so as to make it impossible to discover why it was that Symonds was "forced" to inform on Vaughan. Yet the fact that they are discussing "unrecognized passion between male persons" suggests that this is a moment ripe for sexual disclosures. At the same time, if Symonds's disclosure of Vaughan's "story" seems merely a fortuitous association of ideas, it might also be a warning to Conington that he has already experienced and successfully resisted an attempted seduction by a teacher. Certainly, Symonds's account of Conington's reaction ("he shrank into himself") indicates that the tutor experienced the revelation as a rejection of his own advances. By advising Symonds of the seriousness of such charges, moreover, Conington reveals his own vulnerability to sexual scandal.

According to the *Memoirs*, Symonds was making every effort to overcome his same-sex desire at this time, in an attempt to conform to social pressures and his father's wishes. In turning on Vaughan, then, he can both purify himself of illicit desire and keep his latest suitor, Conington, at a safe distance. Symonds's trip back to Clifton to reveal Vaughan's secret to his father makes melancholy reading, as Symonds guiltily reflects that "I had become the accuser of my old headmaster, a man for whom I felt no love, and who had shown me no special kindness, but who was after all the awe-inspiring ruler of the petty state of Harrow" (112).[54] His position is made more difficult by his own implication in Vaughan's desires: "I felt a deeply rooted sympathy with Vaughan. If he had sinned, it had been by yielding to passions which already mastered me. But this fact instead of making me indulgent, determined me to tell the bitter truth. At that period I was not cynical. I desired to overcome the malady of my own nature. My blood boiled and my nerves stiffened when I thought what mischief life at Harrow was doing daily to young lads under the autocracy of a hypocrite" (112).

Making Vaughan the sacrifice to his own self-loathing (evident in the phrase "the malady of my own nature"), Symonds displaces his unmanageable desires onto someone else, whose punishment might enable him to resolve his own sexual crisis. Like Conington, Symonds's father is ready to believe the worst of Vaughan: "It took as little to convince my father as it had taken to convince Conington. The evidence was plain and irrefragable" (112). Dr. Symonds writes to Vaughan demanding his resignation from the school and threatening a scandal if he refuses to comply. Despite pleas for mercy from Vaughan's wife, Dr. Symonds, acting the role of mid-Victorian moral policeman, is adamant, and Vaughan is forced to resign. The scandal is, however, superlatively hushed up: Symonds comments that "Vaughan then had to withdraw from Harrow; and he did this with consummate skill. No one knew the reason of his sudden abdication except Conington, my father, myself, and a few undergraduates at Cambridge and Oxford" (112).

For Symonds and Conington alike, incriminating Vaughan is preferable to confronting the transgressive aspects of their own sexual desires.[55] The so-called unspeakable vice is, it turns out, utterable only when it implicates someone else. Symonds himself could not speak out about his own sexuality but was only able to denounce the actions of a man who had shown Symonds "no special kindness," a phrase that apparently alludes to the headmaster's preference for Pretor over Symonds as an object of desire. Indeed, one can interpret the later autobiographical account as an attempt by Symonds to justify his actions and to reclaim his lost agency in the affair by appropriating the secret of his sexuality as his own once again to disclose. The subsequent portions of the *Memoirs* make clear that this crisis would return to haunt Symonds in later life. The autobiography attempts finally to lay to rest the guilt at having denounced a fellow invert.

Ironically, Symonds writes that the chief good that came out of the Vaughan affair was his improved relationship with his father. Indeed, it appears that he had in effect revealed his own sexuality to Dr. Symonds through the ruse of disclosing Vaughan's secret: "No veil remained between us. He understood my character; I felt his in sympathy and relied upon his wisdom" (116). Despite this "sympathy" for his son's sexual "character," however, Dr. Symonds immediately advises him to end his relationship with the socially inferior Willie Dyer, pointing out that his involvement in the Pretor-Vaughan affair made him vulnerable to sexual scandal. In obedience to his father's wishes, Symonds "gave up Willie Dyer as my avowed heart's friend and comrade. I submitted to the desirability of not acknowledging the boy I loved in public. But I was not strong enough to break the bond which linked us or to extirpate the living love I felt for him. I carried on our intimacy in clandestine ways and fed my temperament on sweet emotion in secret. This deceit . . . brought me cruel wrong" (117).

Over thirty years after the event, Symonds dramatically interrupts his narrative to announce that he can hardly bring himself to continue with his autobiography when he recalls his previous crimes against the law, not of society, but of his own passion: "Here I feel inclined to lay my pen down in weariness. Why should I go on to tell the story of my life? The back of my life was broken when I yielded to convention, and became untrue in soul to Willie" (117).[56] Being "untrue in soul to Willie" is a remarkable articulation of Symonds's moral collapse under the pressure of his father's will, which he views in hindsight as an unforgivable and crippling capitulation to conventional public morality. If meeting Dyer had been "the birth of my real self," then ending the relationship in the wake of the Vaughan affair signifies the tragic death of that self ("the back of my life was broken"). Significantly, Symonds's sexual desire becomes once more "clandestine" and "deceitful" following his father's prohibition of his affair with Willie. More important, the stigmatizing of his idealized affection for Willie as something socially and morally disgraceful — parallel, at least in his father's eyes, with Vaughan's scandalous seduction of his pupils — returns Symonds to the secretive exploration of his sexuality that he had tentatively begun to reject as an undergraduate at Oxford.[57]

Indeed, "the secret which I carried" takes on a complex significance in these chapters, referring most tellingly to Symonds's sexual self-knowledge but also invoking his troubling discovery of Vaughan's sexual exploitation of his pupils. The "telling" of Vaughan's "story," which, as I have suggested, is a euphemistic phrase for the denuncia-

{ *The Secret Which I Carried* }

tion of his former headmaster, prefigures the telling of his own story in the *Memoirs*, in which he attempts to speak out on the subject of his own conflicted desires. Yet the Vaughan episode had established such telling as an incriminating and punitive form of discourse, plunging both speaker and victim into a dangerous region of secrecy and scandal. If, as the *Memoirs* suggests, Symonds came to view the telling of Vaughan's story as the betrayal of a fellow invert, then he doubtless recognized that his memoirs were potentially a source of sexual self-betrayal, tainted by his earlier involvement in revelatory sexual discourse.

"Little Hints and Fragments": Shorting's Revenge

Symonds's attempt to split his sexual self into two distinct personae — one secretive and sinister, the other aesthetic and idealized — is a recurring feature of his autobiographical narrative. This self-division explains the radical discontinuity between his contempt for Vaughan and Pretor — both of whom are stigmatized by their scandalous pederastic relationship — and his reverence of Conington and Willie Dyer, who are primarily associated with discreet textual pleasure. Here we see emerging the binary oppositions, between "good teacher" and "bad teacher," "good friend" and "bad friend," that define the moral structure of the *Memoirs*. The same structure of displacement, whereby the idealized self can be defined only in terms of its demonized opposite, recurs in a later context, in which Symonds develops a contrast between his own adoration of another choirboy, Alfred Brooke, and the predatory sexuality of a rival at Oxford, named Shorting.

Yet, lest we attribute this narrative logic to the unconscious workings of Symonds's mind, he is remarkably aware of the projection of his idealized sexual desire onto external objects. For example, in describing his passion for Alfred Brooke, in whom he creates an essentially imaginary being to fulfill a long-unsatisfied erotic fantasy, Symonds writes self-critically that "my conception of him, contaminated by my own unwholesome fancy, would have vanished like a vision at the first touch of physical and moral contact. But this I shrank from for a score of unpractically prudent reasons. And I believe that the picture I have drawn of him as the dream object of my permanent desire is a gross libel upon the flesh-and-blood being he was" (128). Symonds's self-awareness of the extent to which Alfred is a product of his *erotic* imagination contrasts strikingly with the role played by his darker doubles, in particular Shorting, the new friend "who was destined to exercise a good deal of influence over my life. . . . We soon became intimate and I discovered that he shared my Arcadian tastes" (117).

The shadow of what Symonds calls his "dark and brooding self" is projected in this section of the narrative onto the figure of Shorting, who, like Vaughan, is reviled for the lack of inhibition with which he proceeds to satisfy his sexual "tastes." Symonds's own reluctance to initiate "the first touch of physical . . . contact" with the object of his desire — a reluctance portrayed vividly in the sonnet "Angelo Fusato" — is contrasted with the aggressive lust of Shorting, described disapprovingly as "the troublous friend, who had chosen the broad way of self-indulgence" (120). Symonds's response to such figures as Vaughan and Shorting is complex and divided: repulsion is certainly registered, but so too is fascination, sympathy, and a degree of envy at their lack of sexual inhibition.

Symonds tellingly describes his divided reaction as Shorting, like Vaughan, "plagued me by his influence — by the sympathy I felt for him, my horror of his course, the love I nourished in my bosom for a man I could not respect" (120). The names of Vaughan and Shorting increasingly constitute a litany of self-reproach for Symonds, whose peace of mind was shattered by his involvement with these two men. Shorting, like Vaughan, is for Symonds a cautionary figure representing the shameless indulgence in homosexual passions that he was increasingly determined to deny to himself. Significantly, he links the two men's names together while explaining his inability to pursue his sexual passion for Alfred Brooke to a satisfying conclusion: "A respectable regard for my father, an ideal of purity of conduct, a dread of the world's opinion forced upon me by Vaughan's and Shorting's histories, combined to make me shrink from action" (127). The word "shrink" — echoing Conington's shocked reaction to the disclosure of Vaughan's story — suggests the loss of sexual potency that accompanies Symonds's emotional withdrawal.

As Symonds describes it, the denial of his sexual desire for Brooke has a crippling effect on his emotional life but does not, oddly enough, prevent him from graduating with first-class honors from Balliol. In the autumn of 1862, he is elected to a fellowship at Magdalen College, where he immediately takes up residence and begins to receive pupils. One of these is Shorting, whom Symonds agrees to coach in philosophy on condition that the tutorials are held in Shorting's lodgings because, according to Symonds, Shorting planned to take advantage of his newly acquired access to Magdalen by pursuing the college's choirboys. As he gradually becomes established in his new environment, Symonds learns of two distressing rumors that affect him. The first is that Alfred Pretor, his friend at Harrow, is spreading the story of "Vaughan's troubles" at Cambridge.[58] The second is Shorting's emerging plan to revenge himself on Symonds for the latter's lack of cooperation regarding the Magdalen choristers. It does not take him long to discover the form that this revenge was to take:

> I was in London, staying with A. O. Rutson at 7 Half Moon Street, when the storm broke on Monday 24 November. A letter from Cobham brought me news that Shorting had sent a document defamatory of myself, and containing extracts from my private correspondence and my poems, to six of the Magdalen fellows. His object was to prove that I had supported him in his pursuit of the chorister Goolden, that I shared his habits and was bent on the same path. All my letters of expostulation and reasoning with him he had destroyed, and had cut out and pieced together little hints and fragments which gave a plausible colour to his charges. [131][59]

Once again, it is a series of texts that produces a crisis in Symonds's life—a crisis so closely related to the earlier disclosure of Vaughan's "story" that the significance of the two episodes cannot be grasped if they are considered in isolation from each other. It was by means of a letter that Symonds had discovered Vaughan's relationship with Pretor at Harrow; and it is by means of Symonds's own incriminating letters that Shorting attempts to ruin his reputation at Oxford. It is difficult, in fact, to determine whether Symonds's outrage is directed primarily against Shorting's assault on his name or against Shorting's violation of the integrity of his texts. Shorting shows little respect for Symonds's writings, having "cut out and pieced together little hints and fragments" from the letters, the rest of which he "destroyed," offering to the Magdalen fellows no more than "extracts from my private correspondence and my poems" as evidence of his sexual misdemeanors. In a curious way, this destruction of Symonds's texts anticipates the barbarous editing of Horatio Brown — with the difference that Shorting employed his scissors to ruin Symonds's name, and Brown, to protect it.

The scandal effectively ended Symonds's career at Oxford, though he protested his innocence of the charges brought forward by Shorting — "my conscience was absolutely clear" (131) — and was eventually acquitted by the fellows of his college.[60] More important, Symonds describes how, in the aftermath of the scandal, "my health failed suddenly; and I have never been a strong man since. Shorting indeed had his revenge. He was of so strange a nature than [sic] even could he have foreseen all the trouble he was bringing on me, and the ruin of my health, I believe he would not have desisted from his dastardly action" (133). This was not only Shorting's revenge, but Vaughan's as well. For much as Symonds had contributed to the downfall of one practicing homosexual who enacted the desires that Symonds experienced himself and with which he "sympathized," he suffered a similar fate at the hands of another such figure of uninhibited desire. The two incidents become closely connected in Symonds's autobiography, and the lingering resentment toward Shorting for the "dastardly action" that had done such damage to his reputation is closely related to his guilt at the ruin he and his father had inflicted on Vaughan. This is not to claim that Shorting was acting consciously as Vaughan's avenger in this crisis. Indeed, if Shorting represents anything in this narrative, it is the uneasy conscience of Symonds himself, enacting a textual retribution that perfectly fits the crime.

Unsurprisingly, the Shorting affair was carefully concealed from the public, just as the events involving Vaughan had been. In his "biography" of Symonds, Horatio Brown inserted one of his many misleading editorial passages, which referred to the episode without indicating that it involved any taint of homosexual scandal:

> I must briefly refer to an event which proved of most serious consequence to a man of Symonds's sensitive and febrile temperament. A quondam friend sought, by means of garbled letters, to damage Symonds's character at Magdalen. He entirely failed in his object. But the unexpectedness of the blow, and the treachery of a man he had trusted, the annoyance at home, the odious necessity of defending himself, so preyed upon his nerves and brain, worn

{ *The Secret Which I Carried* }

by a perpetual internal conflict, and excited by the recent strain of two fellowship examinations, as to precipitate a physical crisis which was already imminent.[61]

Though, in Brown's version, the outcome of the crisis—the collapse of Symonds's health—remains the same as in Symonds's account, the causes have been radically altered. Brown's reference to the "garbled letters" produced by Shorting's editorial violence conveniently disguises his own distortion of the course of events as described in the *Memoirs*. At the time of the crisis, Shorting was not a "quondam" friend of Symonds but one of his most intimate associates: a man for whom Symonds had "nourished" a "love." Moreover, Shorting's attack on Symonds's reputation did not "entirely fail" but resulted in the loss of Symonds's Magdalen fellowship and, indirectly, in his departure from England as an invalid. Most important, the sexual motivation of the attack and the sexual causes of Symonds's vulnerability to blackmail are both erased from Brown's account, an omission that crucially misrepresents a central event in Symonds's life and sexual development.[62]

The Shorting affair was not to be the last of Symonds's defeats in the face of Victorian morality and hypocrisy for which he had, in private, little respect. The long series of embarrassing and scandalous episodes that threatened the secrecy of his sexuality brought with them the need for frequent self-protective subterfuges. Among the most striking—and unacknowledged—ironies in Symonds's *Memoirs* is that Symonds himself would eventually become sexually involved with one of his pupils, Norman Moor, in a manner disturbingly similar to Vaughan's relationship with Pretor. Symonds's strong erotic and aesthetic attraction to Moor is manifested in the description of his "very remarkable face, rather long but finely cut, with deep-set dark eyes under level, marked brows, low white forehead, and a storm of flaky dark hair, laid in heavy masses on a somewhat small skull, and turning at the tips to dusky gold" (193). It was for Moor's sake that Symonds took steps to get a teaching appointment at Clifton School, where he delivered the series of lectures on Greek literature that would eventually be published as *Studies of the Greek Poets* (1873–76), the work that made his reputation in English literary circles. It was also the relationship with Moor that inspired Symonds's most productive period of writing poetry. Hence, he writes with enthusiasm that "it was Norman's influence which led me to take a step decisive for my literary career" (193). And yet, as Symonds presents it in his memoirs, this was a step, however "decisive," in the wrong direction.

"The Black Box Is Hidden Away": Symonds's Textual Secrets

Symonds's own pederastic relationship with Norman Moor brought to a crisis his long-recognized "sympathy" with the passions that had ruined Vaughan. As such, the relationship led him to suspect the very textual sources of same-sex desire that he had discovered in Plato. Though Symonds doesn't comment directly on the similarities between his affair with Moor and Vaughan's sexual interest in his pupils at Harrow, the resemblance is always lurking in the background: Symonds's desire, like Vaughan's, is excited by his pupil's inexperience, innocence, and ignorance, and there is a strong connection between his pedagogical involvement in his pupil and his sexual interest: "My intention to educate Norman and to stimulate his intellect, which seemed to me slack and indolent, soon assumed predominance. I began to coach him for his essays, and to read passages of good Greek and English authors with him. This led to little sweets of intimacy" (196). As with the Greek iambics that Symonds had brought to Vaughan's office (leading to caresses that, from Vaughan's point of view, would have seemed "little sweets of intimacy" but, from Symonds's, were "disagreeably suggestive"), a shared enterprise of reading results in erotic interactions.

Symonds's desire to influence Norman Moor's intellect becomes inextricable from his unspoken desire to stimulate the boy's body (also, perhaps, "slack and indolent"). Anxious to establish the purity of his motives for becoming involved with a pupil, Symonds writes that "without diminishing in passion for the boy, I turned my thoughts steadily and with a will to forming his taste and training his intellect" (200), while refuting a specifically sexual motive with the claim that at no time "did any one of those things take place between us which people think inseparable from love of this sort" (211).[63]

{ *The Secret Which I Carried* }

Symonds's disclaimer of a sodomitical relation between teacher and pupil has the reverse effect of highlighting the sexual nature of their intimacy. And yet, while his previous obsessions with Willie Dyer and Alfred Brooke are portrayed, in different ways, as emotionally unsettling disruptions of his work, his "passionate friendship" with Moor enables him to work at his most productive level. Similarly, whereas his involvements with Vaughan and Shorting proved disastrous for his academic career and peace of mind, Moor "helped to emancipate my intellect and will, so that I date from it my entrance into a new phase of activity, the fruits of which soon afterwards began to show themselves in a full stream of literary performances" (194).

Chief among these "literary performances" were Symonds's homoerotic poems, many of which remained unpublished because of their explicitly homosexual themes. In the letter to Dakyns in which he first mentions Norman Moor, Symonds provides his friend with an inventory of his recently written poetry, commenting on the difficulty of making his "monument of Love Heroic" known to the public.[64] Dakyns was clearly impressed by the poetry—so much so that Symonds sent him the manuscript of another major poem in the series, "Eudiades." Yet even as he depicts the poetry as a turning point, Symonds writes despondently in the *Memoirs* of the new diversion for the sexual energies that could not find an outlet in his own relationships: "I began to make verse the vehicle and safety valve for my tormenting preoccupations. A cycle of poems gradually got written, illustrating the love of man for man in all periods of civilization. Of these the two best are perhaps 'A Cretan Idyll' and 'Eudiades' " (189).[65]

By using the passive formulation "gradually got written," Symonds minimizes his active role in the production of incriminating poetry and implies that he himself is less than wholly responsible for its authorship. His claim that his poetry was a "safety valve" for his sexual passion similarly suggests a passively hydraulic model of sexual desire that, while it characterizes much of the writing in the *Memoirs*, is particularly evident in Symonds's discussion of his poetry. Symonds's anxiety about publishing his verse was shared by those friends who did not concur with Dakyns's enthusiasm for its homosexual themes. With one such friend, Henry Sidgwick, Symonds "thoroughly investigated the subject of my poems on Eros. His conclusion was that I ought to abandon them, as unhealthy and disturbing to my moral equilibrium. I assented. We locked them all up in a black tin box. . . . Having done this, Henry threw the key into the river Avon" (195).

In interpreting this scene, we may draw profitably on Koesten-baum's point that Symonds, in a number of his works, "used keys and locks to explain the difficulty of disclosing homosexuality to the reading public." [66] A letter to the symbolist poet Arthur Symons, for example, refers to Symonds's prose poem "In the Key of Blue" in familiar terms of concealment: "Of things like this, I have always been doing plenty, and then putting them away in a box. The public thinks them immoral." [67] In the above passages, Symonds seems unnaturally calm about what amounts to the confiscation and destruction of his poetry, which from his own viewpoint constituted his most important work. However, this indifference is explained by the revelation that the literary expression of his desire means less than its physical enactment with Moor: "There was something absurd in all this [that is, in Sidgwick's disposal of the poems], because I felt myself half-consciously upon the point of translating my dreams and fancies about love into fact" (195). Symonds here anticipates finding a more satisfactory escape than he had yet discovered from the prisonlike confines of the "black box."

Norman Moor came to represent the much-desired transition from textual encodings of desire to their physical satisfaction. In a diary entry included in the *Memoirs*, however, Symonds expressed some doubt as to whether the conversion from "fancy" to direct sexual experience could be made: "Norman ascends like a star, but a troublous planet. And the prospect of these lectures to the 6th form involves a whole change of life. The black box is hidden away. The art which for three years has been so continuous a safety valve is now shut off. Can I pour the old wine into these new bottles?" (196). This extended (and mixed) metaphor suggests the continuous reproduction of secrecy in Symonds's texts — the box that is the receptacle of the secret poetry itself becomes an object of secrecy that is "hidden away." The language of suppression and concealment that runs through most of Symonds's comments about his poetry is soon augmented, however, by terms more expressive of violence, which suggests the extent to which Symonds's same-sex desire, imprisoned (by himself and by others) in the "black box" of Victorian respectability, had become a source of anguish and fear: "Befooled am I, besotted, to live thus a poem when I have strangled my written poems. . . . I believe in self-deception now. I carry in my heart what I am afraid to analyse — even to define — what I hardly acknowledge to myself" (196). The "secret" that had previously been externalized — hidden in a box — is now portrayed as something internal that Symonds claims to "carry." Moreover, Symonds here attributes to himself the repressive agency he had earlier ascribed to Sidgwick, the key agent in the scene of censorship. The intimate relationship between poetry and sexual experience is reversed, as Symonds laments that the "death" of his "written poems" has made it futile to "live thus a poem." His own role in the suppression of his poetry is clarified and expanded in a letter of January 1869 to Dakyns about his homosexual series: "Those poems must be stifled somehow. . . . I shall try to exterminate them by writing on other matters."[68] In March of the same year, Symonds wrote to his sister Charlotte concerning "John Mordan": "I had written a Volume, of about 10,000 lines, — a row of tales — wh[ich] had occupied me for the last 3 years — all on one terrible & tragic subject (not that all were terrible & tragic). Well, these I put into the iron box I left with you at Clifton when I went to Hastings, locked it, threw the key into the Avon, & put the box itself beyond my own control. There immured [they] will lie until I have force to burn them or until I am dead the only fancies with wh[ich] nature has blessed me, my only hope of being known as a poet. For in some of those poems I was a poet."[69] Symonds here again comes across as a spectator of his own literary demise, despite the fact that the crucial actions are performed by himself. The pathos of the letter derives from its portrayal of himself as a Jekyll-like split personality, fearful that he lacks the moral strength to control the "terrible and tragic" elements lurking in his identity. Symonds's comment, in his later letter to Stevenson, that the story of Jekyll "touches one too closely" takes on poignant meaning when considered in relation to Symonds's suppressed verse. The telling displacement of Sidgwick by Symonds himself as the central agent in the episode succinctly discloses the internalized homophobia of the Victorian literary establishment and Symonds's concomitant sense of himself as a poet manqué who could not attach his name to his homoerotic verse "until I am dead."

Arguably, Symonds emerges as a more heroic, even tragic figure where he struggles to gain the strength of will necessary to abandon his incriminating poetic impulse (as he would later write to Dakyns,

"Illud cacoethes poetandi [that incurable itch for poetizing] is almost extinct in me").[70] The effect is heightened by the plaintive assertion that "in some of those poems I was a poet," which implies that he had in some sense killed himself (as poet) by shutting away his best work in the black box that housed his unpublished verse. The account that appears in the *Memoirs*, by contrast, lends support to my argument that many of Symonds's decisive actions grew out of his desire for acceptance by friends and family, combined with his fear of the consequences of sexual self-revelation. As it is revised in the *Memoirs*, the episode features Sidgwick as a concerned friend, anxious to protect the writer's reputation, but the result is an agonizing (for Symonds) suppression of sexual truth. Sidgwick, in this version, becomes one in a line of "friends," that also include Horatio Brown and Edmund Gosse, whose determination to protect Symonds's name ultimately did him a disservice. For they were protecting not only Symonds's secret but also their own.

The episode of the "black box" is important, moreover, because it indicates Symonds's growing disenchantment with literary expressions of same-sex desire. Although writers such as Plato and Whitman had been liberating and inspirational figures for Symonds, he becomes increasingly cynical in the *Memoirs* about the function of his writing as a "safety valve" that actually inhibits the realization of his sexual desire. For example, his exuberant realization that "the actual historical Greeks of antiquity . . . treated this [homosexual] love seriously, invested it with moral charm, endowed it with sublimity" (99) is gradually replaced by a forlorn recognition of the impossibility of fulfilling, in English society, the desires stimulated by a classical literary education: "The subjects with which I have been occupied— Greek poetry, Italian culture in one of the most lawless periods of modern history, beauty in nature and the body of man—stimulate and irritate the imagination. They excite cravings which cannot be satisfied by simple pleasures" (239).

For Symonds, literature, whether Greek or modern, is at once the stimulant of such "forbidden" passions and "cravings" and the means by which they might be sublimated into "higher" (cultural) activity. Yet this literary sublimation becomes increasingly problematic for Symonds, and his autobiography suggests writing as a temporary and relatively safe distraction from his sexual feelings, rather than a satisfactory resolution of them: "Relief from thoughts which had

{ *The Secret Which I Carried* }

become intolerable, and longings recognized as unassuageable, had to be sought in brain labour" (236). Norman Moor's attraction for Symonds is precisely that he seems to offer a way out of this dilemma, providing Symonds an opportunity to act out his physical desire while avoiding the corrupting pederastic influence of Vaughan. The romantic attention to Moor contrasts favorably with the frustration of Symonds's literary labors, yet is justified by its contribution to his own literary successes and its beneficial effect on Moor's "intellect."

Nevertheless, his correspondence of the period suggests that Symonds came to find his relationship with Moor increasingly unsatisfactory, largely because of his own tendency to intellectualize his sexual passion.[71] In the *Memoirs*, Symonds reflects that "the real malady of my nature was not in the passion I felt for him, but in the self-conscious morbid and sophisticated way in which the passion expressed itself. The passion was natural; and he responded to it naturally, so far as temperament, age and constitution of his emotional self permitted" (213). Significantly, Symonds uses the same phrase — "malady of my nature" — that he employed in his account of the Vaughan affair, even as he attempts to distance himself from Vaughan's pederasty by affirming the "natural" and salutary effects of his own passion for his pupil. The meaning of the "malady" has now mutated to refer, implicitly, to the intellectual obstacles to the realization of his desire, rather than the desire itself. Symonds, apparently, had come to believe that his "problem" — a word he had used for years to describe sexual inversion — was not homosexuality after all but the self-conscious introspection that impeded the satisfaction of desire. Moreover, he recognized that this introspection derived from, or at least was connected with, his literary labors and the dream of an "ideal love" that resulted from his youthful reading of Plato.

Interestingly, Moor himself would later refute Symonds's conviction that the study of the classics by youth had a tendency to corrupt them. Symonds had written to Moor, asking his opinion about the influence of Greek literature on the sexual development of young men, to which Moor replied unambiguously that "a very large proportion of the 'unnatural vice' which they say is so prevalent in public schools has nothing whatever to do with the reading of the classics" (295).[72] Moor went on to argue that the erotic and emotional intimacy formed between boys at public school, far from being a public menace, were potentially a national benefit: "The love of boys for boys is I believe inevitable in our public schools to which we point as our national glory—and not only is it inevitable, but I would go so far as to say it is desirable if it can be kept in an absolutely pure region" (296). Moor here voices the establishment credo that the masculine bonds formed in elite educational institutions became the bedrock of Britain's empire and the foundation of its national prosperity. As Symonds had done in the early stages of his homosexual identification, however, Moor insists on the "absolutely pure region" of idealized same-sex passion as distinct from the pleasures of sensual, physical indulgence that Symonds had witnessed (if not participated in) at Harrow.

Moor's own "case history," which he includes in his letter to Symonds, appears to confirm the conventional Victorian etiology of homosexuality. The story of the "corruption" of a youth by an older person of the same sex, followed by the gradual immersion of an "innocent" in schoolboy homosexual culture, in some ways resembles Symonds's own account of his experience at Harrow: "Corrupted at a very early age by a Harrow eleven boy who came over to Ashborne to play in a cricket match, and invited to his house by him where I stayed two or three days, nights were more to the point, and by him introduced to a sense of what one was made of, for years I never could throw off a perfect lust for being spooned. I regarded every big boy as a possible admirer—and when I got a bit older myself, I regarded every small boy as a possible spoon. A most pandemic state" (296–97). It was, appropriately, a "Harrow boy" who had corrupted him. But Moor evidently felt at home in the explicitly homosexual milieu of public school as Symonds himself had never done. Indeed, the outcome of his story offers an interesting counterweight to the antipederastic misgivings that Symonds had begun to articulate: "The combined influence of Percival and yourself," Moor writes, "did something to cure me of this—but here you see is another case where the paiderastic instinct (if it can be so far dignified as to be called paiderastic) was not in any way caused by the reading of G[ree]k lit[erature], but was rather chastened and directed by a literary education" (297). This might have been specifically calculated to assuage Symonds's growing concerns about the harmful influence of Greek literature: according to Moor, not only did it not corrupt him, it "chastened and directed" him and was in this respect the ideal complement to the influence of Symonds himself, who had helped to "cure" Moor of his "perfect lust for being spooned."[73]

Symonds therefore writes with obvious relief in the *Memoirs* that "in spite of all appearances, and in spite of what I have described myself, he, after the lapse of sixteen years, looked back upon my influence as salutary in the very matter of love between male and male" (212). Moor's letter, unlike most of the epistolary texts in the *Memoirs*, was profoundly reassuring and helpful, convincing Symonds that the results of his "illicit" desire and pedagogical influence had, unlike Vaughan's, been beneficial to others, even if they had proved a source of conflict and unhappiness in himself. It helped to counteract the old traumatic memory of Vaughan at Harrow by offering an example of a beneficial (yet sexual) relationship between teacher and pupil. That the influence of Greek literature—and the same-sex desire that it celebrated—need not be "corrupting" but could serve as a "civilizing" influence on young men was, for Symonds, a profoundly significant vindication of his literary and educational career.

As the preceding discussion indicates, Moor's function in the autobiography is, in part, to justify the coexistence of literary and sexual urges and to represent an idealized outlet for sexual impulses and fantasies that could in actuality find expression only in secretive ways. Yet the ultimate collapse of Symonds's relationship with Moor reminds us that he spent his life grappling, in his writing and elsewhere, with conflicting passions he could neither resolve in private nor express publicly. Moreover, by the time he wrote the *Memoirs*, Symonds viewed the capacity of literature to (as Moor expressed it) "chasten" and "direct" homosexual desire as a source of frustration and resentment rather than the solution to his predicament. Unsurprisingly, the autobiographical project that Symonds believed would bring his sexual self and his literary career into harmony was no more immune than his other writings to the internal doubts and external pressures that had conspired against his attempts to "speak out."

Conclusion: "If Only It Can Be Said"

Less than a year before his death, Symonds again wrote to Dakyns, this time in a tone of dejection that contrasted markedly with the enthusiastic plan to "speak out" that he had articulated only three years previously: "I shall have a great deal to say to you, if only it can be said. I never seem to have lived until quite lately; & just when the times are out of joint for self-externalizing life, I seem drawn into it. It is true I go on writing books, & even poems. But literature has long since lost for me reality of interest. One reads certainly. Copious reading fills the vacuum which remains when feeling & sensation are abeyant."[74] Was Symonds referring, by the phrase "self-externalizing life," to his new attempts at relationships or to the autobiographical project that he was anxious to complete before he died? If the latter, he had evidently become depressed by the slim hopes of his project gaining an audience during his lifetime ("the times are out of joint") and even unsure of the possibility of finding his own voice ("if only it can be said").

The loss of interest in literature expressed in Symonds's late letter to Dakyns conveys the extent to which the tone and subject matter required to address an English bourgeois and presumptively heterosexual audience had become onerous and repulsive to him. His poetry, the only writing in which he believed he had revealed the "truth" about himself, had been securely locked away in an iron box and would never again see the light of day. His reputation as a cultivated and learned critic of Greek and Renaissance culture was intact, but only at the expense of the writing that Symonds felt revealed the voice of his inner self. It is this secret self to which Symonds refers in his letter to Dakyns, and yet to express this self was to risk dissolving it. It was from this trap of comfortable and respectable security that Symonds finally attempted to escape by "speaking out" with confessional candor.

Yet it would be misleading to claim that Symonds was simply a victim of external Victorian authority and repression. Symonds himself played a role in the long concealment of the memoirs from public scrutiny. The contradiction between his desire to "speak out" and the impulse for self-protective secrecy recurs once again in Symonds's instructions to his literary executor, Horatio Brown, regarding the fate of his autobiography. Symonds was confident enough of the importance of his work to pronounce it, in a letter to Brown of December 1891, "a very singular book—perhaps unique, in the disclosure of a type of man who has not yet been classified."[75] Yet he also cautioned Brown about the risks involved in its publication, urging him to proceed with care, in a directive that encapsulates the divided impulses of Symonds's entire career:

I want to save it from destruction after my death, and yet to reserve its publication for a period when it will not be injurious to
my family. I do not just now know how to meet the difficulty. . . . I
have sketched my wish out that this autobiography should not be
destroyed. Still, I see the necessity for caution in its publication.
Give the matter a thought. If I could do so, I should like to except
it as a thing apart, together with other documents from my general
literary bequest; so as to make no friend, or person, responsible
for the matter, to which I attach a particular value apart from life's
relations.[76]

Following Symonds's death in 1893, the manuscript came into the
possession of Brown, who decided against its publication throughout
the period of endemic paranoia about homosexuality just before and
during the Oscar Wilde trials. His response to Symonds's confusing
request for publication with caution was to publish the two-volume
biography of Symonds based exclusively on the memoirs but to avoid
any reference to Symonds's homosexuality. With some circumspec-
tion, Brown justified his approach as follows:

It may be asked why, as an autobiography exists, I have not confined myself to the publication of that. Apart from the ordinary
and obvious reasons which render the immediate publication of
autobiographies undesirable, there is a consideration supplied by
Symonds himself, which induced me to adopt the course I have
taken. "Autobiographies written with a purpose," he says in the
autobiography itself, "are likely to want atmosphere. A man, when
he sits down to give an account of his own life, from the point of
view of art or of passion or of a particular action, is apt to make
it appear as though he were nothing but an artist, nothing but a
lover, or that the action he seeks to explain were [sic] the principal
event in his existence."[77]

The irony of this explanation is remarkable in that it uses Symonds's
own words to justify the exclusion of same-sex desire from the autobiography: the very issue that had motivated him to write it. It
was precisely Symonds's purpose to write an account of his own
life that focused on his homosexual experiences, which had, he felt,
been ignored or concealed in his other writing. Hence, the biography
entered literary history as an example of what one biographer terms

"the respectable and wholly artificial Victorian genre of 'Life and Letters,' with its reverence for its subject and its eagerness to purge the life in question of any irregularities—in short, to sanitize it."[78]

The collusion of Brown with Symonds's desire for caution was, of course, motivated by his own secret agenda. As Koestenbaum points out, "Brown was himself a homosexual; censoring Symonds's work, he intended only to protect a comrade from a disgrace that they both feared."[79] Brown's wish to protect Symonds's secret, however paradoxical it may seem, is remarkably similar to Symonds's motives for disclosing Vaughan's: the urge for self-preservation. Perhaps Brown was concerned that if the memoirs were published, he himself would be tainted with Symonds's homosexuality. Yet the gulf between Symonds's sexual life and his public image was, of course, the very reason why he had felt driven to write the autobiography in the first place. In this way, the aspect of Symonds's life that had demanded the writing of the *Memoirs* was effectively suppressed by the man entrusted with Symonds's literary reputation.

No matter how self-interested Brown's motives may have been, he did succeed in publishing large portions of the memoirs, which, to those who knew Symonds, would have been enough to recognize its sexual theme. When Brown himself died in 1926, the manuscript was left to the London Library, with a fifty-year embargo on its publication. The library committee, chaired by Sir Edmund Gosse, accepted the gift under the specified conditions. Hence, Symonds's secret became, quite literally, the property of the elite literary establishment, with access for the public being extremely limited.[80] Symonds's textual (and sexual) "secret" was one that another box—this one made of green cardboard and housed in the library—would keep concealed from the public for almost a century after his death.[81] When the embargo was lifted in 1976, direct quotation from the manuscript became possible and, in 1984, the memoirs of John Addington Symonds were at last published.[82] The plan he had confided to Dakyns of "speaking out" could finally become known.

CHAPTER 3

Defacing Oscar Wilde

What might be termed the "confessional" significance of Wilde's writing—in particular, the ways in which it can be read as revealing the "secret" of his sexuality—has, in the last decade, become one of the central preoccupations of criticism dealing with his work. Specifically, *The Picture of Dorian Gray* (his only novel), *The Importance of Being Earnest* (his last and most famous play), and *De Profundis*—the name posthumously attributed to the letter he wrote to Lord Alfred Douglas from Reading Gaol—have come under intense scrutiny for the clues they might provide about the relationship between Wilde's aesthetic and sexual practices.[1] That these central writings of Wilde explore, in different ways, the dangers and allurements of same-sex desire has come to seem axiomatic; yet the precise significance of Wilde's sexuality for an understanding of these writings remains opaque. My aim is not to offer a definitive interpretation of the sexual politics of Wilde's writings but rather to attempt two related yet distinct critical interventions. First, I offer a critical reading of several more recent efforts to advance the understanding of Wilde's sexuality in relation to his writing. Second, I question a central premise of this ongoing critical enterprise: that Wilde's sexuality, however it might be defined or understood, is the determining element of his critical responses to Victorian social and literary conventions.

More than any other writer discussed in this book, Wilde has be-come identified with the origins of the modern homosexual: so much so, in fact, that it becomes impossible to approach his writings with an open mind about their sexual meanings. Hence, the preliminary effort must be directed toward challenging our assumptions about Wilde, his sexual desire, and his textual practice. This necessarily in-volves engaging with those critics who have significantly contributed to — arguably, constructed — our understanding of Wilde as primarily a writer about same-sex desire. While not disputing the *relevance* of Wilde's sexuality to the critical understanding of his writings, I ques-tion the assumption that Wilde is to be understood principally as a polemicist or apologist for same-sex desire. Only once this process of critical evaluation is under way can we begin to imagine what other objectives Wilde might be attempting in his writing.

In particular, I endeavor to reinscribe the centrality of aesthetic criticism to the critical project of Wilde's writing. Although most of the critics to whom I refer display a sophisticated awareness of the role of sexual desire and aestheticized self-invention in Wilde's work, only Richard Dellamora has read Wilde's work against the Victorian back-ground of aesthetic discourse and controversy about the aesthetic en-codings of dissident desire in which Wilde's writings were produced.[2] By focusing on Wilde and Walter Pater's subversive appropriation of dominant ideology, rather than suggesting an unquestioning rejec-tion of it, Dellamora emphasizes Wilde's continuity with his Victorian predecessors. The argument of this chapter also draws on Jonathan Dollimore's important insight that Wilde was able to perceive the ideological effects and limits of his society and that his work "recog-nizes the priority of the social and the cultural in determining not only public meaning but 'private' or subjective desire."[3] This critical emphasis on the specific cultural and historical conditions of his art departs from the claim made by Richard Ellmann that Wilde "belongs to our world more than to Victoria's."[4] Wilde's writing, stylistically and thematically, certainly anticipates many aspects of modernist texts; but his aesthetic preoccupations as well as his moral sensibility locate him firmly in the Victorian era. The wish fulfillment of "claim-ing" Wilde for modern definitions of authorship, sexual identity, and textual politics is precisely what I seek to challenge.

To the extent that my use of the term "defacing" in the title of this chapter suggests a violence or disfigurement, this reflects the deep-

{ *Defacing Oscar Wilde* }

seated effects of the "identity" that has been constructed for Wilde by twentieth-century critics and biographers. To offer to "unmask" Wilde only perpetuates the illusion of a "real" self underlying the performance — or appearance — and so props up the notion of "sincerity" that Wilde sought to dismantle. As Dollimore observes, "Wilde's transgressive aesthetic is the reverse: insincerity, inauthenticity, and unnaturalness become the liberating attributes of decentred identity and desire."[5] Unfortunately, what might once have been a mask has now become a face: rather than a contingent, metonymic association between Wilde and same-sex desire, we are confronted with an essentializing, metaphoric "identity" of Wilde as "homosexual."[6] The work of Lee Edelman and Ed Cohen has shown us the extent to which Wilde's sexual "nature" was constructed rhetorically during the trials against the "norm" of late-Victorian, middle-class masculine behavior and is comprehensible only in the context of those culturally specific forms of rhetoric and propaganda. But our sense of Wilde as an aberration has outlasted the context that produced it. And this sense has continued to inform readings of his work that foreground its cultural and sexual difference rather than its continuity with Victorian textual practices and cultural patterns.[7]

With this critical distortion in mind, "defacing" Wilde is employed in the sense used by Paul de Man in "Autobiography as De-Facement." For if, as de Man argues, autobiography, through the figure of prosopopoeia, seeks to construct a subjectivity on the basis of rhetorical configurations, then to expose "the illusion of reference" in autobiography as "something more akin to a fiction" is to "de-face" the identity which has been imagined as lying behind and originating textual meaning. The belief that the writer's desire will inevitably surface in her or his texts is one variation of the still-prevalent credo that textual meaning gives us access to authorial subjectivity.[8] Hence, only when the aesthetic form of autobiography is given priority over its content of self-revelation can the marginal status of the genre be corrected. If, therefore, the project of "defacing" Oscar Wilde should lead the reader to ask, or at least to wonder anxiously, what we propose to substitute for the integrity of the face that is so rudely disfigured, the answer to this question will not be forthcoming. The critical project is, by definition, an attack on the "face" as an index of identity, sign of essential or sexual "difference" (as in Foucault, the homosexual's nature is "written immodestly" on his face) or, of course, as the guarantor of autobiographical truth. The face, as de Man argues, functions autobiographically as a phantasmic construction for unifying discrete elements: " 'Face' then . . . designates the dependence of any perception or 'eye' on the totalizing power of language." The dissolution from which the totalizing effect of the face attempts to protect us is vividly suggested by de Man's metaphoric description: "The face . . . is the power to surface from the sea of infinite distinctions in which we risk to drown."[9]

In this chapter I will aim to dispense with the totalizing effects invoked by the face of Wilde's sexuality—if one considers his life as a whole, Wilde was bisexual rather than exclusively homosexual—arguing that this was but one aspect of a broader, more far-reaching critical project, a program of cultural transgression that is rooted in Wilde's self-construction as an artist. Designated by his own epitaph as an outcast, Wilde's status as at once an insider and an outsider gave him a unique position from which to critique many forms of identity and ideology.

Same-sex desire, in other words, was only one of the ways in which Wilde's life and texts dissent from Victorian orthodoxies and seek to unravel the conventions of both "realist" representation and bourgeois morality. To impute such strategic self-consciousness to his texts is not to deny that Wilde actually experienced and acted on sexual desire for men but to stress that the various strands of aesthetic and literary representation of same-sex desire, including its negation, cannot be traced back to an authorizing homosexual subject or consciousness. Rather, the figure of Wilde-as-homosexual is the totalizing effect that we imaginatively construct from the discrete elements, "the sea of infinite distinctions," perceived in Wilde's writings. That this face is ideologically motivated should be clear from the role of Wilde's conviction and imprisonment for "gross indecency" in the construction of an essentialized identity for Wilde. Indeed, I will show that the 1895 trial proceedings have taught us how to read Wilde's works for signs of his sexual "nature" and so inform even those readings which decry the damaging effects of his conviction and imprisonment on Wilde's life and work.

{ *Defacing Oscar Wilde* }

"Hidden Meanings": Wilde's Art as Autobiography

Basil Hallward's bitter complaint to Lord Henry Wotton in *Dorian Gray* that "we live in an age when men treat art as if it were meant to be a form of autobiography" is one installment of Wilde's defiant insistence on the absolute separateness of art and morals, aesthetic representation and personal conduct. Responding to the severe criticisms of his novel following its first publication in 1890, Wilde argued that his work ought to be judged not on moral criteria but on aesthetic merit. Underlying this point is another claim: that a literary text is not a sound basis for gaining access to or judging the artist's conscious life and behavior. Indeed, Hallward's hostility to the "shallow, prying eyes" of those who would seek to discern his secret desire for Dorian in his art anticipates Wilde's self-portrayal — in his letters to the critics of his novel, during his trials, and in his letter to Douglas from Reading Gaol — as the victim of a truculent public scrutiny.[10]

And yet, notwithstanding such resistance to the intrusive gaze of the reader or spectator, "autobiography," as Wilde's character Gilbert says in "The Critic as Artist," "is irresistible." In the context of the dialogue, the statement means that the pleasure of reading other people's self-disclosures is paramount: "When people talk to us about others they are usually dull. When they talk to us about themselves they are nearly always interesting."[11] The unspoken corollary is that the temptation to *reveal* secrets, in order to satisfy this collective passion for "watching [the] troubled soul in its progress," may lead the artist into an exciting yet dangerous confrontation with public opinion and morality.[12] For instance, the artist Basil Hallward worries about his portrait of the beautiful Dorian, fearing "I have put too much of myself into it."[13] Consequently, Wilde's novel seems both to exhibit and to encourage a certain guardedness toward self-revelation, as though wary of the powerful impulse to confess desires that threaten to destroy the reputation of the artist. Basil goes on to assert that "every portrait that is painted with feeling is a portrait of the artist, not of the sitter. The sitter is merely the accident, the occasion. It is not he who is revealed by the painter; it is rather the painter who, on the coloured canvas, reveals himself." The aftermath of the risky self-revelation that occurs in art is, in Basil's case, a counterreaction of self-protective (not to say melodramatic) secrecy: "The reason I will not exhibit this picture," he tells Lord Henry, "is that I am afraid that I have shown in it the secret of my own soul."[14]

What Basil is suspicious of, it turns out, is less the revelation of his secret itself—whatever it may be—than the unsympathetic scrutiny that is practiced by a public trained to look for signs of moral and sexual deviance. Allon White's account of what he terms "symptomatic reading," an intrusive form of interpretation in which the reader or spectator's "attention shifts from the truth-value or verisimilitude of a statement to the dark motive of its utterance," helps to account for the spectatorial and reading practices producing Basil's (and Wilde's) unease.[15] White traces the growth of "symptomatic reading" back to the fin de siècle, arguing that the textual obscurity of much early modernist writing should be viewed as a self-defensive reaction to new, psychologically more aggressive methods of interpretation. Thus Basil Hallward's refusal to exhibit his picture enacts a key modernist drama also performed by Wilde: the agonistic encounter between the public's new dexterity in symptomatic reading and the artist's evasive strategy of concealing himself, in particular his sexual behavior or desire, from the curious "public gaze."

With this in mind, the emphasis on autobiography as an "irresistible" practice or technique shifts from the work of the artist/author to the interpretation of the reader/spectator. Wilde's own work uncovers another meaning of Gilbert's words: that it is impossible to resist the temptation to *interpret* art as a form of autobiography, however careful the author may have been to exclude personal references and however irrelevant they might seem. As a method of interpretation applied to his own writings, autobiography was alternately, perhaps simultaneously, desired and rejected by Wilde. As he wrote to a friend in 1894 concerning *Dorian Gray*: "It contains much of me in it. Basil Hallward is what I think I am: Lord Henry what the world thinks me: Dorian what I would like to be—in other ages, perhaps."[16] Significantly, of course, Wilde's hint at his self-representation in the novel is immediately qualified by a self-fragmentation that renders his identification with his characters chimerical. This gesture identifying each of his characters in turn as a "mask" has the paradoxical effect of defacing the autobiographical origin of the novel.

In Basil's anxiety that his picture may produce an especially dangerous form of self-disclosure, there is also an important reference to Wilde's creative resistance to the autobiographical interpretation of his works. If, for Basil, the "shallow, prying eyes" of the invasive critic could be defended against only by a vigilant and even paranoid secrecy—the absolute refusal to exhibit one's work in public—Wilde himself responded with an opposite, and arguably more effective, strategy: to be so visible, outspoken, and self-contradictory, in both his literary utterances and his social performances, that nobody knew which remarks could be attributed to Wilde "himself." Through his calculated embrace of inconsistency and paradox, Wilde defied his readers and critics to construct a coherent "face" from the contradictory fragments of meaning he disseminated. When that face was, during his trials, finally and fatally constructed, its monstrous appearance was a direct consequence of the frustration of his enemies at having failed to identify him before.[17] Even the reviews of *Dorian Gray*, hostile as they generally were, failed to recognize how self-conscious and sophisticated Wilde's purpose was. Perceiving the novel as a failure to conform to established standards of moral conduct, rather than a strategic rejection of aesthetic conventions, his critics missed its true transgression. Only with the abortive prosecution of Queensberry for libel was it officially recognized that Wilde had in fact been living the "sins" that had been attributed to his characters, at which point Wilde's fictions could be viewed as nothing other than the sign and representation of his own "perversion."

It was during his trials that the symptomatic reading of Wilde's work reached its apotheosis. Unsurprisingly, the character of Basil Hallward was interpreted most pejoratively to cast suspicion on Wilde himself. The chief lawyer for the prosecution sought to show, with unmistakable sexual import, that "the affection and love of the artist of *Dorian Gray* might lead an ordinary individual to believe that it might have a certain tendency." Reading aloud to the court the passage containing Basil Hallward's impassioned account of his first meeting with Dorian, the prosecution asked Wilde accusingly if he "consider[ed] that that description of the feeling of one man towards a youth just grown-up was a proper or an improper feeling."[18] The prosecution's central objective was to prove that Wilde himself shared the "feeling," the "affection and love," expressed by his fictional character.

Wilde's defense responded by exploiting this vagueness in the prosecution's suggestions and challenging the tenuous link between

Basil's "admiration" for Dorian and Wilde's own alleged sexual "perversion": "Hidden meanings have been most unjustly read into the poetical and prose works of my client," stated Edward Clarke, alluding in particular to "a prurient construction which has been placed by his enemies upon . . . *The Picture of Dorian Gray*."[19] Clarke's attack on the "hidden meanings" and "prurient construction" was inevitably subordinated to his pragmatic aim of gaining an acquittal for his client. Yet we might do well to remember that it was the prosecution during the trials that sought to read the novel as indicative of Wilde's own sexuality, whereas Wilde's defense and Wilde himself sought to disavow such a confessional "construction." Bearing in mind the context of this disclaimer, to what extent might the search for homosexual inscription in Wilde's work be underwritten by a methodology of interpretation that is, in its effect if not its intentions, punitive and even condemnatory?

In considering this question, we find an intriguing parallel between the legal deployment of Wilde's written texts to demonstrate his own homosexuality during his trials and more recent theoretical work that explores the compulsory visibility and legibility ascribed to transgressive desire as part of a cultural regime of sexual surveillance and control. The most influential account is Foucault's narrative of the emergence of the homosexual as a "species," a figure defined exclusively by his sexuality, which "was everywhere present in him: at the root of all his actions because it was their insidious and indefinitely active principle; written immodestly on his face and body because it was a secret that always gave itself away."[20] The homosexual inscription specified by Foucault echoes Basil Hallward's statement of the impossibility of concealing a debauched life from the world: "Sin is a thing that writes itself across a man's face. It cannot be concealed. People talk sometimes of secret vices. There are no such things. If a wretched man has a vice, it shows itself in the lines of his mouth, the droop of his eyelids, the moulding of his hands even."[21]

The tendency to envisage Wilde's work and life as representing or embodying a homosexual identity that was constituted only during and after his trials appears in the work of even the most sophisticated of Wilde's critics. Rehearsing Foucault's model of a discursive shift in the history of sexual identities, whereby the behavioral "aberration" of the sodomite became the "species" of the homosexual — that is, a range of transgressive sexual acts became crystallized into

{ *Defacing Oscar Wilde* }

an essentialized sexual identity, sharply defined against the "norm" of masculinity—Lee Edelman innovatively likens this to a change from a metonymic (contingent) to a metaphorical (essential) conceptualization of same-sex desire. It is this historically specific metaphorical reference of sexuality, Edelman argues, that induces—or perhaps demands—the careful scrutiny of homosexual "signs," whether textual or bodily, as the index of an essential sexual identity, of which the "signs" are taken as merely secondary and derivative representations. Sexual and textual acts become meaningful insofar as they indicate that which is imagined as motivating and explaining them—Foucault's "insidious and indefinitely active principle" of sexual inversion. The role of textual production in this process is crucial, because it is through its persistent association with writing and textuality, Edelman believes, that homosexuality comes to denote "a secondary, sterile and parasitic form of social representation that stands in the same relation to heterosexual identity that writing occupies in relation to speech or voice."[22]

This ambivalent link between homosexuality and writing is formulated in the neologism "homographesis," used by Edelman to identify both "a normalizing practice of cultural discrimination" of sexualities and, in his brilliantly revisionist argument, "a strategic resistance to that reification of sexual difference."[23] The cultural and homophobic demand for what Edelman terms "a visible analogue of difference" is apparently satisfied by a further, specific association of homosexuality with effeminacy—whereby the "sameness" of the male gender, shared by homosexuals and heterosexuals alike, can be overlaid with a difference of inversion, a visible stigma that differentiates the "normal," heterosexual male from the "deviant" homosexual. And yet, by installing the notion of "difference" within the fields of sexuality and textuality, Edelman in his use of "homographesis" simultaneously calls into question the legitimacy of heterosexuality and speech as the natural—that is, at once privileged and dominant—categories. Hence homosexual desire is both threatening to the autonomy of heterosexual identity and desire and necessary for its normative status and hierarchical ascendancy. If heterosexuality is privileged only in relation to an abnormal, pathologized "other," it requires that difference to sustain the fiction of its own status as natural. As Edelman remarks in a later essay, "precisely to the extent that the homosexual . . . disturbs the epistemological security afforded by the logic of sameness and difference as these are grounded in perception, the dominant culture demands that homosexuality be read back into—be construed, that is, as readable within—the system of visualization."[24]

In pursuit of the Foucauldian argument that the visibility of sexual difference is required and in fact produced by the same heterosexual culture that also prohibits and fears it, Edelman recognizes the radical perversion of dominant culture, as well as the productivity of such "difference" at the rhetorical nexus between textual and sexual politics.[25] For Edelman, the ideological force of this visualization and inscription of difference may be realized and so resisted by a rhetorical, figural reading of "natural" categories, including those of desire. Edelman invokes *The Picture of Dorian Gray* to show that a literary text, at the moment of textual/sexual recognition, may actually be constitutive of that "natural" condition which it appears merely to be reproducing. For example, Lord Henry Wotton's speech tempting Dorian to seize the pleasures of life—again suggesting, but not specifying, sexual pleasures—before it is too late, "produces the very 'nature' or self that it seems to reveal."[26] This results in Dorian formulating his own identity on the basis of an imaginary reconstruction of prior experiences that had either lacked special significance or carried a quite different meaning before Lord Henry's speech.

Allowing that Wotton's speech to Dorian dramatizes an identity being constituted by the intervention of an external influence that produces self-recognition—or rather misrecognition of the self as natural—what gives it a specifically sexual significance? For Edelman, the relevance of sexual difference to this scene is suggested by the unstable identification between Dorian and the picture, part of a realm of difference opened up by the fissures in identity produced by the mutating painting. From the outset of the novel, it is clear that the painting represents Basil's aesthetically idealized and erotically influenced vision of male beauty, rather than Dorian "himself." Dorian, however, narcissistically misrecognizes the picture as his own image: "When he saw it he drew back, and his cheeks flushed for a moment with pleasure. A look of joy came into his eyes, as if he had recognized himself for the first time."[27] As Edelman points out, Basil and Lord Henry both contribute to the "crystallization of his identity," which is achieved "through the misrecognition of his homograph (figured in the painted image and the verbal portrait of an autonomous self)."[28] Dorian immediately appropriates the perfect beauty figured in Basil's portrait as belonging to himself: "The sense of *his own beauty* came on him like a revelation. He had never felt it before. . . . [H]e stood gazing at the *shadow of his own loveliness*." [29] Though the word "shadow" serves as a warning of his delusion, Dorian involuntarily designates his own image as that which has been desired and depicted by Basil. This instance of misrecognition propels both the subject and the creator of the painting into the ultimately disfiguring relationship between desire and representation itself.

Dorian's identification with Basil's painting can be read as an "autobiographical moment" in Wilde's text, not in the sense that it refers directly to the author but because it invokes the *structure* of self-reference. As de Man writes: "The autobiographical moment happens as an alignment between the two subjects involved in the process of reading in which they determine each other by mutual reflexive substitution. The structure implies differentiation as well as similarity, since both depend on a substitutive exchange that constitutes the subject." Dorian's subjectivity is constituted, that is, when he misreads the painting as "himself" and thereby enacts a "substitutive exchange" with Basil, mediated by the visual text. The picture, which Basil initially claims "reveals" his secret, is henceforth appropriated by Dorian as the bearer of his own. Therefore, each man's subjectivity is constituted as a secret, both of which are intimately linked by the shared medium of visual representation.[30] Because this subjectivity is based on misrecognition and thus prevents the tracing of this specular structure back to an autobiographical "subject," neither Basil nor Dorian can be identified as the author of or in the text.

The rhetorical blending of visual and verbal metaphors—a conflation associated, by Edelman, with homographesis as a mode of resistance to reified (that is, culturally inscribed) sexual difference—occurs in Wilde's novel when the painting is attributed with an uncanny power of *narrative* representation: as, for example, when Dorian refers to the decayed painting just before showing it to Basil as "a diary of my life from day to day" that "never leaves the room in which it is written." [31] The description of the painting as a confessional narrative that reveals the secret of Dorian's life displaces Basil's anxiety that "I have shown in it the secret of my own soul." [32] It also anticipates the legal exploitation of *The Picture of Dorian Gray* as a narrative that, read symptomatically, could be used to construct the scandalous "secret" of Wilde's life and hence to incriminate its author of "gross indecency." The slippage between visual and verbal representation that characterizes *Dorian Gray* is therefore Wilde's most effective strategy for resisting the essentializing attribution of a sexual "truth" to himself on the basis of his literary texts. The vagueness with which Dorian's transgressions are described ultimately suggests that "sin" has no decidable referent at all in the novel: that it functions — as the painter's art functions for Pater — to provoke the subjective attribution of meaning by reader or spectator. As Wilde wrote in a letter defending his novel, in words that might be taken to heart by his modern critics: "Each man sees his own sin in Dorian Gray. What Dorian Gray's sins are no one knows. He who finds them has brought them."[33]

The identification of this novel as one that reveals its author's homosexuality therefore hinges, for Edelman, on a reading of the novel suggested by the questioning during the first trial by the defense lawyer for the Marquis of Queensberry. Edelman argues that the "deployment of the trope of legibility" in Wilde's novel — related to the account of sin as something "that writes itself across a man's face" — had contributed to "the disturbing effect it had on its contemporary readers: Dorian's clear implication in a world of 'unnatural vice' fails to produce the appropriate inscription of difference upon his body." But as my juxtaposition of Basil's statement with Foucault's suggested, this "clear implication in a world of 'unnatural vice' " can be asserted only once one has chosen to read the nature of Dorian's "sin" in a specific, sexualized way. There is, in fact, nothing "clear" about Dorian's "vice" at all. Though the painting, as Edelman observes, is "written over with the markings of difference generated by Dorian's illicit actions," the assumption that these are *sexual* actions was initially produced by the hostile and insinuating reviews of the novel and then consolidated during the trials.[34]

Similarly, one can agree with Edelman that "Dorian's necessarily unstable identification with the picture of himself . . . [is] posited through and across the differences the picture opens up within the notion of 'identity' as such." But the assertion with which Edelman supports this insight is far from self-evident: "Prominent among those differences, of course, is the question of sexual difference — a question that led to an intriguing line of questioning during the Marquess [sic] of Queensberry's trial for libel." Edelman's "of course" neatly disguises the fact that the "prominence" of sexual difference to notions of identity is precisely what is in question and is largely generated by the focus of the trials, rather than being the self-evident focus of the novel. Reading Basil's speech about "sin" from *Dorian Gray*, Edward Carson, the defense lawyer, asked Wilde, "Does not this passage suggest a charge of unnatural vice?"[35] Wilde would have placed the responsibility for this "suggestion" on the reader's imagination, not on the author's intention or, indeed, the text's own meaning.

Hence, this "intriguing line of questioning" is not a hostile response to a self-evident and already prevailing "prominence" of sexual difference in Wilde's novel but is itself a discursive construction of the modern conception of "sexual difference," according to which certain sexual practices could be attributed to a deviant sexual "identity" and might be "discovered" in the textual productions of homosexual authors. Where Edelman assumes an already existing system of sexual difference used by the lawyer to entrap Wilde into being identified as "homosexual," one can see this conception of difference actually being produced in the course of Wilde's trials. Perhaps because he is committed to Foucault's premise of a "discursive shift" that occurred earlier in the century, Edelman is content to view Wilde's confrontation with the legal discourses as merely an example or confirmation of a "reification of sexual difference," rather than the moment at which that difference is actually constituted.

Indeed, Edelman makes no mention of the fact that the initial charge made against Wilde, which led to the trial of Queensberry for libel — "For Oscar Wilde, posing as a somdomite [*sic*]" — invokes a preessentialized, specifically metonymic or contingent relation to sexuality. Both the use of "sodomite" to denote someone who practices "unspeakable" sexual acts, rather than suggesting an innately "different" sexual nature, and the claim that Wilde was "posing," which alludes to "aspects of behavior that were defined as affectation or mimicry," can be seen to invoke the *metonymic* relation to sexual difference allegedly already displaced by the time of Wilde's trials.[36] We must assume that the Marquis of Queensberry, lacking access to the term "homosexual" in his attack on Wilde, used "sodomite," which was still, in 1895, the current term of abuse deployed by sexual bigots.

If one acknowledges that Queensberry was using "sodomite" as a current rather than a deliberately anachronistic term, then a new interpretation of the Wilde trials emerges: the first trial, in which

Wilde prosecuted Queensberry for libel, was testing the legitimacy of Queensberry's charge. The terminology here is crucial: because Queensberry had accused Wilde only of "posing" as a sodomite, the task of the defense was "to show that Wilde was the kind of person — or at least that he had (re)presented himself as the kind of person — who would be inclined to commit sodomy."[37] Moreover, as Ed Cohen argues, the defense — which would soon thereafter switch roles with the prosecution — sought to personify Wilde as a specific kind of sexual being, whose "perverse" sexual acts represented an essentially deviant sexual personality. By acquitting Queensberry of libel, the legal system prepared the way for the subsequent prosecution of Wilde as a sexual predator who, as Cohen shows, was constructed as "the negation of the middle-class male norms."[38] The ideological production of Wilde as one whose entire identity and body were constituted and marked by his "perverse" sexuality is a concrete historical indication, of much greater significance than an abstract "discursive shift" in terminology, that sexual difference was coming to be identified in new and explicitly political ways. Edelman's theorizing of the rhetorical processes by which sexual difference can be produced and made legible for widely divergent ideological ends is brilliant and incisive; yet his application to Wilde's novel of the Foucauldian paradigm of the homosexual becoming a "species" in the mid–nineteenth century obscures the fact that what is at stake in the work and trials of Wilde is precisely the shift to an essentialist definition of Wilde as one *likely or inclined* to commit "acts of gross indecency."

It was to this essentialized and totalized identification of him as a sexual deviant that Wilde would later respond in his prison letter. Indeed, the purpose of Wilde's *De Profundis* was to "deface" the image of him that had already been created, by retelling the story of his involvement with Douglas and disowning many of the characteristics by which he had been stereotyped. Ironically, Wilde's strategy in this letter was to conduct a double defacement by displacing many of the most hateful characteristics with which he had been stigmatized onto the figure of Douglas, addressed as "Bosie," whom he was to cast as the true villain of the piece. Whereas the autobiographical moment of *Dorian Gray* occurs with Dorian's idealized misrecognition of himself as the image in the picture, Wilde's letter demonstrates a similar structure with the reverse effect: Wilde disowns the hideous image that had been attributed to him by refusing identifi-

{ *Defacing Oscar Wilde* }

cation with the "double" whose sins had been placed to his account. This resembles, of course, the conclusion of Wilde's novel, in which Dorian's culminating refusal to recognize the picture as himself leads to his self-destruction. Yet, appearing between these opposing but equally tragic versions of specularity is Wilde's most engaging and extravagant representation of the disturbances produced by duality and misrecognition — *The Importance of Being Earnest*. This work, suggestive of the ways in which the contradictions and fissures that haunt identity might produce a comic rather than a tragic outcome, mocks the singular notion of authentic identity that has been viewed as the key to "autobiography," while it invites analysis for its creative anticipation and dramatization of the catastrophic events that would be explored in Wilde's prison letter.

Imagining Disaster in *The Importance of Being Earnest*

The period in which *The Importance of Being Earnest* was written and produced is remarkable for being at once the highest pinnacle of Wilde's career and the immediate prelude to his downfall. The two trajectories, in fact, overlap as Wilde reaches his greatest artistic and popular success at the same time as he becomes ensnared in the web of blackmail and persecution that would combine to bring him down. As Christopher Craft writes of this bizarre historical dovetailing of theatrical and legal performances, "For a brief time (from 5 April when Wilde was arrested for 'acts of gross indecency with another male person,' until 8 May when George Alexander was compelled by public opinion to remove *Earnest* from the boards), the two spectacles ran concurrently." [39] As his letters of the period testify and as *De Profundis* would confirm, Wilde's world, always precarious, was beginning to crumble around him. Queensberry's narrowly foiled attempt to interrupt the opening night of *Earnest* was only one of a series of strategies to discredit and humiliate Wilde before his public. [40]

Four days after the opening night, in fact, when Wilde was still reveling in the almost universal praise for his play, Queensberry left the infamous card at the Albemarle Club, addressed to "Oscar Wilde, posing as a somdomite [*sic*]." [41] This coincidence of the production of *Earnest* and the prosecution of Wilde inevitably demands a reading of the play that explores the parallels and tensions between literary text, dramatic performance, and public prosecution. Somewhere in the midst of this cultural production we might expect, or wish, to find Wilde's "desire": except that the author has become historically merged with his fate to the point where, as Craft points out, "the signifier *Wilde* encodes not homosexual desire per se but rather a whole history of tendentious citation." [42]

Offering a striking example of such "citation" — the way in which Wilde's work is read in hindsight as inevitably tending to the "climax" of the trials — Richard Ellmann writes of Wilde during this period: "He had what Henry James calls 'the imagination of disaster.' Nothing less than total ruin would do." [43] Evidently used by Ellmann to refer specifically to Wilde's engineering of his own downfall, in fulfillment of a self-imposed tragic destiny, James's phrase might be applied with more validity to Wilde's final play. In this work, we witness the "total ruin" of the link between social persona and private desire, a connection that had already been placed under great stress in Wilde's previous works. No less important, the play rehearses the collapse of his famous public self, which his letter from Reading Gaol would attempt to renounce in favor of an exiled, private self.

In *The Importance of Being Earnest*, Wilde took the supreme risk of aggressively subverting and parodying Victorian moral assumptions and dramatic conventions to reflect his own "perverse" philosophy, then crafting them into a comic masterpiece that would seduce Victorian Philistia into laughing at itself. The play exquisitely rebukes and satirizes the quest for discovery of one's origins and struggle for social advancement, on which both of the two most popular literary forms — the melodrama and the bildungsroman — had been, in very different ways, founded. The best part of the joke, perhaps, was that Wilde's own career had been devoted to ascending the English social ladder, so that in scenes such as Jack's first confrontation with Lady Bracknell, there is an element of self-mockery. Wilde, arguably, was able to reinvent the Victorian melodrama by parodying it, killing off its clichés in the gales of laughter that, by all reports, filled the St. James's Theatre during performances of *Earnest*. The very preoccupations of the melodrama — identity, origins, duplicity, evil — were mocked and inverted in Wilde's comedy. Wilde's critique of dramatic and societal conventions, however, was entertaining and flattering to his audience when enacted comically on the stage, rather than disturbing and

{ *Defacing Oscar Wilde* }

threatening to public morality as it had been perceived on the printed page of a "decadent" novel. The radical difference in the popular and critical response to *Dorian Gray* in 1890 and *Earnest* five years later is to be explained not by a shift in public taste but by Wilde's greater skill in manipulating and satisfying that taste. The very transience of the dramatic production, as compared with the permanence of print, allows for greater freedom in presenting controversial themes and ideas. Moreover, the containment of the dramatic production within a public space specifically licensed for various forms of "misrule" and satire lessened the danger of Wilde being held personally responsible for the amoral implications of his play.

This is not to say that Wilde himself created or even expected the outcome that resulted from the persecution of himself and Lord Alfred Douglas by the Marquis of Queensberry. Yet the play does dramatize Wilde's "dandified" and paradoxical aesthetic style taken to the very brink of social disaster, pushing to its furthest acceptable limits the ridicule and rejection of Victorian orthodoxies of self, gender, and class. The evasive strategies employed by the play's two "Bunburyists," Algy and Jack, succeed mainly for two reasons. First, their eroticized, conspiratorial relationship—a mutual support system by which each man will, however reluctantly, conceal the other's secret desire and serve as his alibi—saves them from disaster. Like two veteran actors, Algy and Jack, no matter how they berate and criticize each other "behind the scenes," do not betray the other in public. Each man understands the precarious social and sexual vulnerability of the other and strives to protect him from exposure or embarrassment.[44] Yet they seek to protect not secret identities, but double lives: their purpose is freedom of action rather than integrity of selfhood.

The second factor that explains their success—and also accounts for the different outcome of Wilde's own transgressions—is the improbable stupidity and blindness of the other characters. Algy and Jack are two cunning, secretive men operating in a world populated by somewhat mechanical figures. Even Lady Bracknell, who is shrewd and perceptive enough in her economic and social inquisitions, suffers from a tunnel vision that prevents her from understanding the specificity of others' motives. Jack's faux naïveté in dealing with her objections to his engagement to Gwendolyn lures her into believing that she is addressing a simpleton, while she automatically attributes her own mercenary philosophy to all others. The humor of the play derives largely from our pleasure—and surprise—at witnessing Algy and Jack narrowly escape the impending and potentially ruinous collisions with the social world, as well as the charade of respectability that they create around their misdemeanors. At the same time, if the Victorian audience was allowed to participate vicariously in Jack and Algy's freedom, it was in large part because they didn't recognize its purpose.

Secrecy in *The Importance of Being Earnest* is a game played for amusement, to fight off the ennui incumbent on life in respectable bourgeois society, in which the object is a frisson of illicit pleasure taken in successful evasion of discovery. During the early scene between Algy and Jack in which the host interrogates his guest about a cigarette case, for example, Jack complains that "you have no right whatsoever to read what is written inside. It is a very ungentlemanly thing to read a private cigarette case." [45] When Algy—persisting in the "ungentlemanly behavior" of probing Jack's private life and treating the cigarette case, a symbol of refined masculine life, as though it were a "case" in the legal sense—eventually discovers from the inscription that his friend is, like himself, "a confirmed and secret Bunburyist," the empty circularity of secrecy is startling. [46] By discovering Jack's material "secrets" (the cigarette case, the alias, the inscription), Algy confirms merely the obvious fact that Jack has a secret life. The nature or content of that secret life is, as Lady Bracknell would say, "immaterial": Algy bonds with Jack merely because both have constructed alter egos to facilitate the pursuit of unspecified (and implicitly prohibited) pleasures. Indeed, the diffidence with which these men react to the discovery of each other's secrets undermines the notion that their private lives might be in any way scandalous.

Yet the "prop" of the cigarette case—which functions as a material sign of the "empty" code of secrecy circulating between Jack and Algy in the play—becomes far more significant as an important piece of evidence in Wilde's legal case. Under a distinctly "ungentlemanly" interrogation by Queensberry's defense, Wilde confessed that he had given silver cigarette cases, worth about four pounds each (a suspiciously large sum in 1895), to numerous young working-class men, which the defense suggested were given in payment for sexual favors. Wilde's blasé response that "it is my custom to present cigarette cases"—a statement that, effacing as it does any private motive for these gifts, perhaps contains an ironic allusion to the public spectacle of his play—did nothing to lessen the damaging interpretation placed on these acts of "generosity."[47]

Algy, transgressing the codes of gentlemanly conduct by behaving like a prosecuting lawyer, calls as a witness his servant, Lane, who "produces" the cigarette case left behind by "Ernest" and thus "explodes" his double life as "Jack in the country and Ernest in the city." As a member of the working class, the servant Lane plays a role similar to that of the working-class men who, coached as witnesses by the Marquis of Queensberry, would betray Wilde's secret. As a servant, moreover, Lane is in a situation of economic dependency on Algy, whose power to compel Lane to produce this material evidence of Jack's double life is purely derived from his authority as Lane's employer. Yet the salver on which Lane produces and then removes the case indicates a deliberate professional and sanitary distance from it, as though he were afraid of contaminating (or being contaminated by) so sordid a piece of incriminating material. Equally, the introduction of the case on a tray, coming so soon after the similar presentation of the cucumber sandwiches, encodes the object as something at once elegant and to be consumed—as in a sense it is "consumed" by the incriminating interpretation that Algy places on it. Having decided that the case signifies Jack's status as "a confirmed and secret Bunburyist," Algy instructs Jack to "produce your explanation, and pray make it improbable."[48]

Similarly, but in much less comic circumstances, Wilde would be called to account for the circulation of these innocuous but incriminating objects, which apparently betrayed his sexual liaisons with working-class young men. The same object used as evidence to convict Wilde had already appeared as a piece in the puzzle of Ernest's "secret" identity. The crucial difference, of course, is that in the trial, the cigarette case reveals a "secret" that is no longer "empty"; on the contrary, it is used by the opposition as evidence of the crime of "gross indecency with another male person."[49] Hence, the legal discourse also "consumes" the object within a system of signification, inviting Wilde to "produce" his own "explanation" of the object. But the lawyers did not, like Algy, mischievously request an "improbable" explanation; indeed, the very implausibility of Wilde's claim that the cigarette cases were spontaneous gifts contributed to his eventual conviction. It was as though Wilde had mistaken the court for a theater: because it was his "custom to present cigarette cases," he assumed this "custom" gave him the prerogative to explain himself in an improbable way. The theatricality of the trials has often been noted, and in one sense, the cigarette case remains a prop, merely recurring in a different context. As Ellmann writes of the transition between play and trial, "Wilde set the stage for the next act, in which evil would masquerade as fatherly feeling and social orderliness, and good make do with the humiliating guise of the criminal."[50] Yet the implication that Wilde was in control of the proceedings—that he himself "set the stage"—is misleading. In contrast with his earlier theatrical ventures, the trials would construct Wilde as a melodramatic villain, the "improbability" of whose testimony would serve to entrap him.

The loss of "authorial" control over the interpretation of his works that culminated with his trials had already begun during the writing and production of *Earnest*. As is widely known, Wilde originally wrote the play as a four-act comedy, offering it to the actor-manager George Alexander of the St. James's Theatre but suggesting that he probably would not want to take the play because it didn't suit his acting style. Faced with impending losses due to the disastrous failure of Henry James's *Guy Domville*, however, Alexander gladly accepted Wilde's offer but asked Wilde to cut the play from four acts to three. Himself financially destitute, Wilde was in no position to negotiate with the actor-manager—he had sent Alexander the initial scenario with a request for an advance of £150 if he liked it, then receiving a check for £300 when Alexander decided to stage the play. Having made the cuts, Wilde was banished by Alexander from the rehearsals and went off to Algiers with Douglas. When he returned to London for the dress rehearsals and opening night on 14 February 1895, the play was substantially different from the one he originally wrote. Wilde's regret at his loss of control over his work was, characteristically, expressed in humorous form after the first performance, when he remarked to Alexander, who took the role of Jack: "My dear Alec, it was charming, charming. . . . And do you know, from time to time I was reminded of a play I once wrote myself called *The Importance of Being Earnest*."[51]

In considering the significance of Wilde's economically motivated revisions as symptomatic of his loss of control over his life and work, the central episode of importance is the deleted "Gribsby episode."[52] One of the major differences between the three- and four-act versions is that the latter contains a scene in which a London solicitor,

Gribsby, comes with a writ for the arrest and detention of Ernest, whom Algy is currently impersonating, for a huge unpaid bill for dinners at the Savoy. The deleted episode, as John Glavin shows, is crucial in delineating the power struggle between Jack and Algy, forcing a desperate Algy to beg for financial assistance and to confront the potentially disastrous consequences of his much-vaunted "Bunburying." The Gribsby episode, according to Glavin, represents a decisive victory for Jack, who will henceforth be in control of events, and the remainder of the original play revolves around the discovery of his identity (and, as Glavin doesn't mention, it is Jack, rather than Algy, who finally attains the cherished name of Ernest).[53]

Glavin's interpretation, however, doesn't take into account that the huge debt, for the nonpayment of which Algy is nearly arrested, has in fact been run up by Jack under the alias of Ernest. In other words, the scene represents not a moral victory for Jack but a manipulative strategy by the protagonist, who conveniently displaces his own excesses onto his friend, soon to be identified as his brother. Algy has walked into the trap himself, of course, by surreptitiously adopting the name and identity of Ernest for the purpose of wooing Cecily (Jack's ward), without considering the possible consequences. Jack emerges from the episode as merely a more successful trickster than Algy, not as his moral superior; and when Jack finally writes the check to Gribsby, paying off "Ernest's" debt, this act is not one of generosity but a wealthy man clandestinely paying off his own account.

The significance of the Gribsby episode for the present argument is that it provides a little-known example of the play of secrecy that remains central to Wilde's aesthetic practice and is manifested in his literary techniques of displacement and concealment. For example, Wilde's lament to Bosie in his prison letter that "the sins of another were being placed to my account" and that he was the victim of "the absolute transference, deliberate, plotted, and rehearsed, of the actions and doings of someone else on to me" is a reworking both of the transference of Jack's "actions and doings" onto Algy and of the displacement of the burden of guilt from Dorian Gray to his painting.[54] Interestingly, the language in which Wilde complains of his fate to Douglas suggests the preparation and production of a literary, specifically a dramatic, work, one of which he was not the author but merely a character at the mercy of an unscrupulous design.

Unlike the earlier instance of transferred guilt in *Dorian Gray*, however, the Gribsby episode has no bearing on the moral standing of either Jack or Algy. Rather, the episode enacts a comic inversion of Wilde's defense of *The Picture of Dorian Gray*: "The real moral of the story is that all excess, as well as all renunciation, brings its punishment."[55] For the crucial point about the episode is that there is no punishment for transgression: disaster is is narrowly averted, and the near scandal is assimilated into the game of control between Jack and Algy. As in *An Ideal Husband*, Wilde's previous play, in which Robert Chiltern's dubious political dealings in the past are ultimately rewarded by his likely elevation to prime minister, Jack and Algy emerge from the trials of "Bunburying" not only unscathed but socially enhanced as well. As such the play represents Wilde's fantasy of maintaining control of an increasingly perilous situation and of keeping his critics and creditors at bay with a deus ex machina. "Ernest's" life of excess has consequences, irrespective of who must face them—the bill has mounted, someone has to pay it—and the Gribsby episode is certainly a reminder of those "real" effects in a play that can otherwise seem like a sustained escape from realism. This is lost in the three-act version, in which, as Peter Raby writes, "we enter a kind of Arcadia or Illyria and never leave it. There are no extraneous or threatening elements such as Gribsby and his writ might have posed."[56]

As the Shakespearean critic C. L. Barber reminds us, however, such "threatening elements" are in fact crucial to the genuine theater of misrule, in which "license is not simply a phase in a complacent evolution to foreknown conclusions: it means, at some level, disruption."[57] If the presence of danger actually enhances the intensity of the play's comic celebration of fantasy, inversion, and escape, then the Gribsby episode, with its sudden introduction of imminent economic ruin, makes us participants in, instead of merely spectators of, Wilde's drama. The disruption of the holiday license enjoyed by the play's Bunburyists adds to the dramatic power of the action. Though Jack eventually pays the bill, averting disaster, the chilling threat of debt, arrest, imprisonment in Holloway, and disgrace, once invoked, cannot be entirely dismissed. Indeed, it is our retrospective knowledge of the scene's similarity to Wilde's own ensuing disaster, rather than the tone of the scene itself, that creates its somber overtones. Mr. Gribsby, at one level a stock comic character, troubles us because of his likeness to the various unyielding and ruthless officers of the

{ *Defacing Oscar Wilde* }

law that Wilde would encounter during his trials and imprisonment. The stolid inflexibility of Gribsby's approach to law enforcement too closely resembles that of the lawyers who prosecuted Wilde to be wholly amusing, his words of warning to Algy containing a disturbingly veiled threat: "I am merely a solicitor myself. I do not employ personal violence of any kind. The officer of the Court whose function it is to seize the person of the debtor is waiting in the fly outside. He has considerable experience in these matters. . . . But no doubt you will prefer to pay the bill?"[58]

The jarring realism of the scene is soon restored to absurdity, with Gribsby commenting on the need to arrive at Holloway Prison before four o'clock to gain admission, as though they were checking in at an exclusive hotel, and Algy's dismay at the "ridiculous" prospect of being "imprisoned in the suburbs for having dined in the West End."[59] The threat of financial ruin and social disgrace, however, was perhaps the most terrifying and real one to middle-class Victorians, and the mere suggestion of its possibility in a comedy might have darkened the jovial mood of much of the play. Alexander's decision to cut the episode may have contributed to the play's immense popularity and commercial success, but at the cost of a confessional complexity of tone revealed in the longer version. The four-act version is more evenly balanced between humor and pathos, whereas the three-act play, as Glavin points out, veers toward farce.

Yet one should not make the assumption that the financial ruin threatened by Gribsby is merely a metaphorical *substitution* for the sexually related disgrace ultimately inflicted on Wilde. In the deleted Gribsby episode, Wilde's own pressing financial anxieties found their way into his drama: the fear of being arrested for debt was looming increasingly large for Wilde, who had been served several writs during the period in which he completed *Earnest*. Ellmann misses the point, therefore, when he asserts that, in the Gribsby scene, "Wilde even parodied punishment, by having a solicitor come to take Algernon to Holloway Prison . . . not for homosexuality, but for running up food bills at the Savoy."[60] To assume that the only issue of real concern to Wilde at the time of *Earnest* was his sexuality is to dismiss the seriousness of the threat represented by debt. By reducing this scene to a "parody" of punishment, Ellmann reads Wilde's last play in the light of circumstances that came after it, rather than those in which it was produced. Insofar as Wilde imagined disaster, it was the prospect of financial ruin that haunted him, and when he came to describe his relationship with Douglas in *De Profundis*, it was his lover's expensive tastes and financial irresponsibility, far more than Douglas's sexual recklessness, that provoked his bitter attacks.

Crucially, most of Wilde's key decisions concerning the writing and production of *Earnest* were made from financial motives. Wilde left London for Worthing, where he wrote the majority of the play, to save money and escape his creditors; he could not even visit London during this period because of the expense of the trip and the risk of being detained there. His urgent request for an advance from Alexander on receipt of his scenario of the play, followed by his agreement to revise the play according to Alexander's specifications, derived from his financial difficulties. Indeed, Wilde published the popular three-act version, based on Alexander's typescript, with Leonard Smithers in 1899, when, following his release from prison, he was again strapped for cash. The manuscript of his original four-act version of the play, along with all his other manuscripts, had been auctioned off while he was in prison, after he had been made bankrupt by Queensberry, and Wilde no longer had access to them. Hence, the publication of Alexander's version, rather than Wilde's four-act play, was the direct result of Wilde's financial crisis.[61] Most significant, it was only for lack of funds that Wilde, after the opening of his play, stayed in London long enough to receive the insulting card left at his club by Queensberry, for had he been able to pay his hotel bill, he would have left the country before returning to his club. One hardly needs more evidence that financial ruin haunted Wilde and shaped the production of his last play. With the creation of Gribsby, Wilde makes his characters' extravagances suddenly real, their actions punishable, and their indiscretions potentially scandalous. In prison, it was his lost material possessions that Wilde elegized most eloquently in his letter to Douglas.

We are reminded, by the apparent banality of the "crimes" for which Algy/"Ernest" is arrested—in effect, he is going to be imprisoned for eating too much—of the similar emptiness of the "secret" represented by the cigarette case, an object that took on a sexual meaning only during the trials. The determining element, in each case, is consumption. Though the attention given to greed in the Gribsby scene may seem exaggerated, we might remember that excessive appetite has been the besetting vice throughout the play. Algy is apparently the chief culprit: eating all the cucumber sandwiches intended for his Aunt Augusta, foisting himself on Jack as a dinner guest, insisting that the latter become more "serious" about his meals, and (in the four-act version) devouring the pâté de foie gras sandwiches and champagne that Jack has prepared for his own delectation, before being treated by Cecily to a second lunch of six lobsters.

Following the discovery by the women in the play that "Ernest" is a fiction, which results in the cancellation of both their marital engagements, Algy consumes muffins in order to console himself, for which Jack condemns him as "perfectly heartless." In short, Algy incessantly eats food intended for other people and so usurps their right to nourishment. In a society where so many social gatherings are organized around the eating of food, greed emerges as a failure to accept the social contract, as encoded in the orderly rituals of public consumption.[62]

And yet, as we come to recognize, the greed represented by the outstanding debt is not really Algy's. Jack, who has seemed to demonstrate so much more restraint in his eating habits—merely nibbling on a piece of bread and butter when visiting Algy in his rooms in London and making do with the leftover muffins—actually has the most rapacious appetite of all. In a sense, then, it is Jack, rather than Algy, who is exposed in the Gribsby episode as a secretive, extravagant consumer. The vice that the alias of Ernest allows Jack to indulge—and perhaps Bunbury serves the same function for Algy—is apparently a lust for expensive delicacies. Certainly eating, as a form of oral gratification, is plausibly related to sexual pleasure, especially of the kind Wilde preferred, according to his biographers. Christopher Craft argues that "gluttony . . . by axiomatically transposing sexual and gustatory pleasures . . . operates as a screen metaphor for otherwise unspeakable pleasures."[63] As Ellmann similarly claims: "Sins accursed in Salomé and unnamable in Dorian Gray are transposed into a different key and appear as Algernon's inordinate and selfish craving for— cucumber sandwiches. The substitution of mild gluttony for fearsome lechery renders all vice innocuous."[64]

Is gluttony really so "innocuous" to Wilde? Such a view cannot be sustained by a reading of Earnest that takes De Profundis as the frame of reference. One is reminded by Algy's greed, in particular, of the fierce accusations made by Wilde against Douglas's "appetite for luxurious living" (443). Wilde criticizes Douglas throughout the letter for his immoderate appetite, complaining that "your interests were merely in your meals and moods. Your desires were simply for amusements, for ordinary or less ordinary pleasures" (427). Most important, Wilde reminds Douglas throughout the letter that it was he, Wilde, who had to foot the bill for his greedy lover's rampant consumption of luxurious edibles (neglecting to mention, however, that he himself was a participant at most of these dinners). Although Craft clearly takes gluttony seriously in his reading of the play—he doesn't, like Ellmann, dismiss this "vice" as "innocuous"—its significance, for his argument, derives only from its alleged metaphorical function as a "screen" for otherwise unmentionable sexual acts. The idea that gluttony itself might be a key to the play, not as a "screen" for unrepresentable sexual acts, but as a central instance of the exorbitant and selfish consumption that Wilde later attributed to "Bosie," has not yet been advanced, either by Craft or by other critics.[65]

Craft observes of Wilde that "it was his regular practice to dine luxuriously with his lovers prior to sex, thereby enjoying *in camera* the same metaphor he would display on stage in *Earnest*."[66] What Craft describes here, however, is not a metaphor but a sequence of events. In effect, the centrality of sex in this sequence is established only by the critic's own invocation of "metaphor" and use of the word "prior," which instantiate eating as merely a preliminary and formal "foreplay" to the definitive act of sex. In other words, the attribution to eating of a metaphorical function for the "screening" of sexual pleasure derives from the unwarranted assumption that sexuality must be of more "importance"—must be more essential to the "self" that practices such oral acts—than eating. I seek to challenge that priority by foregrounding the promiscuous, greedy incorporation of consumable objects that is primarily signified—in Wilde's last play, as well as in his letter to Douglas—by eating, as well as figured in the actions of the selfish and irresponsible young men who are, in various ways, related to one another as literary figures.

As several thematic resemblances between the play and the letter might suggest, the intimate, occasionally hostile, and complexly erotic bond between the two central male characters in *Earnest*—especially in the four-act version—represents comically some aspects of the relationship between Wilde and Douglas. Intriguingly, Wilde's original choice of name for the character who eventually became

Algernon Moncrieff was Lord Alfred Rufford.[67] As the younger of the two men, Algy/Alfred clearly takes on Douglas's role as the more rebellious and headstrong character, whose easy familiarity with a double life allows him to identify the other as a "secret Bunburyist" and whose appetitive behavior is a constant source of distress (and expense) to the senior partner. If Wilde was still able to produce humor about the uneven relationship in *Earnest*, it was a joke that had turned very sour by the time he penned his letter from Reading Gaol.

Wilde could not, of course, directly represent a sexual relationship between two men on the Victorian stage.[68] In true melodramatic fashion, the climactic discovery of the sibling relationship between the two men neatly (by which one means *too* neatly) resolves the issue of their eroticized liaison; they are now allowed to embrace and address each other lovingly with impunity. That the original name of the younger man should have been similar to that of Wilde's own lover only makes the connection with Wilde's life seem more tantalizing. But this apparently confessional aspect of the play can mislead us with regard to the "desire" that the play explores and eventually "explodes": not sexual desire, per se, but desire for social status and for elegant dining. The spectrum of antisocial practices that paradoxically uphold society extends from Lady Bracknell's predatory economic instincts to the ungoverned appetites of Algy and Jack.

As Wilde originally wrote it, the central relationship in the play bore a much stronger resemblance to that between Wilde and Douglas. For example, in the four-act version, Jack later protests against the insistence of Lady Brancaster (Wilde's original name for Gwendolyn's mother) that he must first "produce at any rate one parent, of either sex," if he wants to be considered as a husband for Gwendolyn: "After all what does it matter whether a man has ever had a father and mother or not? Mothers, of course, are all right. They pay a chap's bills and don't bother him. But fathers bother a chap and never pay his bills. I don't know a single chap at the club who speaks to his father." To this, Algernon replies: "Yes. Fathers are certainly not popular just at present."[69] Douglas's father, the Marquis of Queensberry, was certainly not popular with either Douglas or Wilde and was indeed bothering them with his demands that the friendship end. Moreover, Queensberry's refusal to pay Bosie's bills or continue his allowance meant that Wilde had to pay them instead. Hence, the relationship between the two men in the play reflects some of the dilemmas and obstacles faced by Wilde and his lover in their conflict with unwelcome paternal authority.

Wilde's revisions to the play—both at the instigation of George Alexander before the first production and following Wilde's release from prison as he prepared the first published edition in 1899—resulted in the elimination of most of the confessional elements from the drama. Certainly, the initial scenario offered to Alexander was only the most embryonic version of the play, differing radically from the three-act version produced at the St. James's (the scenario, unlike the first manuscript draft, was in three acts). The Gribsby episode was, as we have noted, among the scenes deleted as Wilde condensed the four-act play into three acts. Jack's quasi-paternalistic interest in Algy's welfare, though undermined by his own indulgence in a form of "Bunburyism," permeates the early drafts, underscoring the difference in age and experience between the two men. Hence, the original Jack and Algy more closely resemble the pederastic male couple derived from the model of Greek culture, on which Wilde based his own relationships with younger men.

By contrast, the later versions evacuate Jack's greater maturity and moral concern, replacing it with something more pragmatic: a fear that he, Jack, will have his social position and wealth undermined by Algy's excesses. Given Wilde's earlier and ongoing literary interest in the theme of obsessive relationships between men, especially between an older and a younger man, the original four-act version is the more consonant with this preoccupation. It treats male intimacy—an important source of the play's significance yet one that is fraught with dangers and tensions—as more than simply a source of humor. Alexander's version, by contrast, exploits the humorous possibilities of two "Bunburyists" with widely diverging temperaments, while erasing many of their more subtle differences and eliminating much of the emotional and erotic significance of their relationship.

If, as Lord Henry Wotton claimed in *Dorian Gray*, "the one charm of marriage is that it makes a life of deception absolutely necessary for both parties," then *Earnest* suggests that the life of deception habitually practiced by its protagonists will continue beyond their official "happy ending" of matrimony.[70] As we know, Wilde's own marriage helped to establish him as a respectable figure in society, while he covertly sought sexual activity with men. As long as the *forms* of

{ *Defacing Oscar Wilde* }

society are respected, the play indicates, society will not take revenge on the individual bent on a "double" or "secret" life of pleasure. Yet the downfall of Wilde shows either that he was not fully aware of what those "forms" were and pushed his flouting of them too far or, more plausible, that those forms were themselves in flux, policed and enforced by sharp-eyed professionals and obsessive moral vigilantes rather than amusingly blinkered aristocrats.

Wilde's dramatic fantasy perhaps belongs to the Age of Restoration comedy, in which society was indeed ruled over by the likes of Lady Bracknell, a snobbish yet irresistibly endearing matriarch, rather than the Marquis of Queensberry, a quintessentially Victorian paranoiac. Lady Bracknell's is not the crusading voice of moral probity but the pragmatic one of social "surfaces." As she remarks of an evening of musical entertainment that Algernon has planned for her, "I'm sure the program will be delightful, after a few expurgations."[71] The assertion of control she wishes to exercise over the "program" is designed to appease the tastes of her audience, not to protest obscenity. In this respect, it resembles the intrusive role of Alexander, whose "expurgations" of Wilde's play perhaps made it more "delightful" in the eyes of many theatergoers but also diverted the audience away from its confessional and erotic design.

"Desire without Limit": Wilde's Dissident Confession

For the remainder of this chapter I will argue that Wilde, in the sexual and aesthetic crisis brought on by his conviction and imprisonment for homosexual offenses (or "gross indecency with another male person," as the legislation termed it) constructed in the figure of his erstwhile lover, Lord Alfred Douglas, a character to whom he could attribute responsibility for the terrible events that had befallen him. That the crisis was in part an aesthetic one is suggested by his declaration that "everything about my tragedy has been hideous, mean, repellant, lacking in style" (490). The "Bosie" of De Profundis, I maintain, is less an actual historical personage than a literary creation of Wilde's, to be compared with Jack, Algy, or Dorian Gray. The difference is that Bosie functions *explicitly* in this confessional narrative as a "double" or alter ego for Wilde himself, on whose behalf Wilde "confesses" the events and transgressions leading to his imprisonment. Moreover, Bosie is described as the true "author" of Wilde's tragedy and hence deserving of blame for its appalling outcome and aesthetic defects. Though Bosie's explicit "crimes" are his failure to communicate with Wilde while Wilde was in prison and his incompetence as a reader/translator of Wilde's texts, Wilde also projects onto his erstwhile lover his own sense of failure as an artist.

Douglas's chief flaw, according to the letter, is his refusal to acknowledge his role in the catastrophe suffered by Wilde: "That from beginning to end you were the responsible person, that it was through you, for you, and by you that I was there, never for one instant dawned upon you" (448). Yet Douglas's uncanny power to remain free and innocent (at least in the eyes of the law) links him with other characters created by Wilde who evade the consequences of their transgressions: in a comic vein, Jack and Algy succeed in protecting their social positions despite their misdemeanors; and in a seriotragic mode, Dorian Gray long defers the physical, if not the moral, degeneration resulting from his clandestine acts. If the figure of "Bosie" resembles Dorian more than Algy, this is because it was his novel's hero to whom Wilde had attributed the insidious power to destroy the life and the work of an artist; and it was from the self-conscious position of the ruined artist that Wilde wrote his prison letter.

The stylistic and tonal differences between the prison letter and *The Importance of Being Earnest* seem, on the surface, far more prolific and significant than do their similarities. Even their titles seem to polarize the two works: the mock pomposity of the play's title is undermined by its paradoxical subtitle, "A Trivial Comedy for Serious People." The whole tone of the play seems flippant, irreverent, insincere — that is precisely where its subversive power lies. In fact, the play continues Wilde's transgressive project of challenging binary oppositions by inverting them:[72] "triviality" becomes, according to the play's inversion of Victorian values, more important than "seriousness," whereas "earnestness" is ruled over by superficiality. By contrast, *De Profundis* — which Wilde wrote after *Earnest* but which was separated from it by the traumatic events of the trials — has long been interpreted as laying bare the hidden depths of Wilde's soul, having been written at the great crisis in his life and deriving ostensibly from his suffering and repentance. Precisely because *Earnest* is so often considered the culmination of Wilde's genius, his most perfect work, his prison letter seems to follow like a flawed and uncharacteristically confessional utterance.

Yet, as I have shown, Wilde's last play—especially the four-act version—can be read in a way that foregrounds its confessional significance. Moreover, it is hard to miss the strong moral themes in many of Wilde's writings or to ignore the almost obsessive preoccupations with guilt, repentance, and salvation that run through the major works. Even the so-called society comedies that brought him such magnificent success demonstrate a deep exploration of the power of the past to determine the present: in particular the destructive force of morally ambiguous or corrupt actions that come back to haunt the protagonists is among the most persistent and important features of Wilde's dramatic writing. If we read *De Profundis* alongside the other plays before *Earnest*—or indeed with the four-act version of *Earnest* in mind—then it becomes less of an anomaly; like these plays, the letter dramatizes the conscience of one who has committed actions that he (or she) regrets and who is torn between a desire to blame those who share the guilt and a need for individual redemption through imaginative engagement with suffering.

Of course, Wilde's literary characters were, with the exception of Dorian Gray, permitted to return from the brink of disaster and resume life in respectable society. Their crises were not fatal; indeed one might say that the crises ultimately enhanced the position of the protagonist. For example, in *An Ideal Husband*, Sir Robert Chiltern's enforced confrontation with his shady political past seems to be leading toward public disgrace and private catastrophe, as he is blackmailed by the equally Machiavellian Mrs. Cheveley. Yet, as a result of some improbable events and a last-ditch defensive speech by Lord Goring, he is forgiven by his wife and emerges as the likely next prime minister of Britain. Ironically, it is Goring himself, the resolute defender of male privilege, whose "career will have to be entirely domestic." For Chiltern, the outcome of corruption is the enticing prospect offered by his wife: "For both of us a new life is beginning."[73] Wilde himself, though he makes frequent calls for "the new life" in his letter to Bosie, was permitted no such rebirth.

De Profundis is linked to *Earnest* in another respect: Wilde's lack of control over the form of its first presentation to the public. Wilde wrote the letter on prison notepaper between January and March 1897, shortly before his release from Reading Gaol. He was not permitted to send the letter to Douglas before his release from prison, but one of his first acts as a free man was to present the manuscript to Robert Ross, instructing him to make two typed copies of the letter before sending the original on to Douglas. Fearing that Douglas would destroy the original letter, Ross instead sent him one of the typescripts, which its recipient appears to have discarded or destroyed without reading. Following Wilde's death in 1900, Ross published excerpts from the work in 1905 that gave no indication of the fact that they were taken from a letter to Douglas. Indeed, Ross's preface to the 1905 edition strongly hinted that the excerpts were taken from a letter to himself.[74] In lieu of George Alexander's cuts, then, Wilde's prison letter was posthumously expurgated by his literary executor and erstwhile lover, Robert Ross, who gave the ponderous title to the first edition.[75]

The excerpts of the letter selected by Ross for publication after Wilde's death were intended to depict Wilde's spiritual crisis and conversion and were published with the explicit purpose of rehabilitating Wilde's reputation among the British public. The gambit succeeded, as the majority of critics found in the expurgated letter a new moral seriousness, remorse, and sincerity, which suggested that Wilde had seen the error of his "perverse" ways. As one critic wrote, "The book is beautiful in all its misery, and worth a million of the dishonest self-revelations of the men who write about their souls as if their bodies were mere pillow-cases."[76] Yet Wilde's own suggested title of *Epistola: In Carcere et Vinculis*, echoing the papal decree, suggests a more playful approach to the quasi-spiritual confession. Among the first critics, only George Bernard Shaw detected a note of ironic, mocking humor more consonant with Wilde's previous reputation as a literary trickster for whom sincerity, or even suffering, was merely a convenient "mask." Though Wilde wrote in the letter that "behind Sorrow there is always Sorrow. Pain, unlike Pleasure, wears no mask" (473), Shaw insisted on "the comedic view of De Profundis. It is really an extraordinary book, quite exhilarating and amusing as to Wilde himself, and quite disgraceful and shameful to his stupid tormenters. There is pain in it, inconvenience, annoyance, but no real tragedy, all comedy." Shaw went on to attack the popular reception of the book, which he claimed had the effect of "degrading the whole affair to the level of sentimental tragedy."[77]

Yet not all the other critics considered *De Profundis* to be sincerely confessional. E. V. Lucas expressed a skeptical view of Wilde's continued "posing" in an autobiography that others found convincing and authentic. Whereas William T. Stead wrote Ross to offer his "thanks for having permitted us to see the man as he really was," Lucas complained that the tone of *De Profundis* "is not sorrow but its dexterously constructed counterfeit" and argued that Wilde's "artifice was too much for him; his poses were too insistent—had become too much a part of the man—to be abandoned."[78] Apparently Lucas had missed one of the central tenets of Wilde's aesthetic creed: that the "mask" or "pose" is not distinct from the "real man" but that social behavior, indeed human personality itself, is a series of masks without any essential or consistent "identity" or face underneath. In his criticism, Lucas refuses to consider that the difference between the "genuine emotion" of sorrow and its "counterfeit" might be impossible to determine. Indeed, if to express an emotion is immediately to place it under suspicion of insincerity, then a literary confession such as Wilde's is certain to appear counterfeit.

And yet Lucas's attack on *De Profundis* is more helpful critically than is Stead's praise of it. Lucas's claim that Wilde is constructing another pose in his letter at least avoids the delusion that we have, through the mediation of the text, attained access to "the man as he really was." Of course, Lucas implied that Wilde's confession was a failure, in that he *ought* to have shown his true self and his not doing so was another example of his perverse lack of sincerity. A more affirmative rendition of the same idea was given by G. S. Street, who in his review of *De Profundis* observed that "people who heartily admire [Wilde's] style, so limpid and graceful, so brilliant in its unforced elegance and adornment, think that here the use of it is a token of insincerity. Surely, rather, its absence would have been. It had grown into his nature; he could not write differently without an effort."[79] This remark transforms one of Wilde's central dicta—"Truth is entirely and absolutely a matter of style"[80]—into something radically different and utterly un-Wildean: style, in Street's view, has become a matter of *nature*, indeed of identity itself. Lucas suggests a similar concept of style as an index of naturalized "identity" when he claims that Wilde's poses "had become too much a part of the man to be abandoned."

This critical transformation of Wilde's antiessentialist position on the importance of style is related to the argument that it was Wilde's "nature"—specifically, his sexual nature—that was being constituted and defined during his trials. Indeed, Wilde's sexual identity was constructed on the basis of his literary style as much as or more than his sexual acts. Jonathan Dollimore, in an impressive reading of what he calls Wilde's "transgressive aesthetic," draws attention to "the perceived connections between Wilde's aesthetic transgression and his sexual transgression," in terms of the "nature," or identity, that was conceived as lying behind it: "In producing the homosexual as a species of being rather than, as before, seeing sodomy as an aberration of behavior, society now regarded homosexuality as rooted in a person's identity; this sin might pervade all aspects of an individual's being, and its expression might become correspondingly the more insidious and subversive."[81]

To view Wilde's "style" as inhering in or directly revelatory of his "nature" is to undercut his protest against essentialist conceptions of the self and to ignore the subversive potential of the link between sexual and textual deviance. According to Dollimore, "Wilde confirmed and exploited this connection between discursive and sexual perversion" in, for example, a famous statement from the prison letter: "What the paradox was to me in the sphere of thought, perversity became to me in the sphere of passion" (466). This connection is expressed more generally in Wilde's assertion in the letter that he was undone as much by textual indiscretion as by sexual transgression. Though explicit hostility toward Wilde's transgressive sexuality was muted in the reviews of *De Profundis*, the assumption that it was revealed by the "elegance and adornment" of his writing remained intact. Wilde's prison letter emerges from the crucible, brought to a white heat during his trials, in which his sexual "nature" and his literary "style" had been merged into a single, "perverse" practice.

Renouncing both the traditional forms of Victorian autobiography and the constraints of sexual "identity," Wilde used the prison letter to exploit the fluidity of roles and theatrical sense that he had mastered as a dramatist. Although this was, as an ostensibly private letter, "the only work he wrote without an audience,"[82] in the words of Regenia Gagnier, *De Profundis*, in common with a number of classic autobiographical texts, is in fact addressed to a highly specific audience: the only reader, in fact, by whom Wilde felt his confession would be understood.[83] The classical autobiographer often chastens his prior self for immoderate or misdirected appetites. St. Augustine, for example, provides an account of his sexual lust as a young man in order to criticize his rebellion against and to reveal his ultimate acceptance of the higher love for God. The youthful Augustine's appetite for sexual pleasure is associated in the *Confessions* with an errant "perversion" that the mature writer has rejected in favor of divine love. Wilde, however, attacks the younger *Bosie* not only for his excessive sensuality but for his negative influence on Wilde's self-restraint as well.

An even more significant influence on Wilde's confessional writing, however, is the autobiographical poetry of Wordsworth, such as the *Prelude*, in which the poet writes critically, if somewhat vaguely, of his youthful self "that my delights / (Such as they were) were sought insatiably" and describes himself as having been

> often greedy in the chase,
> And roamed from hill to hill, from rock to rock,
> Still craving combinations of new forms,
> New pleasure, wider empire for the sight.[84]

Here it is the "insatiable" quality of desire that is rendered problematic, not the object of the desire itself (which is, in fact, unspecified; were we to identify it as a "love for nature," it would seem merely banal). Nature—and its effect on the poetic imagination—would continue to be the "adult" Wordsworth's chosen source of tranquility and inspiration, but his relationship to nature is described as having changed over time. In the autobiographical poem "Lines Written above Tintern Abbey," for example, Wordsworth recollects "the coarser pleasures of my boyish days" (line 74) and writes that the beautiful forms of nature "were then to me / An appetite: a feeling and a love" (lines 80–81). The self-indulgent effects of such youthful "appetite" are the subject of much of Wordsworth's autobiographical poetry, which contrasts this appetite with the mature poet's appreciation of the "still sad music of humanity" (line 92).[85]

As we have seen, the dangers of excessive appetite link Wilde's final play with his letter to Douglas. In both cases, appetite is derided as greed, and uncontrolled consumption is portrayed as a vice that undermines the possibility of social relationships between subjects. Wilde's writing of this period echoes the Augustinian and the Wordsworthian ideals of an austere, disciplined maturity that is shown as having emerged from a dissolute, self-indulgent youth. When Algy is on the point of being arrested for debt in the original, four-act version of *Earnest*, for example, a horrified Miss Prism remarks, "£762 for eating! How grossly materialistic! There can be little good in any young man who eats so much, and so often," to which Dr. Chasuble promptly adds, "It certainly is a painful proof of the disgraceful luxury of the age. We are far away from Wordsworth's plain living and high thinking."[86] The same quotation, from Wordsworth's "Sonnet Written in London, 1802," is used by Wilde in his letter to Bosie, protesting against his lover's excessive appetite for expensive food and wine:

> My ordinary expenses with you for an ordinary day in London — for luncheon, dinner, supper, amusements, hansoms and the rest of it — ranged from £12 to £20, and the week's expenses were naturally in proportion and ranged from £80 to £130. For our three months at Goring my expenses (rent of course included) were £1340. Step by step with the Bankruptcy Receiver I had to go over every item of my life. It was horrible. *"Plain living and high thinking"* was, of course, an ideal you could not at that time have appreciated, but such extravagance was a disgrace to both of us. [428][87]

Wilde's past life is here reduced to a column of debts, the agonizing process of going over "every item of my life" prefiguring the confessional letter to Bosie, in which he depicts the harmful consequences of indulging Bosie's insatiable appetites: "There was not a glass of champagne you drank, not a rich dish you ate of in all those years, that did not feed your Hate and make it fat" (445). And, yet, Wilde's echo from his play tends to recall a note of humor to the account of Bosie's grotesque appetite that undercuts the seriousness of his accusation. The irony is, of course, that "plain living and high thinking" was the last ideal to be associated with Wilde himself; instead of hypocritically claiming this as his "ideal," Wilde is satirically sabotaging the ideal itself by invoking the comedic context of the suppressed scene from his play.

Wilde's distrust of "appetite" and its destructive effects as indicated in his prison letter seems, on the surface, uncharacteristic and even paradoxical. For Wilde has, at least in more recent years, become identified with a "transgressive aesthetic" that sought, precisely, the disintegration — or, alternatively, the multiplication — of the self through the destabilizing and dangerous force of desire. Dollimore, for example, presents Wilde as one whose "concept of the individual is crucially different from that sense of the concept which signifies the private, experientially self-sufficient, autonomous, bourgeois subject," and he argues that "not only are Wilde's conceptions of subjectivity and desire antiessentialist but so too—and consequently—is his advocacy of transgression. Deviant desire reacts against, disrupts, and displaces from within: rather than seeking to escape the repressive ordering of sexuality, Wilde reinscribes himself within and relentlessly inverts the binaries upon which that ordering depends."[88] Dollimore's insight offers a valuable clue to Wilde's approach to the "confession" in *De Profundis*. Wilde does not bypass the form altogether, as an oppressive and limiting structure, but inhabits and "inverts" it, thereby freeing confession from the "repressive ordering" of subjectivity on which it depends. Precisely because the practice of "confession" seems to presume a preexisting, authentic, suffering self that requires expression, Wilde is able to mimic that essentialist idea of identity and expose it as "entirely and absolutely a matter of style." This counterdiscourse of confession appropriates the very distrust of "appetite" as a source of moral error that had characterized the classical versions of the genre.

Oddly, however, Dollimore does not recognize this transgressive force in Wilde's prison letter. Indeed, instead of extending to *De Profundis* his shrewd insight into Wilde's practice of subverting aesthetic and moral codes "from within," he views the letter as "a conscious renunciation by Wilde of his transgressive aesthetic." Arguing that Wilde, in *De Profundis*, "repositions himself as the authentic, sincere subject which before he had subverted," Dollimore describes the letter as "tragic" in its portrayal of the "defeat of the marginal and the oppositional which only ideological domination can effect; a renunciation which is experienced as voluntary and self-confirming but which is in truth a self-defeat and a self-denial massively coerced through the imposition, by the dominant, of incarceration and suffering and their 'natural' medium, confession."[89]

My reading of *De Profundis* differs from Dollimore's in emphasizing Wilde's resistance to those coercive pressures of ideology with which he was confronted. The prison letter destabilizes the confessional integrity of the individual (sexual) subject by splitting its characteristics between Wilde himself and the figure of "Bosie," thereby revealing the autobiographical invocation of a "past self" as an ideological fiction, at the same time as it makes manifest the eroticized intersubjectivity of "author" and "reader." No less than with the novel and the Victorian melodrama, Wilde takes a familiar genre and destabilizes it from within to create a new form that eludes and thereby calls into question established categories of genre and systems of representation. Wilde does not posit a gulf between his present and past selves—the purported object of the autobiography being, as in the *Prelude*, to bridge this gulf—but constructs an opposition between himself and Bosie that the letter strives to maintain and totalize, attributing to the latter figure, in extreme form, the youthful appetites and "perversions" that previous autobiographers identify with their own, error-prone immaturity. Yet the letter is itself a means of rhetorically undoing that opposition, ultimately recalling the rejected figure of Bosie to rejoin a dual subjectivity founded on shared desires, remembered pleasures, and reciprocity.[90]

Wilde's approach to confession is manifestly imitative and subversive: like Augustine, Wilde dramatizes the shameful recollection of his earlier self-indulgences as a painful but necessary duty. And yet Wilde's tone in the letter is blatantly elegiac, allowing him once again to surround himself imaginatively with the material luxuries now beyond his reach: "The Savoy dinners—the clear turtle-soup, the luscious ortolans wrapped in their crinkled Sicilian vine-leaves, the heavy amber-coloured, indeed almost amber-scented champagne—Dagonet 1880, I think was your favourite wine?—all have still to be paid for" (507). Though the last note of financial responsibility returns Wilde—and his reader—to the traumatic reality of his bankruptcy, the tone of the passage remains strongly invested in recapturing the very pleasures it apparently renounces. By indulging Bosie's desires, Wilde writes self-reproachfully that "I . . . let myself be lured into the imperfect world of coarse uncompleted passions, of appetite without distinction, desire without limit, and formless greed" (463). Again, Wilde identifies "Bosie" as the source of past error that he denounces, while reentering vicariously the lost life of luxury and excess.

The initially radical division between self and other in *De Profundis* can be explained in part by the very crisis of Wilde's life, his trials and imprisonment, that motivated him to write the letter. In one of the most powerful passages, Wilde describes the tormenting monotony of prison existence, suggesting that the letter has grown out of the enforced remembering that his isolation brings: "With us time itself does not progress. It revolves. It seems to circle round one

{ *Defacing Oscar Wilde* }

centre of pain. The paralysing immobility of a life, every circumstance of which is regulated after an unchangeable pattern, so that we eat and drink and walk and lie down and pray, or kneel at least for prayer, according to the inflexible laws of an iron formula: this immobile quality, that makes each dreadful day in the very minutest detail like its brother, seems to communicate itself to those external forces the very essence of whose existence is ceaseless change" (457–58).

That the horrifying experience of this stasis—contrasted with which the "external forces" of change appear all the more attractive—is of central importance to Wilde's act of remembering and writing is affirmed by his advice to Bosie: "Remember this, and you will be able to understand a little of why I am writing to you, and in this manner" (458). As Gagnier writes, Wilde's "self in his letter is a self constructed in a particular imaginative act of resistance against insanity and against the material matrix of prison space and time, that is, confined, segmented space and timelessness."[91] Wilde's letter, as Gagnier points out, reproduces the prison-induced obsession with fragments of time in his descriptions of the outside world and his own past. Characterizing the letter as "a self-serving biography of Alfred Douglas, whose remembered image recreated for him the world outside," Gagnier shows how the material conditions of prison experience continually resurface throughout Wilde's attempts to escape them imaginatively.[92] Hence Douglas, who is invoked precisely to transport Wilde beyond prison, "becomes the imprisoned one, and Wilde, the one omniscient."[93] Wilde seeks to blame his entire catastrophe on Douglas, and his attack on "Bosie" is tantamount to a denial of his own past agency. Hence, Wilde writes of "the fatal friendship that had sprung up between us" (432), as though a tragic destiny outside his control had determined the crisis of his life.

Indeed, the figure of "Bosie" becomes more than an individual lover or reader, more even than the reminder of all the mistakes that Wilde believed he had made: he comes to represent all the malevolent forces that had brought Wilde into disgrace. Behind Douglas's reckless behavior and selfish pursuit of pleasure, Wilde detects a greater, more abstract malignity, "as if you yourself [Douglas] had been merely a puppet worked by some secret and unseen hand to bring terrible events to a terrible issue" (443). Much as Victorian society had attributed a predatory sexual appetite to Wilde and thereby created a monster for the purpose of exorcising its own collective sexual anxieties, Wilde in his prison letter creates in Bosie the demonic, compulsive consumer whose ultimate achievement was to orchestrate the public cannibalizing of Wilde himself.[94]

The confessional import of Wilde's letter emerges not at the points where it reveals his secrets but at those where it demonstrates the impossibility of doing so. Drawing attention to the presence of a scandalous secret shared by himself and Bosie, Wilde defers the disclosure of that secret while inviting the reader or audience to speculate as to its nature. Even though he makes no attempt to conceal his sexual relationship with Douglas, which had become public knowledge, Wilde resists disclosing the deferred secret of identity—or, rather, of mistaken identity—on which the letter's composition depends. If Wilde writes out of a desire for revenge against Bosie, then the inner springs of this revenge will nonetheless remain concealed. It is as though, as Marion Shaw has remarked of late-Victorian confessional narratives, "the secret itself is nothing, or at least not anything that the mind can be brought 'to set to paper'; what is important is the journey to the secret, the act of confession itself."[95]

The rhetorical effect of the letter is, moreover, to demonstrate that there is no "reality" behind the mask—that, however "sincere" the confession might seem, the self it claims to unveil is a stylistic construct. Hence, Wilde's statements that would seem to indicate an authentic, "truthful" basis for his confession must be examined carefully for their self-deconstructing irony. Following his release from Reading Gaol, for example, Wilde remarked, "A man's face is his autobiography; a woman's face is her work of fiction."[96] The relevance of this statement is that it initially invokes a fixed, oppositional logic—contrasting autobiography and fiction, man and woman—only then to collapse this logic into a subversive similitude. The stable gender dichotomy of "manly" sincerity and female artifice is soon undermined by a recognition that there is, for Wilde, no differentiation—either of value or of function—to be made between the autobiography and the work of fiction or between "man" and "woman."[97] Both sets of categories, Wilde's remark discloses, are equally conventional types whose opposition is itself ideological. The autobiography is as artificial as the work of fiction, and the "face," in either case, is a textual production.

Wilde's apparently casual collapsing of cherished distinctions—between male and female, between fictional and nonfictional texts

{ *Defacing Oscar Wilde* }

—should be kept in mind while reading *De Profundis*. As Jerome Buckley observes of Wilde, "In his most characteristic writing from the beginning through *De Profundis*, he himself made no great distinction between the two genres."[98] For Wilde, as later for Paul de Man, the generic status of "autobiography" is founded on the illusory notion of a stable, consistent, and unique self. De Man equates the figure of prosopopoeia—"the fiction of an apostrophe to an absent, deceased, or voiceless entity, which posits the possibility of the latter's reply and confers upon it the power of speech"—with "the trope of autobiography, by which one's name . . . is made as intelligible and memorable as a face."[99] This connection has interesting implications for a reading of Wilde's letter.

Moreover, *De Profundis* is self-evidently an address to an absent person. Indeed, Bosie is not only absent but also voiceless, for Wilde begins his letter by reproaching Bosie for his long silence: "After long and fruitless waiting I have determined to write to you myself, as much for your sake as for mine, as I would not like to think that I had passed through two long years of imprisonment without ever having received a single line from you" (423–24). In the course of his letter, Wilde makes numerous and often bitter references to Bosie's voicelessness. Because Wilde is confined by his imprisonment, he is dependent on Bosie for information from the outside, yet he writes accusingly that "you alone stood aloof, sent me no message, and wrote me no letter" (458). Ultimately, Wilde makes his strongest accusation, the one that comes closest to revealing the motive for his letter to Bosie: "Your silence has been horrible. Nor has it been a silence of weeks and months merely, but of years. . . . It is a silence without excuse; a silence without palliation" (463–64). As Koestenbaum points out, "*De Profundis* is an answer to an unwritten letter, to a desired text's absence."[100] Had Wilde not needed to recapture Bosie's voice and face in the void of prison, his letter would not have been written. Gagnier claims that "Wilde forces the presence of Douglas in the prose in order to make the pre-prison Wilde a reality"; but it would be equally valid to say that Wilde remembers scenes from his past so as to render intelligible and "memorable" Bosie's face and voice.[101]

Yet the letter is not merely a way of filling the silence; it also seeks to prompt a reply. When, toward the end of his letter, Wilde writes with apparent confidence, "As regards your letter to me in answer to this, it may be as long or as short as you choose" (510), the reader is struck by the sheer improbability that the Bosie whose character is depicted in the letter would be inclined to reply to it. In fact, Douglas not only failed to reply to Wilde's letter but refused to read it. This retrospective knowledge of the letter's communicative failure renders the detailed instructions Wilde provides for Bosie's reply even more poignant: "Address the envelope to 'The Governor, H.M. Prison, Reading.' Inside, in another, and an open envelope, place your own letter to me: if your paper is very thin do not write on both sides, as it makes it hard for others to read" (510). The letter here invokes the *fantasy* of Bosie's reply, but this fantasy is never likely to be realized, a failure caused not so much by Bosie's refusal to read the letter or even by the material restrictions placed on Wilde's correspondence as by the function of prosopopoeia to confer the illusion of another's presence and power of reply.

The fictional devices of Wilde's apostrophe are perhaps most apparent in the proliferation of detail regarding his relationship with Bosie.[102] Common sense tells us that most of this information is, strictly speaking, redundant. More than anyone else, Douglas would have known about his and Wilde's life together, including most of the details of their shared extravagances and pleasures. Wilde is not simply repeating the facts of his relationship with Bosie but is also presenting a context for their relationship that differs materially from the one that had become publicly known during the trials. Indeed, a central part of the argument of De Profundis is devoted to proving that the monstrous image of Wilde that was constructed by the prosecution, press, and popular gossip was false, while demanding that Douglas accept his share of the moral, if not the legal, responsibility for what had happened. Wilde's summary of the traducement of him that had occurred during his trials is suitably self-dramatizing and memorable: "At the end, I was of course arrested and your father became the hero of the hour: more indeed than the hero of the hour merely: your family now ranks, strangely enough, with the Immortals: for with that grotesqueness of effect that is as it were a Gothic element in history, and makes Clio the least serious of all the Muses, your father will always live among the kind pure-minded parents of Sunday-school literature, your place is with the Infant Samuel, and in the lowest mire of Malebolge I sit between Gilles de Retz and the Marquis de Sade" (430–31).

Wilde's aim in rehearsing the details of his daily life with Douglas is to trace from its beginnings their "fatal" relationship, in an effort to erase the official narrative: "That version," as Wilde remarked bitterly, "has now actually passed into serious history: it is quoted, believed, and chronicled" (456). Hence, as Wilde tells Bosie at the outset of the letter, "I have to write of your life and of mine" (424) to contest the official story. Motivated not by a desire for deeper self-knowledge or even self-blame but by the need for a revisionist account of his own past, Wilde's letter springs into being as an assault on another's character, not a revelation of his own: as he writes to Bosie, relishing the suffering his text might inflict, "You must read this letter right through, though each word may become to you as the fire or knife of the surgeon that makes the delicate flesh burn or bleed" (425). In its attempt to remind Bosie of their shared pleasures and create in him a consciousness of responsibility for their shared guilt, De Profundis develops into a dual confession in which Wilde, seeking to provoke a response from Bosie, attempts to speak on behalf of both parties.

Blaming Bosie for his central role in the disaster, while also criticizing himself for feebly standing by and allowing Bosie and his father to ruin him, Wilde in effect accuses Bosie of being responsible for the crimes Wilde himself had been punished for: "The sins of another were being placed to my account. Had I so chosen, I could on either trial have saved myself at his expense, not from shame indeed but from imprisonment. Had I cared to show that the Crown witnesses — the three most important — had been carefully coached by your father and his solicitors, not in reticences merely, but in assertions, in the absolute transference, deliberate, plotted, and rehearsed, of the actions and doings of someone else on to me, I could have had each one of them dismissed from the box by the Judge" (452). There can be little doubt that the details of Queensberry's involvement in the cover-up establish the "someone else" alluded to by Wilde as Bosie himself. Yet why, in a letter that does not hesitate elsewhere to direct a welter of abuse at its target, does Wilde balk at pointing the finger of suspicion directly toward the person described as "such an enemy as no man ever had" (452)? The attempt to answer this question will lead us to the central, specular relationship between author and reader that determines the structure of De Profundis.

"Face to Face": Specular Confession in *De Profundis*

In the passage immediately preceding the one above, Wilde reminds Bosie that "I could have held up a mirror to you, and shown you such an image of yourself that you would not have recognised it as your own till you found it mimicking back your gestures of horror, and then you would have known whose shape it was, and hated it and yourself for ever" (452). The description seems to confirm that the culpable other referred to is Bosie and that Wilde's purpose in the letter is to confront him with the horrible truth of his destructive personality and irresponsible behavior. Wilde's letter here functions as the same mirror that it allegorizes. Indeed, the rhetorical effect of the passage is to establish a specular relationship between author and reader, Wilde and Bosie, mediated by the "mirror" of the letter itself. As the letter's constructed reader, "Bosie" is the necessary, inverse reflection of Wilde's originative claim as "author."

Hence, the subjectivity of Wilde constitutes itself not autonomously, by asserting a prior self-presence that his narrative merely reproduces, but rhetorically and derivatively, by addressing the absent "Bosie" as the necessary precursor of his authorial subjectivity, at once filling and revealing the lack underlying that textual role. In this sense, the letter's emphasis on Bosie's immoderate appetites is both an accessory of Wilde's assault on him and a strategically necessary function of Wilde's self-portrayal; Bosie's role as an obsessive "consumer" seems to guarantee that he is destined to occupy the secondary position of "consumer" of Wilde's text, which leaves Wilde free to occupy the more elevated position of the creative originator of texts, the author. But the specular effect of the mirror-as-letter should remind us that Wilde can recognize "himself"—that is, his lapsed social function as author, which the letter attempts to reinstate—only in the mirror "image" of Bosie, his imaginary reader. The "horror" that he attributes to Bosie's "shape" turns out to be the reflection of this textual dependence on the very consumer whose excesses the letter vilifies.

This specular relationship suggests the constitution of an autobiographical subject through lack rather than (self-)presence, dependence rather than autonomy, and self-diffusion rather than unity. De Man describes the rhetorical constitution of subjectivity as "the autobiographical moment," which "happens as an alignment between the two subjects involved in the process of reading in which they determine each other by mutual reflexive substitution." The "self" of the autobiographer, irrespective of whether she or he "declares himself the subject of his understanding," is in fact the outcome of a textual reciprocity, in which the roles of author and reader "both depend on a substitutive exchange that constitutes the subject."[103] De Man's comment that the relationship between author and reader "amounts to the same" as that "between the author *of* the text and the author *in* the text who bears his name" helps to illuminate the substitutive relation between Wilde and Bosie produced by the mirroring effects of Wilde's letter.[104]

Bosie's position as reader is required for Wilde, as author, to constitute himself as (autobiographical) subject. But in the course of this reflexive relationship, a substitution occurs in which Bosie and Wilde stand in for each other, each taking on the role and mirroring the image of the other. The letter, that is, initially attempts to put Bosie in his place by bringing him "face to face" with his own hideous image; but the destabilizing effect of the text/mirror between Wilde and Bosie serves to remind us of the substitutive, rhetorical status of this confrontation. Wilde's autobiographical task of "revealing" Bosie's image to him in the letter is displaced by Bosie's role as a grotesque reflection and complement of Wilde's own degraded image. Thus the letter's ultimate effect is to bring Wilde and Bosie, author and reader, "face to face." Produced by the text, of course, the confrontation is a phantasmic one: both Wilde-as-author and Bosie-as-reader are rhetorically constituted and serve as effects of the text rather than as "persons" who exist outside it and are, as it were, struggling for control of the relationship.

This situation helps to account for Wilde's "perverse" refusal to identify the "someone else" responsible for the "sins" that had, he claims, been wrongly attributed to him.[105] The shadowy figure of guilt evoked by Wilde's language is not "another" at all but the displaced image of his own "face," an image on which he depends for authorial self-recognition. If prosopopoeia is that mode of inscription "by which one's name . . . is made as intelligible and memorable as a face," then the ambiguity of the "name" that is thus rendered memorable (or, indeed, whether the "name" and the "face" will match up) is indicative of a more far-reaching crisis of identity. As the textual figure—the cluster of images and tropes—necessary for the letter's apostrophic fiction, "Bosie" is also the term of inversion—one might say, more accurately, perversion—needed to sustain the text's antitheses between innocence and guilt, creation and consumption, loyalty and betrayal, and originality and imitation on which the narrative logic depends. Yet the abjected figure of "Bosie," who occupies the subordinate position in every binary structure posited by the letter, frequently rises up to usurp Wilde's role (and rule) as "author." The power to create and destroy "character"—a literary prerogative which is taken from Wilde during the trials and which the letter is determined to reclaim—is under constant threat from his own Caliban-like figure of unbridled appetite seeking to control the very narrative domain from which the author attempts to expel him.[106] Bosie's dislike of realism, as Wilde portrays it, is to be demonstrated by his rage at seeing his own face in the "glass" of the letter. Indeed, it seems that Wilde has chosen such "realism" as the appropriate mode of representation in writing of Bosie, whose "defect was not that you knew so little about life, but that you knew so much" and who "with very swift and running feet . . . had passed from Romance to Realism" (425).

Though Wilde's letter follows a similarly antiromantic trajectory, renouncing the niceties of correspondence and affectionate reproach for a stark and merciless demolition of his lover's character, romance remains a muted subtext throughout the letter. Wilde's refusal to name Bosie as the "someone else" whose freedom was bought at Wilde's expense might be interpreted as a romantic, or chivalrous, gesture, a reluctance to incriminate Bosie in the sordid world of crime and punishment. The letter makes clear, however, that Bosie's "innocence" had already been "left far behind": "The gutter and the things that live in it had begun to fascinate you" (425). Wilde's omission is perhaps less protective than dismissive, in the sense that it further excludes Bosie from the text, denies him the intelligibility of a name, and so forestalls the very act of recognition that the letter demands of him. Consequently, Wilde is again situated at the center of the drama, further marginalizing the figure of his reader.

The specular relation between Wilde and Bosie—who emerge as the two "selves" or functions necessary for the constitution of a single, textual subject—recurs in another striking juxtaposition: "I have had to look at my past face to face. Look at your past face to face" (508). "You" and "I" here become aligned with "face to face": the hierarchical relation between author and reader is dissolved in a complete equivalence of two faces, looking at each other, reflecting (on) each other's "past," before linking to form a single, sutured subject. Wilde's assertion of a moral and textual priority over Bosie—through his suffering, Wilde has already achieved the moral insight for which Bosie must strive—is undermined by the symmetry of the rhetorical figure.

Though Wilde begins the letter by emphasizing his difference from Bosie, asserting that "from the very first there was too wide a gap between us" (425), by the end of the letter this "gap" has been eliminated and replaced in the text by a resumption of intimacy. Bosie's appearance as the textual counterpart of Wilde is by no means harmonious, of course; their complementarity is resisted and deferred in the letter, precisely because it deconstructs the singularity of the confessional subject and involves the disclosure of "shameful" secrets. Writing with apparent disdain that "it was only in the mire that we met" (432), Wilde indicates that the textual interdependency between himself and Bosie, which the letter foregrounds, is a source of distress, involving the dissolution of his individualism—the quality in himself that he considers most "Christlike"—as well as the recollection of their sexual relationship, about which he has come to feel ambivalent.

Characterizing Bosie as "the true author of the hideous tragedy" (448), Wilde conflates the series of events that brought him down and the narrative in which those events are related. To be the author of one is, implicitly, to be the author of both, and Bosie's dominance over Wilde in their relationship is symptomatic of his tendency to usurp Wilde's authorial role in the letter. The role of "Bosie," initially consigned to the debased role of passive consumer, is transformed into a nefariously active one, demonstrating in his consumption a stronger will than Wilde can invoke as creator. Hence, Wilde's later claim to "authorship" of his own downfall is revealed as an entirely strategic attempt to find in his ruin a paradoxical form of self-assertion, or even self-creation: "Nobody, great or small, can be ruined except by his own hand" (465).

If, overall, Wilde seeks to share responsibility for the tragedy with Bosie, however, his sole authorship of the letter, as of all his texts, is something that he jealously guards. Bosie's conspicuous failure to write—not only his long "silence" as a correspondent but also his incompetence as a translator of Wilde's work (which Wilde condescendingly terms "the schoolboy faults of your attempted translation of *Salomé*" [432])—makes Wilde's literary success all the more distinctive and triumphant. Though his literary works had been used to incriminate him, it is only as an artist that Wilde feels any control or has any faith in the future. Seeking a meaning in his present plight, Wilde writes that "I hope to live long enough, and to produce work of such a character, that I shall be able at the end of my days to say, 'Yes: this is just where the artistic life leads a man'" (488). Therefore the contrast between Wilde's "artistic life" and Bosie's "sterile and uncreative" (426) existence is one on which the letter depends for its construction of Wilde-as-artist. The clear superiority of the originative author over the imitative reader/translator is at the heart of Wilde's eagerness to point out Bosie's botched translation of his play: it seems to confirm their radical dissimilarity and inequality.

Indeed, the criticism of the translation of *Salomé* is part of a larger pattern, in which Bosie's shortcomings are invariably related to his textual failings: for example, his callous failure to write to Wilde follows on the heels of his indiscreet publication and circulation of Wilde's letters. Wilde links these textual misdemeanors at the beginning of his letter, writing that "you yourself will, I think, feel in your heart that to write to me as I lie in the loneliness of prison-life is better than to publish my letters without my permission" (424). Koestenbaum has argued that *De Profundis* "warns that tragedies come from misreading, miswriting, or mishandling letters," and Douglas emerges as the sinister agent of all these malevolent actions.[107] In particular, Wilde's outraged indictment of the use made of a "charming letter" he wrote Douglas typifies his view of the epistolary text as a dangerous and unstable object:

> Look at the history of that letter! It passes from you into the hands of a loathsome companion: from him to a gang of blackmailers: copies of it are sent about London to my friends, and to the manager of the theatre where my work is being performed: every construction but the right one is put on it: . . . I produce the original letter myself in Court to show what it really is: it is denounced by your father's Counsel as a revolting and insidious attempt to corrupt Innocence: ultimately it forms part of a criminal charge: . . . I go to prison for it at last. That is the result of writing you a charming letter. [441]

Bosie's chief infringement here is of textual propriety: a private letter should not be "published," and Wilde is blaming Douglas for having carelessly let this one slip out of his possession into the hands of "a loathsome companion," as well as challenging the incriminating use made of his letter by the legal system. Bosie has ruined his *Salomé*, the prosecution has corrupted his letters, and the twin sets of "readers" become linked in a conspiracy to distort Wilde's texts beyond recognition. Refuting the legal claim that he "corrupted" Bosie's innocence, Wilde responds by protesting against a more significant corruption, that of his own writing. His attempt to reclaim the meaning of his letter, "to show what it really is," poses a challenge to the authority of the court's interpretive acts. Moreover, Wilde's claim that he went to prison directly as a result of writing a letter to Bosie constructs an aesthetically satisfying parallel with *De Profundis*, the letter with which Wilde prepared himself to emerge from prison at the end of his sentence.

Douglas's epistolary irresponsibility—which culminates in the "silence" that Wilde's letter seeks to fill—emerges elsewhere in the narrative as the source of Wilde's greatest anguish. Wilde writes of being assaulted by the Douglas family: "On the one side there was your father attacking me with hideous cards left at my club, on the other side there was you attacking me with no less loathsome letters" (430). Again Wilde portrays himself as the victim of epistolary violence, prefiguring the legal violence of the trials, the result being that "between you both I lost my head" (430), an image that figures both the loss of rational control and the castration that has been symbolically inflicted on him by the legal system.[108] The letters from Bosie, though described as "revolting" and "loathsome" (429), at least remain private. Wilde's most aggrieved outbursts occur when describing Douglas's disrespect for the privacy of the letter (indeed, his instructions to Bosie about how to write to him in gaol, with its insistence on a double envelope, emphasize his need for privacy). Wilde's protest articulates his horror that the entire British public has been able to "read" him in the press coverage of his trials, as though his subjectivity were an "open postcard" (446) rather than a private letter.

The agonizing loss of privacy, the absence of a "mask" with which to compose his public image, is most vividly dramatized in the famous description of Wilde on the platform at Clapham Junction—which, like the railway station referred to by Lady Bracknell, "might serve to conceal a social indiscretion" but not to cover up a sexual scandal:[109]

On November 13th 1895 I was brought down here from London. From two o'clock till half-past two on that day I had to stand on the centre platform of Clapham Junction in convict dress and handcuffed, for the world to look at. I had been taken out of the Hospital Ward without a moment's notice being given to me. Of all possible objects I was the most grotesque. When people saw me they laughed. Each train as it came up swelled the audience. Nothing could exceed their amusement. That was of course before they knew who I was. As soon as they had been informed, they laughed still more. For half an hour I stood there in the grey November rain surrounded by a jeering mob. For a year after that was done to me I wept every day at the same hour and for the same space of time. [490–91]

The account suggests a dramatist's or actor's nightmare: the total loss of control over one's public, in which the laughing, appreciative audience is transformed into a "jeering mob." The reversal, in this scene, of Wilde's usual pleasure at being the focus of attention — his sudden terror at being visible "for the world to look at" — is directly related to his lack of control over his image, his inability to appear in a guise that would keep the observer at an awed distance, rendered in his humiliating confession that "of all possible objects I was the most grotesque."

This crucial passage is characterized by the way in which Wilde's portrayal of himself as a unique subject drains away and is consumed by the collective will of the crowd, whose activity and growth is proportional to Wilde's stasis and diminution as an "object." It is as though Wilde is turned into a statue, a monument of disgrace, by the calcifying gaze of the hostile mob, which represents the British public. Among that crowd, in Wilde's imagination, is Bosie, who seized all the "opportunities" of publicly humiliating Wilde even after his imprisonment. Wilde's attempt to reclaim agency in his letter — by dramatically reenacting not only what had happened to him at Clapham Junction but also his weeping at precisely the same time every day thereafter — merely underscores his passivity, his reactive role in responding to events and crises that have always, it seems, been "authored" by "someone else." Paradoxically, Wilde's dramatic effort to encapsulate the horrors of prison in a single nightmarish scene ultimately marginalizes him in the confession. The confrontation between Wilde and the crowd works like an allegory of his relationship with Bosie, in which the "spectator" takes control of the action and banishes the "author" to prison and exile. Having been, according to his accusation, removed from the public stage through Bosie's agency, Wilde bizarrely repeats this same process in his letter, in which Bosie's subjectivity becomes more dynamic and influential than is Wilde's.

Consequently, Bosie cannot be reduced to merely the imitative, corrupting reader of the letter when he has played such a central role in the events it describes. Wilde's complaint to Bosie that, in responding to Wilde's tragedy, "you had the sympathy and the sentimentality of the spectator of a rather pathetic play" (448), attempts to turn Bosie back into the passive spectator, rather than the active author-figure he had become. Wilde writes that "had our life together been as the world fancied it to be, one simply of pleasure, profligacy and laughter, I would not be able to recall a single passage in it" (435). The reference to their shared life in terms of a text is indicative of this blurring between textual representation and the events represented. Wilde's life with Bosie is one that has to be written before it can be comprehended, and Wilde is determined to preserve the right to tell the story.

Yet he cannot diminish Bosie's central role, and the blurring between roles of author and reader exemplifies a pattern of substitutive specularity between Wilde and Bosie that reinforces their complementary functions. Despite the letter's repeated portrayals of a stark moral and intellectual contrast—for example, Wilde's frequent attribution to Bosie of "the supreme vice . . . shallowness" (425)—Wilde and Bosie are persistently linked by the letter's figures of comparison and similitude. Wilde constructs a cautionary figure, "he who does not know himself," and writes that "I was such a one too long. You have been such a one too long" (425), indicating that if Wilde's lack of self-knowledge is to be resolved by authoring a confession, Bosie's may be remedied by reading one. Here, the attempt to differentiate between the two collapses in the rhetorical symmetry of the expression. Similarly, Wilde states, "I don't write this letter to put bitterness into your heart, but to pluck it out of mine" (465). We recall de Man's description of the art of prosopopoeia as "a system of mediations that converts the radical distance of an either/or opposition in a process allowing movement from one extreme to the other." [110] This "movement" destabilizes the static, almost emblematic moral opposition between the two figures of Wilde and Bosie wherever it occurs.

In particular, Wilde's effort to establish an antithesis between himself and Bosie is fatally undermined by the specular mediation of the letter itself, posited as an exchange between subject positions. When Wilde advises Bosie, for example, that "you will let the reading of this terrible letter—for such I know it is—prove to you as important a crisis and turning-point of your life as the writing of it is to me" (448), the effect is less to differentiate between the "writing" and "reading" of the text—to distinguish the creative, morally purposeful author from the sterile, indolent consumer—than to connect them with the autobiographical figure of the "turning point." The letter is portrayed as having exactly the same effect on each of them: hence their distinct roles are dissolved into a single process, mediated by their mutual substitution in the text. Wilde writes that "most people are other people. Their thoughts are someone else's opinions, their life a mimicry, their passions a quotation" (479), implicitly contrasting his own, Christlike originality and individualism with Bosie's sterile, imitative nature.

The antagonistic quality to the epistolary relationship between Wilde and Douglas is, of course, highlighted by the bitterness and violence of the language. It is this linguistic violence, above all, that distinguishes the prison letter from the more playful specular involutions of *Earnest*. Wilde writes with disgust of "a letter you had published in one of the halfpenny newspapers about me," which Douglas considered "a wonderful letter . . . a proof of almost quixotic chivalry" (448–49). Douglas's crass insensitivity to Wilde's position is compounded in the letter-related incident for which Wilde reserves his greatest and most prolonged scorn. This occurs when Douglas proposes to publish extracts of the letters Wilde had written to him in an article to be published in the French journal *Mercure de France*: "You had left my letters lying about for blackmailing companions to steal, for hotel servants to pilfer, for housemaids to sell. That was simply your careless want of appreciation of what I had written to you. But that you should seriously propose to publish selections from the balance was almost incredible to me" (453–54).

Wilde's horror is intensified when he learns that the letters Douglas proposes to publish were those written to him by Wilde from Holloway Prison, "the letters that should have been to you things sacred and secret beyond anything in the whole world!" (455). Douglas's violation of Wilde's textual secrecy is compounded by his promiscuous dissemination of Wilde's letters, which are represented, like the painting in *Dorian Gray*, as the receptacle of a dangerous secret. Wilde professes astonishment that Douglas, in whose friendship he had trusted, "proposed to publish [his letters] for the jaded *decadent* to wonder at, for the greedy *feuilletoniste* to chronicle, for the little lions of the *Quartier Latin* to gape and mouth at!" (455). In its combination of outrage and self-pity, this protest anticipates the account of Wilde's public humiliation at Clapham Junction. Indeed, the embarrassing publication of the secret letter logically precedes the display of Wilde's vulnerable body on the railway platform: Douglas's betrayal results directly in Wilde's agonizing exposures. Stripped of his "secret," Wilde is thereby deprived of his most effective mask. Moreover, Wilde's loss of control over — and Douglas's lack of respect for — his letters prefaces his own dehumanizing reduction "in the great prison where I was then incarcerated" to "merely the figure and letter of a little cell in a long gallery, one of a thousand lifeless numbers, as of a thousand lifeless lives" (454).[111] The idea of the letter, then, functions multivalently to incorporate the deferred disclosure of Wilde's secret; the broken contract between Wilde and Douglas; and the penitentiary reduction of Wilde's "identity" to a standardized sign, devoid of all individual style.

Conclusion

With its repeated statements of horror at an unsought and deeply humiliating public exposure, Wilde's letter reveals a strategic resistance to and subversion of the confession. Far from being a repressive or externally enforced concealment of a shameful truth, the "secret" is for Wilde the soil of complex experience and disciplined desire, in which the seed of what he called "individuality" might flourish. Culminating in the recognition that "secrets are always smaller than their manifestations" (506), Wilde's prison letter relentlessly traces this growth of a shared secret into a manifestation whose effects were at once personal, cultural, and multifariously textual. As the climactic cultural manifestation of his secret, his trials and conviction inaugurated a series of events over which Wilde had lost control. The prison letter seeks to reclaim control of his secret and to reinscribe it within a narrative of his own construction. Hence, far from being a work in which Wilde repents of his crimes and confesses his guilty past life, the letter is a celebration of the power of secrecy to free desire from the irritating or tragic incursions of public scrutiny.

Though Wilde's letter denounces Bosie as the "other" from which the confessional subject must establish a safe distance, it is crucial that this denouncement is rhetorically undone by the mediation of the letter and its inscription of the reader as necessary counterpart. This implied reader of *De Profundis*, whatever else he might be, is free, and the letter seeks to punish him for this undeserved freedom, which has been secured at Wilde's expense. Asserting that Bosie belongs to "a race, marriage with whom is horrible, friendship fatal, and that lays violent hands either on its own life or on the lives of others" (440), Wilde conceives of his letter as a form of justified self-defense.

Yet he also depicts with graphic relish the pain that his letter will inflict on his reader. Hoping that his unflattering portrayal of Douglas "will wound your vanity to the quick," Wilde advises him to "read the letter over and over again till it kills your vanity" (424). The language suggests a therapeutic purpose of moral rejuvenation, as though the letter were destroying a diseased organ; but to kill Bosie's vanity, founded on the beauty of his face and the aristocracy of his lineage, is not only to kill Bosie himself but also to eradicate the specular duality he forms with Wilde. If, in the hands of Douglas, the letter produces a series of random explosions, Wilde methodically transforms it into an instrument of disfiguring, defacing, and suicidal violence. By so doing, he deconstructs the singularity of the autobiographical subject and dissents from the power of confession to establish the guilt and marginality of those in whose voices it claims to speak.

CHAPTER 4

A Double Nature

The Hidden Agenda of Edward Carpenter's
My Days and Dreams

In *My Days and Dreams: Being Autobiographical Notes*, published in 1916 but begun as early as 1890, Edward Carpenter "came out" as a homosexual with an unmistakable directness that was, in the words of Noel Greig, "unique in English literature for the time or indeed, for long afterwards."[1] Though it lacked the confessional zeal of Symonds's *Memoirs*, Carpenter's autobiography has almost certainly had more influence on the literary representation of same-sex desire in the twentieth century. Symonds's *Memoirs* (1984) and Wilde's *De Profundis* (1905/1962) — the subjects of the previous two chapters — were both posthumously published works, in which the homosexual "confession" became public long after the authors were beyond criticism or scandal. Carpenter was among the first in England to make his homosexuality an explicit and central part of his public persona. The publication of *My Days and Dreams*, in fact, was at once a key incident in Carpenter's lifelong mission of dealing directly and honestly with the facts of sexuality and a major event in literary history. Yet Carpenter's autobiographical openness was not as straightforward as it appeared, being mediated by the reserve required to avoid the kind of controversy that had culminated in the destruction of Wilde.

In this chapter I will examine the ways in which the dramatic form of self-revelation contained in Carpenter's autobiography was developed as a strategy to avert the sexual scandal that threatened him. The secrecy that had characterized earlier homosexual autobiographies is here renounced for a new aesthetic practice of disclosure, and yet the incriminating memories of the Wilde trials lingered in the ongoing hostility toward public statements of same-sex desire. Carpenter attempts in his autobiography to forge an alliance between his sexual desires and his radical politics that would be productive of what Jonathan Dollimore has termed "sexual dissidence": a combination of specific sexual deviance and other forms of radical political and cultural engagement.[2] And yet Carpenter was unwilling to be cast in the role of hero or martyr and assiduously avoided the kind of public scrutiny and scandal that had befallen Wilde.

Born in 1844, Carpenter followed a remarkably conventional Victorian path for his first thirty years, being educated at Cambridge University, where he was ordained as a clergyman. Appointed as the curate to the "muscular Christian" F. D. Maurice, Carpenter began to feel misgivings about the academic and clerical career that stretched ahead of him. In 1874, he left Cambridge to teach in the university's extension scheme, which took him to northern England and brought him into contact with the working classes. This led him to renounce teaching altogether, and Carpenter ultimately set up home at Millthorpe in Derbyshire, near Sheffield, where he lived for the remainder of his life and, from 1898, cohabited with his lover, George Merrill.

His literary career began in 1873, with the publication of *"Narcissus" and Other Poems*, which, Carpenter writes, "fell practically dead — a few notices, mostly depreciatory, in the papers, a few copies bought by friends, and then it ceased to stir."[3] Though he went on to become internationally famous as a mystical guru-figure for those seeking alternative lifestyles and as a political activist, Carpenter's literary output — including his autobiography and his major poetical work, *Towards Democracy* — has long been neglected by critics and scholars, though there has been sporadic attention to his work on the part of socialist critics and historians of sexuality. During his lifetime, Carpenter became known as an apologist for same-sex desire in his pioneering works *The Intermediate Sex* (1908) and *Homogenic Love* (1894). Sheila Rowbotham and Jeffrey Weeks's careful 1977 study of Carpenter's sexual politics, along with the prominence given to Carpenter by Jeffrey Weeks in *Coming Out*, his classic study of homosexual history, helped to establish Carpenter as a major figure in the history of sexuality in modern England.[4] More recently, the complex relationship between Carpenter's homosexuality and his socialist politics has received attention in a collection of essays exploring his place in Victorian radicalism.[5] Eve Kosofsky Sedgwick has discussed Carpenter in the context of the English admirers of Walt Whitman, a group that included Symonds and Swinburne as well.[6] Others have examined the influence of Carpenter on the work of major twentieth-century novelists, in particular E. M. Forster. Indeed, Forster's posthumously published novel, *Maurice*, originated in a visit paid by Forster to Carpenter and Merrill at Millthorpe. The contribution of Carpenter to modern discourses and representations of same-sex desire has, however, been largely eclipsed by the greater prominence of his contemporary, Oscar Wilde.

The various drafts of Carpenter's autobiography in existence testify to the slow and tentative evolution of the work.[7] Carpenter wrote the early portions of the autobiography in the 1890s, before the conviction of Oscar Wilde made the revelation of a homosexual orientation in print impossibly risky. In part because of the Wilde trials and the atmosphere of suspicion that followed them, in part because of his own uncertain development toward sexual self-consciousness, Carpenter delayed publication of his autobiography for a generation. Whereas Symonds had composed his *Memoirs* in a relatively short time (1889–93), Carpenter's autobiography took shape over a quarter of a century, which is reflected in the informal and diffuse structure of the work. As Carpenter presents it in his preface, the composition appears to have been an almost random affair, devoid of any clear purpose or urgency: "As it happened, in the summer of 1890, when staying in London, I used to make the garden my resort for writing purposes; and one day in July of that year I started some autobiographical notes. In a very casual way, and with long intervals between, the notes have been continued down to the present time" (7).

The long period of composition tended to undermine the literary construction of a consistent autobiographical self, favoring the roughly chronological succession of recollections, ideas, and self-insights that could be supplemented at any time. Carpenter himself admitted that "the volume . . . has been composed in somewhat disjointed fashion" (7). When juxtaposed with the emotional and rhetorical intensity of Symonds's *Memoirs*, *My Days and Dreams* is also somewhat reserved and vague about the details of Carpenter's sexual history. When we consider the necessity of self-protection, Carpenter's sexual evasiveness is less surprising than his willingness to reveal his sexuality in published form at all. Yet there are various discrepancies between the accounts of events described in the autobiography and the versions that emerge from other, in some cases unpublished, sources. These inconsistencies alert the reader to the fact that Carpenter's project is to present a specific and selective version of his life in the autobiography, one designed to enhance his respectability and lessen the potential of a scandal over his homosexual confession. Carpenter represents the emergence of his sexuality in terms of a "double nature," which allows him to understand both male and female longings, experiences, and secrets. Though this double nature is encoded positively, the autobiography demonstrates the persistence of duality in a somewhat less utopian sense, distinguishing Carpenter's own sexual "nature" from those which threaten the privilege of "masculine" agency and desire. In particular, Carpenter's anxiety to differentiate his own sexuality from "effeminacy" indicates the pressure of conventional gender categories, as well as the cautionary construction of Wilde as an effeminate stereotype, on his representation of same-sex desire. I begin by discussing the factors motivating Carpenter's decision to write and publish an autobiography and then examine the key themes and figures of duality that combine to form the "hidden agenda" of the narrative.

Carpenter and *The Intermediate Sex*

Carpenter began his autobiography with the purpose of revealing his homosexuality to an audience that knew him primarily as a Socialist activist, Whitmanesque poet, pacifist, and "back to nature" enthusiast. For most of his life, Carpenter had acted directly and written forcefully against what he perceived as the oppressive sexual hypocrisy and puritanism of Victorian society. In 1894 Carpenter published a series of pamphlets entitled *Sex-Love*, *Woman*, and *Marriage*, which collectively sought both to challenge the widespread Victorian belief in the superiority of men over women and to attack the fear that a tolerant atmosphere for the expression of sexuality would undermine the ethical and institutional structure of civilization. These publications were followed, in early 1895, by the pamphlet *Homogenic Love*, which Carpenter claimed in his autobiography was "among the first attempts in this country to deal at all publicly with the problems of the Intermediate Sex" (195).

Carpenter had reached an agreement with Fisher Unwin to publish the first three pamphlets under the title *Love's Coming-of-Age*. But because of the panic surrounding the discussion of sexual topics following the trials of Oscar Wilde in 1895 — and the fact that Carpenter had already published an essay on homosexuality — the publisher withdrew from the agreement, forcing Carpenter to seek out other publishers for his book. When all that he approached refused to publish it, he returned to the Labour Press in Manchester — the original publisher of his series of pamphlets — which issued the book in 1896. In *My Days and Dreams*, Carpenter made a direct link between the difficulty of publishing his book and the decade's most spectacular scandal: "The Wilde trial had done its work: and silence must henceforth reign on sex-subjects" (196).

Ironically, the controversial pamphlet *Homogenic Love* was not included in the 1896 edition of *Love's Coming-of-Age*. Later editions of the volume, however, did address the subject of same-sex desire in a chapter called "The Intermediate Sex," a condensed version of Carpenter's book of the same name that was published in 1908. *The Intermediate Sex* was one of the most significant defenses of homosexuality to be published in English, a work in which, as Richard Dellamora has recently pointed out, "Carpenter attempts to validate homosexual desire by enlisting it in the service of the evolution of the race."[8] The autobiography, Carpenter hoped, would build on the work of this volume by providing a personal narrative of sexual development and liberation, a narrative focused on the pivotal role of same-sex desire in the emergence of one individual from the dark ages of unconscious Victorian rigidity in matters of gender and sexuality.

In his chapter entitled "The Intermediate Sex" included in later editions of *Love's Coming-of-Age*, Carpenter set out to contribute to the work of sexologists such as K. H. Ulrichs and Albert Moll who had pioneered the investigation of the sexual characteristics of *Urnings* (Ulrichs's term for homosexual men). Carpenter's central argument was that "intermediates" formed a large proportion of humanity and combined the strengths of men and women. Possessing what he termed a "double nature," intermediates were able to communicate freely with both men and women, thereby enjoying "a certain freemasonry of the secrets of the two sexes."[9] Like Symonds, Carpenter sought to disprove the common belief that all intermediates were characterized by a highly visible and "not particularly attractive" inversion of gender behavior. Hence, Carpenter designates as "the extreme specimens" those who occupy the outer limits of the intermediate sex, somewhat stereotypically describing the male of this kind as "a distinctly effeminate type, sentimental, lackadaisical, mincing in gait and manners, something of a chatterbox, skilful at the needle and in woman's work, sometimes taking pleasure in dressing in woman's clothes."[10] In effect, Carpenter is trying to achieve tolerance for the "normal" or "healthy" intermediates at the expense of the extreme types, whom he caricatures and denigrates as "effeminate." It is important to his purpose to establish the atypical nature of this behavior and to demonstrate that "by far the majority of [*Urnings*] do not exhibit pronounced effeminacy."[11]

Whereas the effeminate intermediate reveals "a tendency towards the feminine, large at the hips, supple, not muscular, the face wanting in hair, the voice inclined to be high-pitched, etc.," the "normal" intermediates are "not distinguishable in exterior structure and the carriage of body from others of their own sex."[12] This differentiation between various degrees of intermediacy introduces a paradox into Carpenter's argument that is never resolved satisfactorily. For the stated purpose of the essay is to introduce the discussion of intermediates into public discourse, to challenge the "veil of complete silence" that has been "drawn over the subject, leading to the most painful misunderstandings." One of the obstacles to public awareness of intermediates is that "these folk tend to conceal their true feelings from all but their own kind, and indeed often deliberately act in such a manner as to lead the world astray." Though Carpenter here laments the necessity of secrecy for intermediates because of "the want of any general understanding of their case," he goes on to express his distaste for those "intermediates" who do, in fact, make their sexual difference unmistakably clear, preferring those who keep their "double nature" to themselves, who belong "mentally and emotionally to the other [sex]" but physically to their own.[13] In other words, Carpenter argues simultaneously for and against the visibility of intermediates,

{ *A Double Nature* }

as though acknowledging that they would be tolerated only if they conformed to the behavioral conventions of gender identity.

In *My Days and Dreams* Carpenter discusses the intermediate sex in personal terms, as one who is himself an example of the "type." Yet Carpenter is, unsurprisingly, careful to place himself in the middle of the spectrum and to distance himself from those who occupy its extremes. In conformity with his claim that intermediates "are often purely emotional in their character," Carpenter emphasizes his emotional intimacy with other men, rather than his experiences of physical sexuality.[14] At times, the physical desire for other men that Carpenter was willing to acknowledge in his personal correspondence is displaced in the autobiography onto others, such as his working-class lover, George Merrill. Indeed, Carpenter's attraction to working-class men — an attraction he shared with Symonds, Wilde, and Forster — derives in part from the perception of their greater virility and physicality. Being closer to nature, he hypothesized, working-class men are also less alienated from their own bodies and less inhibited sexually. Carpenter's pride at "hav[ing] lived almost entirely among the working masses" (13) discloses not only his social solidarity with but his physical desire for men of the laboring class. The greatest challenge to this masculine identification comes, paradoxically, with the influence of Whitman, whose sexual "conversion" of Carpenter threatens to feminize him.

In an early chapter of *My Days and Dreams*, Carpenter explains his reasons for abandoning his career as a Cambridge don for a rural life of frugal subsistence and physical labor. He then moves beyond his search for an alternative lifestyle to reveal the struggle to confront his sexual desire in a context of phobia and repression: "And behind it all there was that other need — which I have already mentioned more than once — that of my affectional nature, that hunger which had indeed hunted me down since I was a child. I can hardly bear even now to think of my early life, and of the idiotic social reserve and britannic pretence which prevailed over all that period, and still indeed to a large extent prevails — especially among the so-called well-to-do classes of this country — the denial and systematic ignoring of the obvious facts of the heart and of sex" (94). Carpenter's self-portrayal as a kind of victim, "hunted down" by his sexual desire, links him with other Victorians, such as Symonds, who had represented their secret sexuality as a source of guilt and anxiety. Carpenter writes that, from his earliest days, "I felt myself an alien, an outcast, a failure, and an object of ridicule" (13–14), a feeling that is explicitly connected with his emergent sense of sexual difference. Carpenter seeks in the autobiography to assert that a homosexual identity had developed in his earliest years and that he had no control over its course, which supports the claim in "The Intermediate Sex" that "even in the most healthy cases the special affectional temperament of the 'Intermediate' is, as a rule, ineradicable."[15] This assertion does not entirely correlate, however, with the earlier "self-analysis" produced for Symonds and Ellis, in which he wrote that "at the age of eight or nine, and *long before distinct sexual feelings declared themselves*, I felt a friendly attraction toward my own sex."[16] In the self-analysis, Carpenter states that his childhood was free from sexual desires, also admitting that "my own sexual nature was a mystery to me."[17] Hence, the emergence of sexual self-consciousness appears both more gradual and less imperative in the self-analysis than it does in the autobiography. If, as one critic argues, "the hidden agenda in Carpenter's account of sex-love was a defence of homosexuality," then this defense was built on a specific version of the events in Carpenter's life that would later be revised.[18] As Carpenter subsequently came to realize, to defend homosexuality as innate and "ineradicable," it was necessary to demonstrate that he himself had always been of this disposition.

In *My Days and Dreams*, as well as in "The Intermediate Sex," Carpenter writes that his program of reform included the sexual liberation for society at large and a Socialist platform advocating social and sexual equality for women and the working classes. For Carpenter, the general Victorian distaste for and ignorance about the "facts" of sexual desire were the fundamental obstacles to a widespread acceptance of homosexuality: Carpenter began *Love's Coming-of-Age* by claiming, in language that would find an echo in *My Days and Dreams*, that "the subject of Sex is difficult to deal with. There is no doubt a natural reticence connected with it. There is also a great deal of prudery."[19] Against considerable resistance from his fellow Socialists, Carpenter sought to make freedom of sexual choice and expression a central tenet of the radical/utopian political agenda being developed in the late nineteenth century. In his autobiography, Carpenter traced the links between his own developing political views and his growing awareness of sexual desire for men, exploring the connections between the oppression of women, homosexuals, and the working classes. For example, he sympathizes with the disastrous effects of sexual "denial" on the mental and physical health of women, arguing that one reason for the sexual deprivation experienced by women was the widespread ignorance of the existence of men of "the intermediate type," who were often disinclined to marry.

The narration of his own sexual history is crucial to this project, as Carpenter tells us that though he valued the friendship of women, they had never been a source of mystery or erotic attraction to him, because "the romance of my life went elsewhere" (96). He had written rather more bluntly in the self-analysis that "my feeling, physically, towards the female sex was one of indifference, and later on, with the more special development of sex desires, one of positive repulsion." The hostility toward heterosexual relations is more outspoken in the anonymous self-analysis, in which Carpenter could forgo the tact required of a published autobiography. Carpenter then explicitly identifies himself as an example of the "intermediate type" for whom marriage held no attraction (or, as he put it earlier, "the thought of marriage or cohabitation" with a woman "has always been odious to me") and reveals the peculiar emotional problems resulting from his sexual "temperament":[20]

My isolation was in a sense my own fault—due partly to reserve and partly to ignorance. When at a later time I broke through this double veil, I soon discovered that others of like temperament to myself were abundant in all directions, and to be found in every class of society; and I need not say that from that time forward life was changed for me. I found sympathy, understanding, love, in a hundred unexpected forms, and my world of the heart became as rich in that which it needed as before it had seemed fruitless and barren. [97]

Whereas for Symonds—who had discovered the writings of Ulrichs and Hirschfield while working on his *Memoirs*—the idea of sexual community was a largely utopian concept, Carpenter describes entering an actual human society defined by a shared sexual preference. This discovery is crucial to Carpenter's sense of himself as a sexual being. Moreover, Carpenter's sexual utopia includes members of "every class of society," establishing a link between sexual freedom and social integration. Same-sex relationships were appealing for

Carpenter in part because he believed they allowed him to transcend class and other social barriers.

Equally significant is the description of his life *before* the discovery of his homosexuality as "fruitless and barren." Carpenter uses imagery of conception, gestation, and birth to link his sexual self-discovery with his literary creations and to establish both aspects of his life as part of a natural cycle. An underlying motive for this choice of imagery is a reaction against the popular conception of homosexuality itself as "fruitless and barren," a form of sexual activity defined as "unnatural" because it resulted in no physical reproduction. As Carpenter wrote in his self-analysis, "I cannot regard my sexual feelings as unnatural or abnormal, since they have disclosed themselves so perfectly naturally and spontaneously within me." [21] It is Carpenter's literary affirmation of the naturalness of same-sex desire that would become his crucial message and chief legacy to later and more famous homosexual writers.

Carpenter's openness about his homosexuality in the autobiography was achieved only after a long period of careful introspection. Having surmounted some of the practical obstacles to living openly in a same-sex relationship, Carpenter remained extremely cautious about expressing his own desire in literary form. Though his friends knew of his cohabitation with Merrill, the general public had little inkling of Carpenter's sexual preference, for it was quite possible to write on homosexuality without being identified as an invert — providing one did so in appropriately objective language. As any careful reader will discover, Carpenter's *My Days and Dreams* is not really a confessional autobiography in the sense that Symonds's *Memoirs* is. For whereas Symonds makes his tortured account of his secret sexual history the central theme of his unpublished narrative, Carpenter places his sexual history in equal relation to other aspects of his life, particularly his political involvement in the Socialist movement, and thereby diminishes its centrality to his development. This suggests that the secretiveness of Symonds's homosexual life, as depicted in the *Memoirs*, is largely what gives it a special thematic significance: the "secret life," in other words, was a fundamental component of the literary and cultural construction of Victorian homosexuality. By renouncing a secret life, Carpenter was in effect refusing to live his sexual identity as it had been defined by Victorian culture. At the same time, the notion of a double nature attracted Carpenter because of the prospects it offered for social and sexual freedom.

This is not to belittle the courage that such self-disclosure would have required. Rather, it is to point out that Carpenter revealed his self-discovery as an "intermediate" in an autobiography that was by no means exclusively focused on his sexuality. Carpenter was not cryptic in his sexual self-disclosure, but neither was he aggressive or polemical. Whereas Symonds's autobiographical project developed into an urgent, "confessional" account of his sexual history—one that he had been building up to throughout his literary career—for Carpenter the case was almost reversed. *My Days and Dreams* strikes the reader as even anticlimactic in its sexual revelations, alternately circumspect and nonchalant in its discussion of Carpenter's desires and experiences.

This suggests another, perhaps more subtle context of secrecy to *My Days and Dreams*. Carpenter's evasiveness does not conceal the central "fact" of his homosexuality, but it does obstruct the reader's access to details about his sexual history and particularly the specific forms of his desire. Perhaps intended to demonstrate that sexual difference did not have to be the central preoccupation in the lives of "intermediates," Carpenter's autobiographical reticence has the additional effect of suggesting his "normality" as against the off-putting effeminacy and promiscuity of "extreme" inverts. The aforementioned case history that Carpenter submitted for anonymous inclusion in Symonds and Ellis's *Sexual Inversion* is significantly more revealing about the specifics of Carpenter's sexual desire: "My ideal of love is a powerful, strongly built man, of my own age or rather younger—preferably of the working class. Though having solid sense and character, he need not be specially intellectual. If endowed in the latter way, he must not be too glib or refined. Anything effeminate in a man, or anything of the cheap intellectual style, repels me very decisively."[22]

By contrast, we find out very little about Carpenter's sexual impulses through reading his autobiography—certainly far less than we discover about Symonds's from the *Memoirs*—other than the fact that he is an "intermediate type" who lived for many years with another man, George Merrill. But the erotically active, even promiscuous, male body is identified in *My Days and Dreams* with the working-class Merrill, whose ability to provoke desire in Carpenter is balanced by his tendency to bring unwelcome attention to the sexual dissidence of the Millthorpe community. Whereas Symonds displaces the unacceptably physical aspects of his own sexual desires onto other figures who are demonized as sexual predators, Carpenter idealizes Merrill as a working-class liberator of the bourgeois, intellectual life from which he sought to escape. Merrill's role in *My Days and Dreams* takes on autobiographical significance as the incarnation of Carpenter's ideal of masculine comradeship, drawn both from the Socialist movement and the "Greek" influences of Whitman's poetry.

The relationship with Merrill, besides being a source of great happiness to Carpenter, served a complex range of sexual and political desires and ideals, which become clearer in the context of Carpenter's preference for same-sex relationships that cross class boundaries. In the following section I will explore in some detail Carpenter's appropriation of the concepts of "democratic comradeship," or "comrade love," that constituted the heart of Whitman's homoerotic message as it was received in England.[23] Though Whitman's influence on Carpenter is mediated by texts, it is described in terms of a physical and emotional interpenetration. As two of the central figures in *My Days and Dreams*, Whitman and Merrill both take on roles as Carpenter "doubles," performing functions in the narrative that he is unable or reluctant to attribute to his own persona.

❧❧❧

"The Seed of New Conceptions":
Whitman, Carpenter, and *Towards Democracy*

"It was not till (at the age of twenty-five) I read Whitman—and then with a great leap of joy—that I met with the treatment of sex which accorded with my own sentiments" (30). Thus Carpenter introduces the vital figure of Walt Whitman into his autobiographical narrative, allowing for no misunderstanding about the sexual force of this influence. Whitman's role in Carpenter's sexual self-discovery is pivotal to the narrative of *My Days and Dreams*, coming to the surface in a crucial scene of "conversion" that occurred, like that of Symonds, during a private act of reading. Carpenter was already a fellow of Trinity Hall, Cambridge, in the summer of 1868, when another fellow of the college came into my room with a blue-covered book in his hands (William Rossetti's edition of Whitman's poems) only lately published, and said: "Carpenter, what do you think of this?" I took it from him, looked at it, was puzzled, and asked him what he thought of it. "Well," he said, "I thought a good deal of it at first, but I don't think I can stand any more of it." With those words he left me; and I remember lying down then and there on the floor and for half an hour poring, pausing, wondering. I could not make the book out, but I knew at the end of that time that I intended to go on reading it. In a short time I bought a copy for myself, then I got *Democratic Vistas*, and later on (after three or four years) *Leaves of Grass* complete. [64]

This fortuitous encounter with Whitman is a turning point in Carpenter's life story: "From that time onwards," he writes, "a profound change set in within me" (64). His reading of Whitman's poems, he claims, set in motion "a current of sympathy," carrying Carpenter "westward, across the Atlantic" (64), and ultimately leading him to renounce his privileged position at Trinity Hall and as deacon to F. D. Maurice, for a life of sexual transgression, political activism, and relative material poverty. The courage gained from his recognition of a kindred spirit in Whitman, the narrative makes clear, altered the course of his life.

Whitman's *Leaves of Grass* was, in this sense, Carpenter's "fatal book," much as the *Phaedrus* and the *Symposium* had exercised a life-changing influence on Symonds. Rather than being a wholly new influence, however, the transforming power of Whitman's text is specifically attributed by Carpenter to the voice it gave to his own "strangely unspoken . . . and unexpressed" (77) sexual desires.[24] As Carpenter describes it, the encounter with Whitman's text is a scene of recognition: "What made me cling to the little blue book from the beginning was largely the poems which celebrated comradeship. That thought, so near and personal to me, I had never before seen or heard fairly expressed" (65). This word "comradeship," so central to Whitman's homoerotic lexicon, here signifies the acknowledgment of desires that had long been felt but remained unarticulated by Carpenter himself. On returning from a trip to Europe, Carpenter writes, "It suddenly flashed upon me, *with a vibration through my whole body*, that I would and must somehow go and make my life with the mass of the people and the manual workers" (77; emphasis added). At this juncture, Carpenter's same-sex desire merges with a utopian political objective: to escape his stifling, bourgeois surroundings and find a haven in what he hoped would be a less restrictive and more sympathetic environment.

That Carpenter also sought sexual contact with working-class men becomes the inevitable subtext of this disclosure. Throughout *My Days and Dreams*, in fact, Carpenter's same-sex desire is strongly supported by his commitment to social democracy and his wish to reject the trappings of his class privilege. Leaving Cambridge because of "a deep want of sympathy between myself and the whole mental attitude, mode of life, and ideals of the university, and of the gilded or silvered youth who lived and moved within it" (77), he enlists instead as a teacher for "the University Extension Lecturing Scheme" (78) in the north of England, a milieu radically at odds with the urbane and monied world of Cambridge, but one in which he could join a working-class community in the industrial towns. Carpenter does not comment in *My Days and Dreams* on the relation between these two turning points in his life; nor does he register at this point his sexual preference for working-class men. To do so might have made the link between his homosexuality and his physical urge to join the "manual workers" suspect in the eyes of his Socialist colleagues, while giving additional ammunition to his more hostile critics. As the critic Samuel Hynes observes of this period, the established order was "a network of imperatives and prohibitions holding a traditional society together. From the established inside point of view, any attempt to cut one strand of this net must loosen others and so if the exponent of sexual knowledge is also a Socialist he is not simply a man with two separate advanced ideas but a doubled threat to the social order." [25] Carpenter sought to lessen this threat of his "double nature" by minimizing the sexual component of his socialistic beliefs.

Carpenter was not alone in associating homosexuality with utopian social change, as is apparent from a letter written to him by Symonds on 21 January 1893. Attempting to solicit Carpenter's contribution to *Sexual Inversion*, on which he was collaborating with Havelock Ellis, Symonds wrote in a distinctly Whitmanesque vein: "The blending of Social Strata in masculine love seems to me one of its most pronounced, & socially hopeful, features. Where it appears, it abolishes class distinctions, & opens by a single operation the cataract-blinded eye to their futilities. In removing the film of prejudice & education, it acts like the oculist & knife. If it could be acknowledged & extended, it would do very much to further the advent of the right sort of Socialism."[26] What exactly Symonds meant by the "right sort" of socialism (or, indeed, the wrong sort) remains a mystery; it is not a subject he explores in his other writings. What is clear is that Symonds shared Carpenter's impulse to challenge the social structure by following same-sex desire across class divisions and that he, too, had derived this democratic philosophy from Whitman. Symonds's sexual relationships with Swiss peasants and Italian servants in some ways mirrored Carpenter's relationships with working-class men in England: both writers sought to break free from the social and sexual restraints of Victorian class orthodoxy.

Along with Whitman's influence came the exposure to different cultures that would precipitate Carpenter's self-imposed exile from Cambridge. Sensing in the early 1870s that "a crisis was approaching" (66), he set out for Italy, where he was stimulated by the aesthetic and cultural riches of Europe. Among the "healing influences" that Carpenter found abroad was Greek sculpture, which, he writes, "had a deep effect . . . which, adding itself to and corroborating the effect of Whitman's poetry, left with me as it were the seed of new conceptions of life" (67). The eroticized language of this passage is reminiscent of Symonds's account of being "impregnated" and "inspired" by Greek literature and suggests an important link between same-sex desire and cultural reception.[27] Carpenter eventually moved beyond the emphasis of Victorian aesthetes on ideal representations of masculine beauty by taking the dramatic step of joining working-class communities and living with a man from the lower classes. Yet Greek sculpture served as an inspiration for such a daring move precisely because of its radical difference from bourgeois Victorian civilization: in *My Days and Dreams* he praises "the Greek ideal of the free and gracious life of man at one with nature and the cosmos—so remote from the current ideals of commercialism and Christianity!" (68). On his return to England, Carpenter found that "a change had taken place in my mental attitude which would make my return to the Cambridge life impossible" (68).[28]

According to Carpenter's autobiography, it was Whitman's influence that led directly to his estrangement from Cambridge, his renunciation of Holy Orders, and his move to the north of England to live among the "manual workers." Another, equally significant result of his immersion in Whitman's poetry was that he began to write verse of his own and to consider the possibility of a literary career. This transitional stage in his history is represented in terms of the divide between inner and outer selves which is manifest in much Victorian autobiographical writing and which takes on a specifically sexual significance in Symonds's *Memoirs*. Perhaps unsurprisingly, Carpenter's "inner" self is portrayed as the authentic one, doing battle with the limitations imposed by the socially determined "outer" self: "While (in other things as well as in literature) my inner scarcely conscious nature was setting outwards in swift current from the shores of conventionality, under the influence of its new genius [that is, Whitman], into deeps it little divined, my external self was still busy in a kind of backwater, and working hard if by any means it might attain to a creditable or even a possible existence in these channels!" (66).

The parenthetical reference to "other things" suggests that the reorientation of Carpenter's life involved his sexuality as well as his writing. Of course, the "backwater" refers both to the respectable middle-class existence and sexual conformity that Cambridge represented and to the canonical tradition of English poetry that had, hitherto, been Carpenter's study. In fact, the influence of Whitman, his "new genius" and liberator of his "scarcely conscious nature," crosses between sexual self-discovery and literary inspiration, to the point where the two areas of life are hard to distinguish. Wayne Koestenbaum's description of Symonds's *Memoirs* as "a work remarkable for recognizing no border between growth as writer and growth as homosexual" might be applied with equal validity to *My Days and Dreams*.[29] The stages of Carpenter's "experimentation," as represented in the autobiography, cannot be viewed in exclusively literary or sexual terms, for the two realms are closely and continuously interrelated. Attaining the freedom to write is a necessary step for Carpenter in the process of coming to terms with same-sex desire. The difference is that whereas Symonds felt that he had failed as a poet seeking to articulate a prohibited desire, Carpenter believed he himself had succeeded.

Carpenter's struggles to find his voice as a poet and to articulate his same-sex desire were parallel ones, and the solution to one problem would, he recognized, be the solution to both. His first publication, *"Narcissus" and Other Poems*—a strikingly un-Whitmanesque

{ *A Double Nature* }

volume of 1873 that Carpenter himself claimed held "nothing of any moment" (71) — inaugurated his efforts to "speak out" about homosexuality and to combat the secrecy that seemed to paralyze all attempts at representing homosexual desire: Carpenter writes poignantly that "it was as if a magic flame dwelt within one, burning, burning, which one could not put out, and yet whose existence one might on no account reveal" (77). Like Symonds, Carpenter struggled with the problem of expressing impermissible desires in verse; the difficulty both writers faced was how to communicate desire honestly, in such a way that it could be recognized by those who were sympathetic, without incriminating the writer.[30] When Carpenter had made the break from Cambridge and the University Extension, settling down with Albert Fernehough at Bradway (the farm near Sheffield where he lived before moving to Millthorpe), he began to write the verses that would eventually become the first part of his major work, *Towards Democracy*. This Whitman-influenced epic poem signified Carpenter's break from literary tradition and also registered his attempt to live openly with a working-class "comrade."

Even before Carpenter's discovery of "the keynote which harmonized these disjointed utterances" (99), his poetic fragments are attributed with the invaluable function of emotional and erotic release: "The sufferings of these years, the emotional distress and tension which I had experienced, poured themselves out in poetical effusions, outbursts, ejaculations — I know not what to call them. . . . I wrote just what the necessity of my feelings compelled — formless scraps, cries, prophetic assurances — in no available metre, or shape, just as they came. In no shape that they could be given to the world; but they were a relief to me, and a consolation" (99). Carpenter's quasi-orgasmic language inevitably imbues his literary output with sexual significance, and his poetry served, as had that of Symonds, as the only form of "safety valve" available to him before he gained the physical satisfaction of his desires. The "emotional distress and tension" that Carpenter believed had resulted from sexual repression ("the conditions which brought about — to a comparatively late age — the absence of marriage, or its equivalent, were a fruitful source of trouble and nervous prostration" [97]) are, paradoxically, the source of his early poetry, and sexual repression is thereby linked to literary creation. Yet this early verse is described as immature and transitional, emerging like his secretive desire itself in "no shape that . . . could be given to the world." Where, for Symonds, the impossibility of physically realizing his sexual desires led to disenchantment with the safety valve of poetry, Carpenter's breakthrough as a poet would follow directly from his sexual liberation.[31] The point at which Carpenter's stifled "feelings" found expression in physical sexuality is not stated in the autobiography, but *Towards Democracy* (evidently the "joyous utterance" he refers to) emerges as a kind of sexual journal in which erotic desire and release are at once recorded and celebrated. More than any other of his works, *Towards Democracy* demonstrates Carpenter's creed of the primacy of sex in the search for human happiness:

Sex still goes first, and hands eyes mouth brain follow;
from the midst of belly and thighs radiate the knowledge
of self, religion, and immortality.[32]

Early in the poem, Carpenter displays his passion for democracy in an extraordinary image of interracial sexual embrace, adding another dimension to the relationship between his desire and politics:

O disrespectable Democracy! I love you. No white
angelic spirit are you now, but a black and horned Ethiopian — your great grinning lips and teeth and powerful brow
and huge limbs please me well. . . .
You fill me with visions, and when the night comes
I see the forests upon your flanks and your horns among
the stars. I climb upon you and fulfil my desire.[33]

Carpenter imagines democracy as a willing sexual partner, while the outrageous racial stereotype of the Ethiopian conveys his attraction to democracy as a kind of exotic "otherness," offering a dramatic contrast — not entirely thought out — to his own cultural experience.

Towards Democracy is also replete with images of secrecy and disclosure, as they impinge on the joyous discovery of sex. Carpenter asks his reader, "Have you a terrible secret within / you which must out, yet you dare not reveal it?," then rejoicing when "the doors that were treble-bolted and barred, and / the doors weed-overgrown and with rusty old hinges / Fly open of themselves."[34] It soon becomes clear, in fact, that Carpenter's questions and apostrophes are addressed not to another reader but to himself — specifically, to an earlier self that has not yet experienced the great life change that enables the creation of the poem itself. Apparently addressing himself in the past tense, Carpenter asks:

> Was it really your own anxious face you used to keep
> catching in the glass? was it really you who had so many
> things, one way or another, you wanted to conceal from
> others — so many opinions too to disguise?
>
> All that is changed now.[35]

This moment of recognition suggests the suppression of physical desire as a disfiguring influence. Carpenter is rarely explicit about the fact that what he wanted to conceal from others was his same-sex desire; and yet the similarity of these passages to those in *My Days and Dreams*, in which he writes about the emotional strain of denying his desire, helps to clarify the meaning of the poem.

Elsewhere, the homoeroticism of the poem is unmistakable, as Carpenter, now using a Whitmanesque free-ranging consciousness, writes:

> I enter the young prostitute's chamber, where he is
> arranging the photographs of fashionable beauties and favorite
> companions, and stay with him; we are at ease and under-
> stand each other.[36]

The scene could be taken from *Leaves of Grass*, except for the crucial detail that, in Carpenter's poem, the prostitute is male. Significantly, the poem discloses an aspect of Carpenter's sexual history — that at some point he visited male prostitutes — that goes unmentioned in the autobiography. The significance of *Towards Democracy* as a sexual confession appears elsewhere, as Carpenter first expresses the overwhelming force of his desire as a kind of sexual/textual martyrdom:

> The budding pens of love scorch all over me — my skin
> is too tight, I am ready to burst through it — a flaming girdle
> is round my middle. Eyes, hair, lips, hands, waist, thighs —
> O naked mad tremors; in the dark feeding pasturing flames!

The poem goes on to identify the object of desire as the muscular, working-class male body: "The thick-thighed hot coarse-fleshed young bricklayer / with the strap round his waist." Carpenter later adds to this vision a striking development of the sexual fantasy, depicting a masochistic subjection to phallic control:

The bricklayer shall lay me: he shall tap me into place
with the handle of his trowel;
And to him I will utter the word which with my lips
I have not spoken.[37]

Towards Democracy represents a double achievement, in which
Carpenter simultaneously frees himself from the bounds of conventional poetic form and subverts bourgeois sexual norms. As though
it needed specifying, Carpenter acknowledges his debt to Whitman,
whom he portrays as a messianic prophet:

The savage eternal peaks, the solitary signals — Walt Whitman, Jesus of Nazareth, your own Self distantly deriding you —
These are always with you.[38]

Carpenter's poetic persona thus emerges from a complex array of
sources, including Greek art, Whitmanesque poetics of desire, socialism, and Eastern mysticism. The combination of these influences
allowed Carpenter to achieve a complex form of literary self-representation that, though not fully satisfactory as a substitute for sexual
intimacy, was crucial in the construction of his sexual self.

A turning point in the autobiography occurs with a subtle but significant shift from the language of tension, frustration, and release —
an implicitly male-oriented, orgasmic metaphor that dominates the
narrative before the writing of his major poem — to figures of gestation and birth, based on the quite distinct pairing of *Towards Democracy* as a child and Carpenter as a childbearing mother. Carpenter
writes that "I was in fact completely taken captive by this new growth
within me," adding that when he actually came to write the poem,
"and so it was that *Towards Democracy* came to birth" (106). The depiction of literary creation in terms of childbirth returns us to the androgynous "double nature" that Carpenter believed "intermediates"
possessed, combining male and female attributes in an individual
self. Hence Carpenter's role as a childbearing "mother" to his poem
is developed throughout a long paragraph that deserves quotation at
length:

What sweet times were those! all the summer to the hum of the
bees in the leafage, the robins and chaffinches hopping around,
an occasional large bird flying by, the men away at work in the
fields, the consuming pressure of the work within me, the wonder-

ment how it would turn out; the days there in the rain, or in the snow; nights sometimes, with moonlight or a little lamp to write by; far far away from anything polite or respectable, or any sign or symbol of my hated old life. Then the afternoons at work with my friends in the fields, hoeing and singling turnips or getting potatoes, or down in Sheffield on into the evenings with new companions among new modes of life and work—everything turning and shaping itself into material for my poem. There was a sense to me of inevitableness in it all, and of being borne along, which gave me good courage, notwithstanding occasional natural doubts; and a sense too of unspeakable relief and deliverance, after all those long years of gestation, as of a woman with her child. [107–8]

This extraordinary evocation of an idyllic rural existence combined with the flurry of literary activity is, lyrically, one of the high points of *My Days and Dreams*. Perhaps the most striking aspect of the passage is Carpenter's carefully presented appropriation of a feminine role— or perhaps one should say that his role is androgynous, for apparently he is as comfortable recollecting his participation with the "men . . . at work in the fields" as he is invoking the maternal role of creator and caregiver to his literary child.

So focused is Carpenter on the work "within me" that when the image of birth is finally realized, it comes as no surprise and indeed has been carefully led up to. That the imagery is more than fortuitous is demonstrated when the same metaphor is reiterated in triumphantly describing the completion of the poem in 1882: "The child, conceived and carried in pain and anguish, was at last brought into the world" (108). Carpenter's pride in his "child" appears not to have been dampened by the fact that, on its publication in 1883, *Towards Democracy* "excited very little comment, except as the ravings of some anonymous author" (112). Among the earliest critics was Havelock Ellis, whose unkind dismissal after a first perusal of the work—"Whitman and water"[39]—did not prevent him writing to Carpenter about his poem in less derogatory terms after a second reading: "I think that T[owards] D[emocracy], compared to L[eaves] of G[rass], is (in no bad sense) *feminine*. W[hitman] is so strenuously masculine."[40] This comparison between the works mirrored Carpenter's own thinking about his and Whitman's gendered aesthetic practices.

Though his modern readers would probably challenge this attribution to Whitman of a vigorous and unambiguous masculinity, it appears that Carpenter accepted the gendered differentiation as a way of distinguishing his style from that of his mentor. Given Carpenter's own formulation of the poem as a "birth" and his self-representation in *My Days and Dreams* as a childbearing mother, it would be surprising if he objected to Ellis's comparison, for Carpenter did not consider the "feminine" as inferior, in literary terms, to the "masculine." Indeed, the "double nature" of the intermediate implies no inequality between the male and female attributes, though it does deploy stereotypes of gender roles. On the one hand, as his writings indicate, Carpenter felt a lifelong sympathy for and identification with women, finding that his lack of erotic interest in them allowed him to recognize women as fellow beings who deserved equal rights and opportunities, rather than as sexual objects destined for male control. Yet Carpenter not only expressed aversion at male effeminacy but also described his sexual reaction to women as "one of positive repulsion."

Critics of Carpenter's "feminism" have certainly identified his tendency to reproduce the oppressive structures of gender inequality in his efforts to achieve democratic change. Rowbotham and Weeks, for example, take particular issue with Carpenter's attitude toward working-class women: "There is a point beyond which Carpenter does not probe the boundaries of his class and sex. The new life never reached the working-class women round the Sheffield socialist club as strongly as it did the men." Rowbotham and Weeks argue that the homoerotic feelings that, Carpenter believed, allowed him to transcend boundaries of class and gender actually "confined the radical implications of Carpenter's politics in practice to the working men in his circle. The sexual feelings which brought them together also created a defensiveness against the women which it must have been hard for them not to resent." These critics conclude that, despite their Socialist agenda and well-intentioned efforts to promote democracy, "the extent to which Carpenter and his friends could present a challenge to domestic relationships was reduced because its intensity was limited to one sex."[41] Given Carpenter's distaste for male effeminacy and focus on masculine desire, it seems likely that what he found threatening and repellent in "effeminate" men was not the feminine as such but the *conflation* of gendered attributes.

Indeed, Carpenter was restricted in his thinking about gender by the very notion of an "intermediate sex" that he helped to create. Although he sought to question the dominant Victorian thinking about sexual identities and roles, Carpenter's intermediate sex framework unfortunately reproduced the hierarchy of gendered identities by retaining the notion of a biologically determined gender. As Beverly Thiele points out, "The assumption that sexual behaviour was grounded in biology prevented Carpenter from seeing sexual stereotypes as malleable and socially constructed." Consequently, "the androgynous intermediate sex became just another fixed stereotype," and the caricature of the effeminate homosexual was, for Carpenter, the negative extreme of this stereotype. Carpenter's idealization of the masculine revealed itself not in aversion to women—whom he wrote of, apart from his sexual response, with admiration and respect—but in his distaste for the "effeminate" behavior of some male homosexuals. If "Carpenter's extreme types of homosexual and lesbian were parodies of gender stereotypes," then Carpenter himself sought to appropriate the less problematic position of the "Uranian," the term used to designate those who "combined the body of their own sex with the soul-nature of the opposite." [42] Androgyny, for Carpenter, might be experienced emotionally and intellectually but should not be manifested physically as effeminacy. Even though Carpenter's sexual desires are not made specific in *My Days and Dreams*, his attraction to the labor movement is in part influenced by stereotypes of working-class masculinity as being virile, potent, and unintellectual (Carpenter's other prejudice being against "anything of the cheap intellectual style").

Hence, Carpenter was willing to occupy a "feminine" role only in the context of literary creation and exclusively in relation to writers such as Whitman, whom he considered more original than himself. Yet he did this by reclaiming the "feminine" as a source of cultural value and power, not as a diminished version of the masculine. Though this might strike us as a contradictory position, it actually served his strategic purpose of establishing a creative androgyny that did not manifest itself as offensive effeminacy. In his account of the influence of *Leaves of Grass* on *Towards Democracy*, for example, Carpenter portrays the books as complementary masculine and feminine creations, while affirming his own integrity and originality as an artist:

Whatever resemblance there may be between the rhythm, style, thoughts, constructions, etc., of the two books, must I think be set down to a deeper similarity of emotional atmosphere and intension [sic] in the two authors—even though that similarity may have sprung and no doubt largely did spring out of the personal influence of one upon the other. Anyhow our temperaments, standpoints, antecedents, etc., are so entirely diverse and opposite that, except for a few points, I can hardly imagine that there is much real resemblance to be traced.[43]

Carpenter's disclaimer here is perplexing, given his previous insistence on the crucial influence of Whitman on his own aesthetic practice. He attributes the close affinity between himself and Whitman to an emotional kinship rather than to mere stylistic agreement, only then to offer what is effectively a denial that the likeness between the poets is there at all.

As soon becomes clear, this is less a modest disavowal of literary originality on Carpenter's part than the assertion of an aesthetic practice no less valid and perhaps less strident than Whitman's own. Acknowledging that the American poet's "full-blooded, copious, rank, masculine style must always make him one of the world's great originals," Carpenter insists on the complementary merits of his own poem: " 'Towards Democracy' has a milder radiance, as of the moon compared with the sun—allowing you to glimpse the stars behind." The inevitably feminine associations of the moon offer a contrast to the "masculine" sun but do not suggest an inferior value. Indeed, the greater visual perception Carpenter attributes to the influence of the moon—it allows us to "glimpse the stars behind"—reflects well on the visionary qualities of his poem. Carpenter's last attempt to attribute widely differing qualities to the two poems results in another comparison that is by no means unfavorable to himself: "Tender and meditative, less resolute and altogether less massive, [Towards Democracy] has the quality of the fluid and yielding air rather than of the solid and uncompromising earth."[44]

In "Note on Towards Democracy," and My Days and Dreams, Carpenter is careful to work through his relation to Whitman and the ideal of same-sex desire offered in Leaves of Grass, especially "Calamus," in a way that distinguishes his own artistic identity. Admitting that "these influences lie too far back and ramify too complexly to be traced," he insists rather defensively that "I do not think I ever tried to imitate [*Leaves of Grass*] or its style."[45] Carpenter's eagerness to distinguish himself from Whitman by ascribing "masculine" and "feminine" roles to each does not mean he was unaware of the high valuation of the "masculine" in literary culture or the possibly damaging effects to his own reputation of being associated with the "feminine" (only one step away, for a nineteenth-century male poet, from the stigma of effeminacy that he abhorred). Yet if at one level his acknowledgment of Whitman's masculine force is an act of homage to his avowed literary master, it also instantiates the "feminine" as a positive cultural value, particularly in the context of poetic creation, in which the moment of inspiration is depicted as a "natural" conception.

Acknowledging his debt to Whitman is an important item on Carpenter's agenda in *My Days and Dreams*. The autobiography is an appropriate place for the expression of this influence, which is not merely of a literary kind—the token gesture of gratitude to an inspirational writer—but central to Carpenter's self as it is constructed in his autobiography. Carpenter portrays himself as having been inspired by Whitman—indeed, in the Greek sense, "impregnated"—with the "seed of new conceptions," resulting in the "birth" of his major poem. Ultimately less interested in representing himself as feminine or Whitman as masculine than in defending the production of poetry that foregrounds same-sex desire, Carpenter presents his earlier life as "barren" and "fruitless," as when he writes that he was only able to achieve his greatest poetic utterance after "a period of seven years in numerous abortive and mongrel creations."[46]

According to *My Days and Dreams*, without the discovery of Whitman's blend of democratic enthusiasm and homoeroticism, Carpenter's life would have followed a more conventional and less satisfactory course. At the same time, the autobiography has as its objective the representation of an individual self, which entails some degree of separation from Whitman's influence. Whitman is therefore represented as Carpenter's hypermasculine alter ego, at once validating and complementing his own aesthetic and erotic agendas. The apportioning of distinct gender roles to himself and Whitman serves this purpose of self-differentiation and prepares the ground for a subsequent reversal of gender roles between Carpenter and George Merrill.

The relationship with Merrill becomes possible, however, only with Carpenter's involvement in the Socialist movement, which allows him to explore his sexual attraction to working-class men.

"Meddling with the Sexual Question": Carpenter's Socialist Secrets

The central chapters of Carpenter's autobiography describe, in compelling detail, his growing involvement in socialist thought and activism. Significantly, the account begins with a reading experience that reproduces the rhetoric of previous autobiographical encounters with "fatal" texts: "In a vague form, my ideas had been taking a socialistic shape for many years; but they were lacking in definite outline — that definition which is so necessary for all action. . . . The instant I read that chapter in [Henry Mayers Hyndman's] *England for All* — the mass of floating impressions, sentiments, ideals, etc., in my mind fell into shape — and I had a clear line of social reconstruction before me" (114). The influence of *England for All* is described in retrospect as comparable to that of *Leaves of Grass* or the *Bhagavad-Gita* in its concrete effects on Carpenter's life. Whereas Whitman's text had provided a focus for Carpenter's sexual stirrings, and the sacred treatise, a key to his mystical poetic "utterances," Hyndman's book, which he first read in 1883 (the same year, he points out, that the first volume of *Towards Democracy* was published), crystallized his political thinking and launched him on an intensive program of political activism: "From that time forward," Carpenter writes, "I worked definitely along the Socialist line" (115).[47]

In *My Days and Dreams*, Carpenter relates that in 1886 he helped to found the Sheffield Socialist Society, an organization that provided the foundation of his social and political life for many years afterward. A whole chapter of the autobiography is devoted to the activities of the society and especially to Carpenter's delight at discovering "that wonderful enthusiasm and belief in a new ideal of fraternity" (128). "Fraternity," another key term recurring throughout the autobiography, is closely linked to the conception of "comradeship" that Carpenter had appropriated from Whitman. Though the chief stress

{ *A Double Nature* }

of the latter term is erotic and romantic, "fraternity" is used by Carpenter to imply the intimacy sought even in primarily political contexts. Both concepts, in fact, combine the personal affection cherished by Carpenter with a larger vision of social democracy and equality, the fusion of sexual desire and radical political action that Carpenter idealized. One should not imagine, of course, that Carpenter's pleasure in fraternity was an abstract experience, based solely on a utopian vision of the future. Even while socialism "enshrined a most glowing and vital enthusiasm towards the realization of a new society" (126), his political involvements also afforded him direct contact with working-class men who, as we have seen, embodied his own sexual ideal.

Of course, the social and sexual advantages of Carpenter's involvement in the Socialist movement were offset by several less desirable consequences. In the first place, Carpenter's political activism made him more vulnerable to attack from critics who were all too willing to misunderstand the purport of his political agenda. Second, the Socialist movement was itself reluctant to acknowledge same-sex desire as the means of overcoming class distinctions that Carpenter, drawing on Whitman's philosophy of "adhesiveness" and "comradeship," believed it to be. This contradiction resulted in some significant omissions from the autobiography. Though several of the friendships he formed in the movement developed into sexual relationships, Carpenter makes no mention of these involvements in *My Days and Dreams*. In his autobiography, Carpenter is vague about the nature of his relationships with his comrades, in part to protect the movement from the stigma of homosexuality. Indeed, the autobiography represents the difficulty of combining same-sex desire and working-class emancipation, the goal toward which Carpenter had spent his life working.

The most striking autobiographical gap, in this respect, relates to Carpenter's relationship with George Hukin, referred to fleetingly (and innocuously) in the autobiography as "no speaker, nor prominent in public—but though young an excellent help at our committee meetings, where his shrewd strong brain and tactful nature gave his counsels much weight" (131). Perhaps the only indications in *My Days and Dreams* that Hukin meant more to Carpenter than his other political comrades are the affectionate reference to "his Dutch-featured face and Dutch build" and the full-page portrait appearing opposite his description in the text.[48] In fact, Carpenter's relationship with Hukin was much more intimate and influential than is revealed in the autobiography. The two men became lovers, and Hukin came to be for several years Carpenter's strongest emotional and sexual tie to the Sheffield society. Because Hukin was also romantically involved with a woman, Fannie, whom he eventually married, this affair was a source of much frustration and anguish to Carpenter, and it is likely that he had this relationship in mind when he refers somewhat cryptically to the "tragic elements in my personal life at the time" (136). It is to Carpenter's unpublished correspondence that we must turn for a fuller understanding of the complex relationship between Carpenter's political involvements and his sexual development.[49]

From his letters, it is clear that Carpenter consulted Hukin on a range of personal and political topics, especially concerning the publication of his controversial writings on sexuality, and that he gave Hukin a copy of *Homogenic Love*, his groundbreaking pamphlet on homosexuality. Hukin's side of the correspondence is still more revealing and suggests that the barriers of class and education that Carpenter desired to transcend by means of the erotic bond of "comradeship" were not so easily removed. A letter of 8 July 1886 shows Hukin expressing his low self-esteem in relation to Carpenter: "I would rather withdraw from than approach any nearer to you. I feel so mean and little beside you: altogether unworthy of your friendship. It is not your fault that I feel so, I know. You have always tried to put me at my ease, to make me feel at home with you. Sorry I can not come nearer to you. How I should like! — yet I feel I can't."[50] By October of this year, Hukin had apparently regained his composure, and the conviction of being loved by Carpenter was the measure of his new self-confidence: "It is so good of you to love me so. I don't think I ever felt so happy in my life as I have felt lately. And I'm sure I love you more than any other friend I have in the world."[51]

As Carpenter came to recognize that his friend's affections were increasingly directed elsewhere and that Hukin would in all probability marry Fannie, he began to adopt a somewhat more paternal attitude toward him. Carpenter took the young couple under his wing in a number of ways, such as giving them a new bed as a wedding gift. Hukin thanked him in a letter, also making it clear that Carpenter still had an important place in his emotional and sexual life:

{ *A Double Nature* }

Thanks for your bed, Ted, which Willie brought in last Monday evng. It's ever so much nicer than the one we had, so much softer, and so wide we might easily lose each other in it if it wasn't for the way it sinks in the middle, which somehow throws us together whether or no. I do wish you could sleep with us sometimes, Ted, but I don't know whether Fannie would quite like it yet; and I don't feel I could press it on her anyway. Still, I often think how nice it would be if we three could only love each other so that we might sleep together sometimes without feeling that there was anything at all wrong in doing so.[52]

There is no indication whether the ménage à trois proposed by Hukin met with Carpenter's or indeed with Fannie's approval; but Hukin, after his marriage, continued to write to Carpenter in a romantic vein, until he was in turn displaced in Carpenter's affections by the arrival of George Merrill. Letters such as one thanking Carpenter for his praise of Hukin's "beautiful face" are interspersed with correspondence about the local response to the Chicago martyrs and other details of the activities of the Sheffield Socialists.[53] The private correspondence between the two men gives some indication of how the Socialist fraternity accommodated Carpenter's sexual interests as well as his political aspirations; yet while his politics are given a central place in the autobiography, his sexual life is reduced to a few footnotes and fleeting references.

There are several explanations for this autobiographical emphasis on the political rather than the sexual aspects of Carpenter's life. In the first place, socialism had by 1916 achieved respectability as a major political movement beginning to establish a parliamentary base, and Carpenter's role in the founding years of the Socialist revival of the 1880s would have been his chief claim to recognition by many readers. Even *Towards Democracy*, a work that was considerably ahead of its time in its frank treatment and representation of homosexuality, was read primarily for its political message. As Chuschuchi Tsuzuki writes, citing a Socialist activist of the period: "*Towards Democracy* . . . became a bible to many young Socialists. 'A little green leather edition was always in our pockets' wrote Fenner Brockway."[54] Not only was Carpenter in the avant-garde as a writer on Socialist subjects, but he was also living openly with his male lover, and many of his Socialist colleagues did not share his conviction that sexual and economic liberation should go hand in hand. Even while privately accepting the moral validity of homosexuality, numerous Socialists saw the political liability of entering the debate publicly. A letter from G. B. Shaw, giving his objections to signing a manifesto condemning the 1885 Labouchère Amendment against male homosexuality, might be cited as an example. "No movement," wrote Shaw of socialism, "could survive association with such a propaganda":

> I can sympathize with E[dward] C[arpenter]'s efforts to make people understand that the curious reversal in question is a natural accident and that it is absurd to persecute it or connect any general moral deficiency with it. But to attempt to induce it in normal people as a social safety valve would be ruinous, and could seem feasible only to abnormal people who are unable to conceive how frightfully disagreeable—how abominable, in fact—it is to the normal, even to the normal who are abnormally susceptible to natural impulses.[55]

Though he dances around the issue somewhat, Shaw's fundamental opposition to political solidarity with homosexuals on the part of the Socialist movement is unequivocal. In a similar vein, Robert Blatchford, editor of the *Clarion* (a leading Socialist journal of the period) and himself a secret homosexual, criticized Carpenter for his efforts to make homosexual liberation a part of the Socialist agenda, arguing that "the time is not ripe for Socialists, as Socialists, to meddle with the sexual question."[56] Carpenter, of course, had already "meddled with the sexual question" in much of his published writing. To write explicitly about his sexual relationships in his autobiography would, he realized, move the controversy onto a more personal terrain and so jeopardize his standing as a leading Socialist and perhaps endanger the public support of the nascent party.[57] Writing his autobiography for publication—in contrast to Symonds, who had abandoned any hope of an audience for his *Memoirs* during his lifetime—Carpenter had the unprecedented opportunity to present the version of his sexual self that he wanted the public to acknowledge. Yet the risks of such a disclosure in the period of panic following the Wilde scandal remained insuperable and certainly contributed to his decision to delay publication of *My Days and Dreams* until 1916. Additionally, Carpenter's reticence can be attributed to his reluctance to incriminate his friends, many of whom were still alive in 1916, by giving details of his sexual involvements with them. Particularly Hukin, after his marriage, might not have relished the revelation of his sexual involvement with a prominent "intermediate."[58]

If Carpenter was open about his cohabitation with Merrill, he is nonetheless careful in *My Days and Dreams* to present his account of his sexual life in strictly monogamous terms, the result being that his other erotic ties are portrayed in terms of an innocuous "fraternity" in the Socialist movement rather than as instances of more directly physical relationships. The friendships could be portrayed with minimal risk, while readers who shared Carpenter's sexual desires would understand the special significance of "fraternity." Carpenter's emphasis on his political activism allows him to acknowledge his intimate relationships with working-class men without admitting any direct implication in "unspeakable" sexual practices. Of course, socialism was itself suspicious and subversive in the eyes of many of his contemporaries. Carpenter remarks of his neighbors at Millthorpe that "my reputation as a Socialist alarmed them" (147), and he offers a humorous account of the resistance that greeted his campaign to join the parish council: "Almost a panic ensued among the larger farmers and the parson as to what we might possibly do or propose. Strange stories were circulated of the Socialist programme, and of the expenses into which the community would certainly be plunged if it were adopted" (158).

There is no indication in *My Days and Dreams* that Carpenter recognized his open sexual dissidence as a source of this "alarm" and "panic." Indeed, it would take an aggressive public campaign against him for Carpenter to realize how nefariously interrelated his political radicalism and his sexual preference could appear. His socialism had given him ample opportunity to follow his sexual desire and also provided Carpenter with a code language of political "fraternity" with which to articulate, in disguised form, the discourse of male intimacy. But the practice of crossing class boundaries in a long-term, same-sex relationship proved more complicated than the theory. Even as *My Days and Dreams* attempts to defend and idealize Carpenter's affair with Merrill, the narrative reveals some of the disruptions and dilemmas to which the affair led.

Before examining Carpenter's relationship with Merrill at greater length, however, we should consider the origins of Carpenter's decision to complete and publish the autobiography, which can be traced back to an important episode that is entirely omitted from *My Days and Dreams*. The assault on Carpenter's reputation by a religious vigilante named O'Brien in 1909 is not discussed in the autobiography, but this series of events provided the impetus for publishing a work that had been started decades earlier. In particular, the omitted episode dramatizes the possibility of a hostile distortion of the Whitmanesque ideal of comradeship that defined both Carpenter's literary career and his sexual development. Whitman's role in *My Days and Dreams* is that of Carpenter's ideal alter ego, whereas O'Brien comes to embody a disavowed "double" of Carpenter, a crude caricature of his own subversive ideology of gender, politics, and sexuality. This disturbing figure was so threatening that he had to be excluded altogether from the published autobiography. An exploration of these events is crucial, however, because it reveals the limits of Carpenter's autobiographical self and suggests the paradox that his literary "openness" is in some ways predicated on a secretive practice of textual evasion.

"Infernal Comradeship": Carpenter and O'Brien

In the tenth chapter of *My Days and Dreams*, Carpenter interrupts the idyllic portrait of domestic tranquility at Millthorpe that he had evoked in previous chapters. Despite the healthy and peaceful lifestyle that a retreat such as Millthorpe afforded, there were, he pointed out, certain disadvantages to being a famous "recluse" with an international reputation as a mystical guru and Socialist prophet: "Still we were liable to incursions. To Job are ascribed the pregnant words (xxxi. 35) 'O that mine adversary had written a book!' And I am afraid that I had in some such way laid myself open to attack. The ubiquitous American who (to adopt the style of Bernard Shaw) only stayed in England to visit Millthorpe and Stratford-on-Avon, was much in evidence. And faddists of all sorts and kinds considered me their special prey" (167).

The textual nature of the vulnerability that Carpenter here hints at is peculiarly apt for the context of autobiographical self-revelation.

The representation of himself as "prey" links the passage to the earlier one in which Carpenter describes being "hunted down" by his own sexual desires. In writing his autobiography, Carpenter again risked making himself "open to attack," and the resulting self-defensiveness is legible in many sequences of the narrative. In an effort to resist the "incursions" of so many people—including "vegetarians, dress reformers, temperance orators, spiritualists, secularists, anti-vivisectionists, socialists, anarchists" (167)—a friend of Carpenter's suggested "that I should put up at the gate a board bearing the legend 'To the Asylum' on it. Then the real lunatics would probably avoid the neighborhood" (167–68).

The informal tone suggests how relatively unscathed Carpenter was by most of these intrusions—indeed there are indications in the chapter that he was alternately flattered and amused by the attention, and even reverence, he received from his admirers. In fact, none of the visitors he describes qualify as "real lunatics" but rather as mild eccentrics who saw in Carpenter a countercultural hero and inspiration. The implication that his neighborhood was visited and he himself victimized by "real lunatics" is not entirely unsubstantiated, however. Because the "incursion" that brought the most dramatic and potentially disastrous challenge to Carpenter's reputation and lifestyle was completely omitted from the autobiography, the narrative of this crucial episode must be constructed from other sources. Yet the omission itself proves significant in terms of Carpenter's cautious and secretive discussion of his sexual history.[59]

To summarize the O'Brien affair: in the early part of 1909, when Carpenter was on vacation in Florence with George Merrill, a series of letters appeared in several Sheffield newspapers, with the signature of M. D. O'Brien. One such letter, headed "Usefulness of Competition," appeared in the *Sheffield Telegraph* and was sent to Carpenter by his friend George Hukin, accompanied by a note alerting him to its possibly serious consequences. The main purpose of O'Brien's public letter was to link Carpenter's Socialist politics as explicitly as possible with his homosexuality and to discredit him by claiming that both were "perversions" designed to subvert the Christian ethos of English civilization. A quotation from the letter reveals the confusion between religious zeal and homophobic mania that characterized O'Brien's attack:

In the last verse of the first chapter of his Epistle to the Romans St Paul says that those who practiced such things as were practiced by some very loving and ultra-sociable people in his day "are worthy of death." Now it is a fact, a fact which I am in a position to prove up to the hilt, that the very same practices which, according to St Paul (and according to the ordinance of god Himself, if St Paul is correct) are worthy of death are held up for the approval, if not for the imitation, of Socialists by one of the ablest, if not the ablest, leader in the Socialist movement. The infernal thing is called "Comradeship," and a very clever attempt to justify, and even glorify, it has been circulating for years among the Socialist party. When the truth on [sic] this matter comes to the light of day it will be an eye-opener for many Christians with Socialistic leanings.[60]

There could have been no doubt in the minds of the letter's readers that O'Brien referred particularly to Edward Carpenter, easily the most prominent of the Sheffield Socialists and a local celebrity as well as something of a national figure as a result of his involvement with William Morris's Socialist League during the 1880s and 1890s. Moreover, as Rowbotham and Weeks point out, Carpenter's homosexuality was something of an "open secret" in the area. This, combined with his public visibility, made him especially vulnerable to attack, such that Carpenter "was in double jeopardy as an advocate of the liberation of homosexual love and as a socialist."[61] O'Brien's defamatory invocation of the Whitmanesque term "comradeship" cut dangerously close to the heart of Carpenter's own idealistic philosophy of same-sex desire.

Unpleasant as this public attack on him in his absence was for Carpenter, there was worse to come. O'Brien was not content to broadcast his opinions through the letter columns of the Sheffield newspapers and had a pamphlet printed that gave further vent to his deep-seated hatred of Socialist politics and his repugnance for male homosexuality. The pamphlet's attack was based on the assumption that these two "perversions" were closely interrelated: homosexuality and socialism were twin pillars of an evil conspiracy known as "comradeship" that aimed to undermine the Christian basis of civilized society. Moreover, unlike the original letter, the pamphlet identified Carpenter as the specific target of the attack. The pamphlet—the full title of which was *Socialism and Infamy. The Homogenic or Comrade*

Love Exposed. An Open Letter in Plain Words for a Socialist Prophet, to Edward Carpenter[62] — has been described by Rowbotham and Weeks as "an extraordinary document" that expressed a range of anxieties about the moral, economic, and political survival of the Sheffield and British populations: "[O'Brien's] real horror was of homosexuality. The imagery is vivid, 'putrid cesspool,' 'cancer,' 'vile Prophets of Sodom and Gomorrah.' Homosexuality is described as a 'disgusting, loathsome, and socially destructive vice.' . . . He was not only concerned about the wealth and morals of the inhabitants of Sheffield, he was personally revolted. 'Embrace and endearment between men . . . the very thought of such effeminate practice fills one with loathing.' It would turn men away from their wives to male 'comrades' and make them unfit for 'the duties of the married state.' "[63]

O'Brien's obsession with what he perceived as the sterility and corruption of "endearment between men" represents the antithesis of Carpenter's enthusiastic emphasis on the natural, healthy, and productive aspects of same-sex desire. Oddly, however, O'Brien's distaste for "effeminate practice" echoes Carpenter's own prejudice against male effeminacy. Despite their profound differences, both men perceive effeminacy as a threat to masculine identity. Although Carpenter's cohabitation with Merrill was, as Sedgwick has observed, an "enduring, quasimarital relationship," it was nonetheless threatening to O'Brien because of its disturbing similarity to the institution of heterosexual marriage.[64] Ancient Greek society, on which Carpenter's ideal of "comradeship" was partly based, recognized homosexual love as existing alongside heterosexual marriage. O'Brien, however, could conceive of the two practices only as being radically inimical, with "comradeship" emerging as a dark threat to the family and society. Hence the "internal comradeship" that Carpenter practiced could not be reconciled by O'Brien with his distorted views of masculinity and Christian ethics.

The sheer vehemence and persistence of O'Brien's attack was enough to unnerve Carpenter and his friends. George Hukin anxiously informed Carpenter of the personal arrival of O'Brien in the neighborhood to spread the word of Carpenter's infamy:

The enclosed pamphlet addressed to you arrived last Sat:. In the afternoon the author of it himself, appeared in the village with a satchel full, distributing them broadcast. He left one here. I did not see him myself, he handed it to F[annie Hukin] at the back door. [George] A[dams] tells me he saw him + O'B[rien] said "you know it's libelous. C[arpenter] could prosecute me. I want him to. I have just been to his house. It's empty. He's left the country, & he'll never dare to come back again." . . . A. is very alarmed & thinks the situation very dangerous for you.[65]

As described by Hukin, O'Brien appears to be haunting Carpenter like a menacing double from gothic fiction. His attempt to provoke Carpenter into a self-destructive retaliation or to intimidate him into living in exile also recalls the Marquis of Queensberry's malignant stalking of Oscar Wilde and Lord Alfred Douglas across London. Carpenter, however, refused to fall into the same trap as Wilde. He replied to Hukin's alarming letter with an impressive mixture of sangfroid and haughty contempt for his antagonist, indicating his determination to ignore the provocation:

O'Brien's explosion is really rather mad — in fact it is so extreme and violent that it overbalances itself, and will not I think carry much weight — though doubtless it will damage me in places; and anyhow it is not pleasant to have him raving about up & down the country. I do not at all think of taking any action — but in a day or two I will write a letter to the Sheffield papers — rather brief, pointing out the madness & sweeping charges in the letters against literary men, schoolteachers, & every thing Socialistic, and inferring that little notice need be taken of it, particularly as all my views are written out in my books & can be read by everybody with much more advantage than the garbled hash wh. he puts forward.[66]

The repeated references to O'Brien's "madness" recall Carpenter's apparently joking remark about a sign to discourage "the real lunatics" from visiting him at Millthorpe. Unlikely as it is that such a sign would have discouraged O'Brien, his absence from the autobiography represents an even more effective form of banishment. Yet O'Brien cannot simply be dismissed from the story of Carpenter's life as an unstable crank. Perhaps the most alarming aspect of O'Brien's accusations was that they caricatured Carpenter's actual views concerning the relationship between socialism and homosexuality. For example, "comradeship" for Carpenter did invoke the power of same-sex desire to cross class boundaries and so result in a more democratic

{ *A Double Nature* }

society. Where Carpenter and his followers advocated such radical cultural change, O'Brien viewed it as pernicious, anti-Christian, and symptomatic of imminent social collapse. Much of Carpenter's literary effort had been spent trying to revitalize a tradition of "comrade love" that had flourished in the ancient world, especially in Greece, but had since fallen into disrepute following the prosecution of the Hellenist Wilde for "gross indecency." In the words of Moncur Sime, writing during Carpenter's lifetime, "Not only does Carpenter realize the importance and value of Comradeship for an age that has passed, but he is surely convinced that some institution founded upon it will rise again, and become a recognized factor of modern life, and even in a larger and more perfected form than prevailed in Dorian society, or in the ancient and pagan world." [67]

Carpenter's apparent confidence that the public's knowledge of his books would serve to expiate him from charges of perversion is somewhat unconvincing. In the first place, the notion that his esoteric writings might "be read by everybody" is itself wishful thinking, given the conservatism of the publishing industry and mainstream reading public during the period. Second, if O'Brien's version of Carpenter's views was "garbled hash," it nonetheless contained the distorted, half-digested fragments of Carpenter's own belief in the interdependency of radical politics and same-sex desire. Such a combination, no matter how it was presented, would come across as subversive, if not incriminating, in the eyes of the British public. O'Brien's attack certainly demonstrated that Carpenter's writings were open to a damaging interpretation he had not foreseen and that the vindication he expected would result from a study of his books — suggested by his appeal to his own writings in his letter to Hukin — was by no means assured. In the end, a major scandal was averted largely because of Carpenter's cool head and the protective counterweight of the solid reputation that he had established in the community over a long period of time. According to Rowbotham and Weeks, the only concrete damage done was that Carpenter was dropped from the parish council at the next election.[68] But there were, as they point out, other, less tangible effects: the O'Brien affair revealed that "the laboriously created world of Millthorpe and friends was vulnerable. There was a moment of real peril. Despite the protection of a private income and his gentleman's breeding Carpenter's freedom was fragile."[69]

The fragility of Carpenter's social position helps to explain his decision to omit the O'Brien episode from his autobiography. The omission is important primarily because O'Brien's attack presented the most radical challenge to Carpenter's humanistic and idealistic vision of "comrade love," at once caricaturing and slandering the potent brew of democratic enthusiasm and sexual passion that, for Carpenter, was the motivating force of his political and personal life. It is not difficult, of course, to understand why Carpenter would refrain from directly confronting or prosecuting O'Brien. He had everything to lose from such an encounter and very little to gain. Unlike the Marquis of Queensberry, whose attack on Oscar Wilde led to the latter's conviction for "gross indecency" in 1895, O'Brien possessed no aristocratic title and wielded no real social power. He was an outspoken and isolated vigilante whose repeated pleas for Carpenter to prosecute him combined, in a startling way, paranoia and vindictiveness and were relatively easy to ignore. Had Carpenter's antagonist been a more socially prominent figure, events might have taken a very different course, and Carpenter would have been compelled—as were Newman and Wilde before him—to take drastic and risky action to fend off potentially scandalous charges.

The relatively short space of time between O'Brien's pamphlet and the publication of *My Days and Dreams* indicates that Carpenter would not have forgotten the episode. On the contrary, his reasons for excluding it had to do with the unfavorable light it might cast on himself and the incompatibility of the episode with the self-portrait he wished to construct in his autobiography. Whereas Whitman's presence in the autobiography vindicated the aesthetic merit of his life's work, O'Brien's would inevitably have tainted his political activity with sexual motives, alienating the general reader whom Carpenter hoped to reach with his message. Yet the publication of the autobiography can be seen as a delayed reaction to the O'Brien affair, an attempt to forestall another, perhaps more serious scandal by making his sexual preference clear. Rather than publishing his views in esoteric and erratically circulated pamphlets, as he had in the past, Carpenter—now a widely respected figure—turned to autobiography in an attempt to consolidate his reputation and diffuse his ideas more broadly. The strategy of renouncing secrecy was a gambit that paid off, eliminating the threat of sexual blackmail by declaring his freedom from shame. Though Carpenter would not refer directly to O'Brien's grotesque caricature of his views for fear of incriminating himself, the conflict had made obvious the need for a clear account of his political creed and sexual preference within the narrative of his own personal struggle for liberation.

It is tempting to interpret the chosen time of publication of *My Days and Dreams*—during the First World War—as an additional instance of Carpenter's desire to avoid excessive public scrutiny of his sexual lifestyle. Of course, the havoc and destruction wrought by the Great War provided tragic evidence of the destructiveness of capitalism and the need for pacifist resistance and international cooperation: Carpenter's statement of his beliefs was timely, in this sense.[70] Yet the fact that there was a war on meant that more risks could be taken with sexual confession: a sexual scandal was much less likely at a time of international crisis, if only because attention would be distracted by world events.

The erasure of O'Brien and his malignant construction of Carpenter's homosexuality is the clearest instance of the secrecy that qualifies and underlies Carpenter's carefully constructed autobiographical disclosures. Rather than presenting himself as a tortured victim with a dreadful secret to confess—a persona he constructs, however, in his major poetical utterances—Carpenter takes the act of self-revelation apparently in his stride, calmly and quietly offering intimate views of the growth of his sexual self-awareness. Yet, concerned not just for his own reputation but for those of his friends and of the Socialist movement as a whole as well, Carpenter was constrained when it came to representing the details about his sexual life. The publication of *My Days and Dreams* was achieved less through reckless courage than by means of a carefully constructed self-representation, in which same-sex desire, though no longer a "secret," continues to be characterized by caution and reserve.

"The Real Problem": Representing George Merrill

An important lesson of the O'Brien affair was that Carpenter's vulnerability to attack derived not merely from his writings on socialism and homosexuality but also from his relationship with George Merrill. This, at least, was the view of George Hukin, who informed Carpenter in a second letter about O'Brien that "G[eorge Merrill] is the real problem with all the stories going about concerning him. I think it would be wise to keep him away for the present. Of course one does not know how much O'Brien knows still one must be careful at present [*sic*]. Strange stories are afloat."[71] The last sentence alluded ominously to the local rumors that Merrill was sexually promiscuous and had attempted to solicit sexual contact with various young men in the Millthorpe neighborhood. Merrill is here portrayed as a subject for narrative that threatens to disrupt the harmony of domestic life. The problem then emerges of how the "strange stories" linked with Merrill might be incorporated within the narrative of *My Days and Dreams*.

Even if we allow for Hukin's jealousy toward Merrill as the man who displaced him in Carpenter's affection, it becomes apparent that Merrill's indiscretion might have increased Carpenter's vulnerability. Merrill's working-class background and lack of formal education made him something of an anomaly in the Millthorpe milieu, which, despite Carpenter's often proclaimed disillusionment with bourgeois civilization, remained solidly upper middle class, attracting visits from members of Britain's Socialist and literary elites. While Carpenter himself was accepted as an endearing eccentric of unmistakably patrician pedigree, Merrill's presence was viewed with suspicion by many of Carpenter's friends and colleagues, such as Henry Salt, who described him as Carpenter's "evil genius." In *My Days and Dreams*, Carpenter addressed the resistance of his friends to accepting Merrill, describing their adverse reaction to the cohabitation:

> If the Fates pointed favorably I need hardly say that my friends (with a few exceptions) pointed the other way! I knew of course that George had an instinctive genius for housework, and that in all probability he would keep house better than most women would. But most of my friends thought otherwise. They drew sad pictures of the walls of my cottage hanging with cobwebs, and of the master unfed and neglected while his assistant amused himself elsewhere. They neither knew nor understood the facts of the case. Moreover they had sad misgivings about the moral situation. A youth who had spent much of his early time in the purlieus of public-houses and in society not too reputable would do me no credit, and would only by my adoption be confirmed in his own errant ways. [161]

Carpenter's explanation in this passage of the resistance, sometimes amounting to hostility, toward Merrill reveals a significant blind spot in his thinking: as Sedgwick points out, his friends' "opposition is chalked up to everything but homophobia."[72] Yet Carpenter was apparently alluding to the sexual transgression in their relationship by the reference to the "moral situation," and he resisted his friends' disapproval. Indeed, in an unpublished essay on Merrill, written several years before *My Days and Dreams* was published, he includes his decision to live with Merrill and "to arrange a domestic life really congenial and suitable to myself" among "the three best things I have ever done."[73] As Thiele points out, moreover, Carpenter's "previous three or four homosexual relationships were difficult and unhappy," so that moving in with Merrill, which occurred when Carpenter was in his mid-fifties, came as a great relief.[74] There is some evidence that Carpenter was influenced by his friends to treat Merrill as less than an equal. Explaining that each of his life changes "met with almost violent opposition from my friends and acquaintances," Carpenter adds that "the domestic change, though in many ways the most natural and inevitable of the three, excited as much [resistance] as the others."[75]

Notwithstanding his own enthusiasm for the living arrangement, the class inequality of Carpenter's relationship with Merrill poses something of a problem in assessing the extent to which he succeeded in living out his democratic philosophy of comradeship. Sedgwick argues in Carpenter's defense that "the openly unequal allocation of domestic roles between him and Merrill seems paradoxically to have been part of a realistic, unwishful, relatively nonexploitive relationship, in which Merrill represented a bond, but not the only bond and not a substitute for other, politically purposeful bonds, with working-class people."[76] Yet this cautious support of Carpenter's relationship reinforces the very imbalance between the men that it tries to refute. Carpenter's description of Merrill as a "youth" is both condescending and misleading—he was not much younger than Carpenter—whereas the statement that Merrill's role was that of "assistant" to Carpenter as "master" serves to keep the economically dependent lover in his (subordinate) place.[77] In general, the description evokes a relation combining that of employer-employee with father-son, rather than one characterized by full sexual and social equality.

The most significant aspect of Carpenter's portrayal of Merrill, left unexplored by Sedgwick in her account, is the extent to which

Merrill's working-class background was itself the source of Carpenter's erotic attraction toward him. Carpenter's class difference from Merrill is ultimately inseparable from his sexual desire. Indeed, it is noteworthy that Merrill so closely represents Carpenter's ideal of "a powerful, strongly built man, of my own age or rather younger— preferably of the working class." In *My Days and Dreams*, Carpenter describes his first meeting with Merrill in a way that emphasizes the attraction that Merrill's humble background exercised over him:

> I had met him first on the outskirts of Sheffield immediately after my return from India, and *had recognized at once a peculiar intimacy* and mutual understanding. Bred in the slums quite below civilization, but of healthy parentage of comparatively rustic origin, he had grown so to speak entirely out of his own roots; and a singularly affectionate, humorous, and swiftly intuitive nature had expanded along its own lines—subject of course to some of the surrounding conditions, but utterly untouched by the prevailing conventions and proprieties of the upper world . . . he was, it may safely be said, never "respectable." [160; emphasis added]

This "peculiar intimacy" and "mutual understanding" between the working-class Merrill and the middle-class, Cambridge-educated Carpenter supports the theory that same-sex desire is able to cross class boundaries. At the same time, one cannot ignore the slightly patronizing tone of Carpenter's description, portraying Merrill as a fascinating social and sexual object in whom he is able to recognize— or onto whom he might project—his own dislike of "respectability." In its tone, the depiction of Merrill in the autobiography resembles the earlier portrait that Carpenter wrote in 1913: "Whatever the drawbacks of [his] early days may have been they brought him the priceless advantage that he never had any education in the modern sense, and grew up totally ignorant of the existence of the Saturday Review or the Spectator and untouched by the moralisings of such goody books as were left in the house by the occasional visits of the missionary."[78]

Carpenter observes that "I still doubt whether I find anyone more natively human, loving, affectionate and withal endowed with more general good sense and tact than he."[79] Merrill was apparently valued by Carpenter precisely because his lack of "education in the modern sense" made him immune to "civilization"; education and books, Carpenter implies, would have ruined his "intuitive nature." Oddly,

Carpenter forgets at this point that the central turning points of his own life history occurred through reading texts and hence were dependent on his literary education. One need not doubt the sincerity of Carpenter's affection to recognize how strategically important Merrill was for his ideology and for the completion of his autobiographical narrative. The working-class background of Merrill not only contributed to his sexual appeal for Carpenter but also offered living proof that humble social origins could produce a "noble" soul, leading to the conclusion that traditional education, like most institutions of civilization, was largely a sham. Issues of power within the relationship are, however, circumvented by this attribution to Merrill of a virtue at once unassimilable by middle-class culture and unspoiled by an elite education, such as Carpenter himself had endured. Carpenter's elevation of Merrill to the status of "noble savage" or free spirit conveniently leaves Carpenter's own social and economic privilege intact and largely unexamined.

It is perhaps facile to criticize the blind spots and contradictions to be found in Carpenter's writings on the politics of class, sexuality, and gender. Carpenter's unique contribution to opening up public discourse on homosexuality, as well as his commitment to achieving equality between the sexes, has long been underestimated, and his courageous stand on controversial political issues has been sadly neglected. His pamphlet *Homogenic Love* was among the first published defenses of homosexuality, yet ironically Carpenter's very public outspokenness can lead us to forget that some discretion was necessary for his survival, just as it was for Symonds's. As Rowbotham and Weeks point out, given the virulently homophobic culture in which he lived and wrote, "Carpenter was probably protected only by the habitual vagueness of his writing on homosexuality."[80] Carpenter was careful, in particular, not to reveal the sexual side to his relationship with Merrill in his autobiography, never repeating his "confession" of physical desire for a working-class man that appeared anonymously in *Sexual Inversion* and poetically in *Towards Democracy*. This discretion is certainly apparent in the statement, which now seems somewhat evasive, that he and Merrill "settled down" together as "two bachelors" (163). Evidently, the reference to the bachelor status of the two men is used by Carpenter to deflect attention from their sexual relationship.[81]

Yet at key moments in the autobiographical narrative, the sexual attraction between Carpenter and Merrill is made implicit, if not explicit. The account of the first meeting between them, for example, contains an unmistakable moment of erotic recognition that overcomes their social distance: "What struck me most . . . on my first meeting with him was the pathetic look of wistfulness in his face. Whatever his experiences up to then may have been, it assured me that the desire of his heart was still unsatisfied" (160). Though it is Merrill's "desire," rather than Carpenter's, that is given prominence, there can be no doubt in reading this account that Carpenter's sexual longing was also "unsatisfied" at the time and that Merrill offered an escape from a life of lonely frustration. That the expression of Merrill's desire is described as a "pathetic . . . wistfulness" perhaps indicates Carpenter's awareness of the guilt and secrecy associated with homosexuality and the difficulty of giving physical expression to a prohibited desire. Though recognizing in the other a potential sexual partner, each man had to proceed with caution and to signify an interest with discreet signs that would be recognized only by someone in search of the same satisfaction.

If Carpenter sometimes objectifies Merrill in *My Days and Dreams* and other writings, presenting him as a superb specimen of "uncivilized" virility, this reflects the specificity of his own historical context, involving limitations of time and place that inevitably condition all discourse about sexuality. To explore the variations of sexual desire is to encounter many manifestations of difference, or "otherness," and the class divide was a powerful attraction to many middle-class homosexuals, including Symonds, Wilde, and Carpenter. His response to Merrill, in fact, offers an important example of the combined idealism and pragmatism that characterizes Carpenter's writings on sexuality and democracy. Domestically, the relationship was convenient for Carpenter in that it allowed him to pursue his creative interests while leaving most of the household chores to Merrill's supervision.[82] Socially and politically, the relationship proved compromising on a number of occasions, most dramatically in the case of the O'Brien episode. Yet the presence of Merrill served, paradoxically, to protect Carpenter from scandal, deflecting the social prejudices and sexual anxieties of his friends and neighbors by presenting a public facade of safely "bachelor" cohabitation.

Even in 1916, when he published *My Days and Dreams*, Carpenter took a substantial risk in declaring that he belonged to the "intermediate sex" or "homogenic type." Carpenter's sexual preference for working-class men was potentially scandalous, because it was for just such transgressive relationships with men of a lower class that Wilde had been convicted and imprisoned. The popular hostility toward same-sex desire was sufficiently strong at the time to discourage E. M. Forster from publishing his homoerotic novel *Maurice*, written in 1913–14: "If it ended unhappily" Forster later wrote in a terminal note, "with a lad dangling from a noose or with a suicide pact, all would be well, for there is no pornography or seduction of minors."[83] Carpenter's autobiography also featured a same-sex romance between men of different classes and ended happily as well, with the writer comfortably ensconced in a loving partnership with Merrill. It is this affirmative emphasis on sexual partnership and domestic happiness that differentiates Carpenter's narrative so markedly from Symonds's *Memoirs* or Wilde's *De Profundis*. *My Days and Dreams*, unlike these earlier autobiographies, unabashedly declares itself as a narrative without a secret and seeks to represent same-sex desire as a source of strength and satisfaction rather than of shame and torment. And yet the self that Carpenter sought to represent was ineluctably shaped by the same conditions that had produced the persecution of Wilde and had engendered the silent suffering of Symonds. At once embracing and eschewing the impossible project of full self-disclosure, Carpenter's autobiography constructs a self that, while willingly confessing its sexual dissidence, is still characterized by the deployment of secretive strategies.

EPILOGUE

Strange Desires

Sexual Reconstruction in E. M. Forster's
Secret Fictions

The importance of Edward Carpenter's intellectual legacy is perhaps best demonstrated by the reception and propagation of his own writings and ideas by his followers and disciples. As I argued in the last chapter, Carpenter's life and work represented an alternative to the disastrous outcome of same-sex desire dramatized by the fate of Wilde, and it is hardly surprising to see his influence at work on twentieth-century writers seeking to represent same-sex desire in literary texts. The work of E. M. Forster—the most famous of Carpenter's friends and admirers—is, as Nicola Beauman observes, "imbued with Carpenter's ideas."[1] Aside from his indebtedness to Carpenter's influence, Forster is also an important figure for considering the relationship between secrecy and same-sex desire in literary modernism.

Forster's visit to Carpenter and Merrill at Millthorpe in 1913 directly inspired the composition of *Maurice*, the novel in which he charts the development of a homosexual protagonist. Following this visit Forster gradually acquired a circle of homosexual friends and colleagues, with whom he shared his writings about masculine love. Forster did not emulate Carpenter's efforts to publish his work on homosexuality, however, instead suppressing his explicitly homoerotic fictions, including the novel *Maurice*. If it seems unfair to blame Forster personally for withholding this work from publication, it is hard to avoid the impression of a retreat from the sexual and literary disclosures of Carpenter, or even of Wilde and Symonds. To many, the public silence of Forster about his homosexuality seems to reinforce the ideology of same-sex desire as a "secret" that leads to the evolution of a complex "double life." Hence, as Richard Dellamora points out: "Forster is often thought of as a man with two careers: the first climaxed with the publication of *A Passage to India* in 1924, after which he ceased to publish new fiction. The second career is a posthumous one as a writer of gay short stories and the novel *Maurice*."[2]

It is the second of these careers, representing Forster's complex and ambivalent relation to his homosexuality, that is usually associated with the influence of Carpenter. Though Dellamora argues that, in fact, "Forster had not two careers but one marked by continual compromise and resistance," it does seem helpful to differentiate between the work that Forster chose to publish in his lifetime and that which he decided to withhold.[3] Rather than describing Forster's "second career" as posthumous, however, it is more helpful to consider it as a secret one: for the homoerotic texts were actually written concurrently with the published fiction—*Maurice*, for example, was written shortly after *Howards End*. Forster's "secret fictions," in this sense, were the works he showed only to his close friends and had no intention of publishing during his lifetime. In this epilogue I want to define the "secret" writing more broadly, however, to include elements of plot and character that were suppressed from the published novels, in particular *A Room with a View*. By considering these excisions, we come to recognize that the boundary between Forster's public and secret literary careers was permeable and often indistinct.

One might argue that Forster's second career originated with his visit to Carpenter at Millthorpe. Though he disavows any direct representation of Carpenter or Merrill in the novel *Maurice*, for example, Forster's willingness to trace the origins of his novel back to Carpenter is itself aesthetically significant. For Forster's generation, the Wilde trials formed a persistent and traumatic background to their renewed efforts to articulate dangerous desires. By contrast, the long, distinguished, and relatively unscandalous career of Edward Carpenter demonstrated that a sexually dissident writer and thinker could remain unscathed.[4] Thus, Forster's literary output is divided in another sense: the secrecy and panic that derived from the appalling spectacle of Wilde's persecution could not be entirely reconciled with the cautious optimism and idealistic faith in democratic "comradeship" preached by Carpenter. For instance, Maurice, the only explicitly homosexual hero of Forster's novels, passes through a phase of self-hate, in which he identifies himself vituperatively as "an unspeakable of the Oscar Wilde sort," before attaining happiness in a Carpenterian relationship with the working-class gamekeeper Alec Scudder.[5] Robert K. Martin argues that the progression of Forster's hero from the aesthetic, platonic version of same-sex desire associated with Clive Durham, to the physical, robust, and cross-class desire embodied by Alec, represents a transition from the ideals of Symonds to those of Carpenter. But Wilde is also an important, if largely unspoken, presence in Forster's novel, an influence that needs to be accounted for.[6] By examining the dual influences of Wilde and Carpenter in Forster's fiction, we can come to understand some of the contradictory impulses at work in the novels and the continued influence of the nineteenth-century aesthetic of sexual secrecy in Forster's work.

Forster was introduced to Carpenter's work in the early 1900s by Goldsworthy Lowes Dickinson, Forster's mentor at Cambridge as well as a close friend of Carpenter's. At this period Forster was struggling with his own sexuality and eagerly embraced Carpenter's enthusiastic approach to the subject of same-sex desire. According to Beauman, it was his introduction to Carpenter's advocacy of sexual freedom, possibly through reading *Love's Coming-of-Age*, that "hurried him forward" to complete *A Room with a View*, the novel on which he had been working sporadically and desultorily for years and which Oliver Stallybrass describes as the Forster novel "with the most complicated pre-natal history."[7] The complexity of the novel's evolution can be traced to Forster's divided aims and conflicted sexuality, his desire to produce an affirmative novel that ended in romantic happiness being at odds with his own sense of sexual blight. The consequent difficulty of imagining a happy sexual future for himself impeded his ability to complete the novel, the drafts of which progress uncertainly from a tragic melodrama to the apparently lighthearted comedy of manners that became *A Room with a View*.

Significantly, this novel is explicitly about the sexual confusion of the heroine, Lucy Honeychurch, who "knew her desires" only after playing Beethoven on the piano, when she experiences a rare sensuality and emotional freedom. Forster links Lucy's sexual unhappiness to the limited freedoms allowed to Edwardian women, writing of their oppressed situation in terms that strongly suggest the influence of Carpenter's *Love's Coming-of-Age*: "It is sweet to protect her in the intervals of business, sweet to pay her honour when she has cooked our dinner well. But alas! the creature grows degenerate. In her heart also there are springing up strange desires."[8] Beneath the compassionate description of women's struggle for emotional emancipation, it is not difficult to recognize Forster's own identification with his heroine, as she struggles against the suffocating respectability of her suburban background and seeks in Italy an emotional and erotic escape. Hence, the pathos of Lucy's situation closely resembles Forster's own, and the novel represents the emergence of his own "strange desires" and his frustrated attempts to comprehend them.

Forster's novel dramatizes his belief that sexual self-knowledge arrives in sudden flashes of insight — sometimes in the form of a moment of bliss, sometimes as a disaster — which may be ignored or denied but which cannot be eliminated. Toward the end of the novel, during a crucial scene, Mr. Emerson observes to Lucy, "It seems to me . . . that you are in a muddle" (222) — using Forster's preferred term to designate sexual confusion — and tacitly reminds us that his son George is not "in a muddle," having become aware of the latent passion between himself and Lucy when they witness the murder of an Italian man in the Piazza Signoria. Though Lucy is vaguely aware at the time that "she, as well as the dying man, had crossed some spiritual boundary," it is only George who recognizes the erotic significance of the event: "For something tremendous has happened; I must face it without getting muddled" (63–64). What has "happened," George eventually discovers, is that he has developed a sexual passion for Lucy and, he believes, she for him; he later announces that "I have cared for you since that man died. I cannot live without you" (187). The association between sexual epiphany and death suggests that, in Forster's imagination, such recognition is invariably catastrophic.

The physical component of sexual passion is never ignored by Forster, however subtly it may be represented. Mr. Emerson's argument that "you can transmute love, ignore it, muddle it, but you can never pull it out of you" contains within it his version of the Carpenterian philosophy that "love is of the body; not the body, but of the body. Ah! the misery that would be saved if we confessed that!" (*Room*, 223). Mr. Emerson, as Beauman points out, is the character in the novel who most closely represents the views of Carpenter about sexuality: "He is the representative of the natural life, in which emotions are freely expressed; and he is set against the forces of . . . respectability."[9] In Forster's novel, it is Emerson who finally breaks down the barrier that Lucy has constructed to contain her sexual desire, allowing her to recognize the sexual epiphany that has occurred, irrevocably, between herself and George: "[Mr. Emerson] had robbed the body of its taint, the world's taunts of their sting; he had shown her the holiness of direct desire" (225). Though completed several years before his first visit to Millthorpe, *A Room with a View* dramatizes Forster's fantasy of being guided by the kind of sexual wisdom embodied by Carpenter and Mr. Emerson. As Mary Lago comments, "George Emerson possesses what Forster had never known: a sympathetic father who is friend as well as parent."[10] By the end of the novel, as Beauman expresses it, "Lucy has achieved everything that Carpenter would have wanted her to achieve."[11] One might also say, with equal accuracy, that Lucy has achieved everything that Forster himself dreamed of achieving: she has acknowledged, and acted on, her sexual desire and has thereby obtained a passionate intimacy with a strong, working-class man.

Forster described his own sexual epiphany in somewhat more somber, less optimistic terms. At the end of 1904, he wrote in his diary that "nothing more will come out of me: I've made my two great discoveries—the religious about four years ago, the other in the winter of 1902—and the reconstruction is practically over."[12] The most plausible reading of this statement is that the "other" discovery refers to the realization of his homosexuality, which was followed by a period of "reconstruction" during which he assimilated his new sexual awareness into a new persona. However, this affirmative interpretation of "reconstruction" does not entirely square with the note of pessimism in Forster's statement that "nothing more will come out of me." In context, "reconstruction" appears to refer to the attempt to disguise or modify his desire in order to adapt—in both his writing and his social behavior—to heterosexual convention and respectable society.

It is important to examine, therefore, the strategies that Forster deploys in his published novels to represent a conflicted interest in same-sex desire. Forster's fictional treatments of heterosexual romance are, in some cases, encoded versions of same-sex fantasies: as Dellamora insightfully expresses it, "Writing from a tacitly homosexual subject-position, Forster frames relations between men and women with an eye to desire between men."[13] In a diary entry of 16 June 1911 (shortly after the publication of *Howards End*), Forster recorded his growing "weariness of the only subject that I both can and may treat—the love of men for women & vice versa"; and this "weariness" is expressed more often in satirical or acerbic portrayals of heterosexual relationships than in positive representations of same-sex desire.[14] The critical exploration of the homosexual themes in the novels Forster published during his lifetime has been uneven but fruitful. For example, Elizabeth Heine has discussed the sexually autobiographical elements of *The Longest Journey*, suggesting that Rickie Elliott's "lameness"—which first delays his marriage and then prevents him from having children—"stands for Forster's own homosexuality," which he believed was, like "lameness," "congenital."[15] In his essay on *A Room with a View*, Jeffrey Meyers focuses on the Reverend Beebe as a homosexual figure who, despite being "first presented in an entirely sympathetic light," is ultimately portrayed as "actually dangerous."[16] Because Forster's revision of *A Room with a View* most clearly demonstrates the vacillation between self-disclosure and secrecy in his representation of same-sex desire, I will briefly discuss the most significant of these alterations.

The early drafts of the "Lucy" manuscripts, which eventually evolved into *A Room with a View*, indicate the extent of Forster's concealment of his interest in same-sex desire. In an early deleted scene, for example, Beebe attempts to dissuade George (who, in this draft, is named Arthur) from marrying Lucy. Informing George/Arthur that "you're what the cads call irresistable [*sic*]," Beebe goes on to give reasons why an alliance between Arthur and Lucy would prove disastrous. Yet the dialogue between them serves instead to indicate Beebe's sexual interest in Arthur and the latter's subtle encouragement of this desire. An exemplary passage detailing Beebe's thoughts about Arthur demonstrates that Lucy's original function is to mediate desire between the two men: "This was love of a kind: he could not doubt ‹it› /that/ though he persuaded himself that true love ‹was› /would be/ purer. But ‹in any case› /be what it might,/ it must be checked, or ‹certain› tragedy awaited them all. 'I can't listen to your outpourings. If you begin again I shall go away. And I think we both want to talk. But first of all you must trust me. Do you believe that I like you?' " It is important to note the ambiguity over whose "desire" is being described here and the distinct possibility that it is Beebe's desire for George/Arthur that "must be checked" if "tragedy" is to be avoided. Failing to deter Arthur from pursuing Lucy, Beebe becomes hostile and resorts to threatening him: "I am sorry that our pleasant friendship has ended thus. We need not proceed to the bandying of words. But I wish to tell you openly that I am your enemy. I shall make whatever ‹means›[?] /use/ I choose of all I know." Beebe's resentment suggests the role of the spurned lover, not that of the protective "friend."[17]

In the course of revising the novel, Forster eliminated this important scene, along with others exploring the intimacy between George and Beebe. Some traces remain in the published novel of Beebe's passion for George, however, such as when Lucy first confesses that she loves George, to which Mr. Beebe responds, "I am more grieved than I can possibly express. It is lamentable, lamentable — incredible" (225). To Mr. Emerson's question, "What's wrong with the boy?" Beebe replies mysteriously, "Nothing, Mr Emerson, except that he no longer interests me" (225). This sudden evacuation of Beebe's "interest" in George is accompanied by an equally sudden loss of authorial sympathy for Beebe, of whom Forster writes that "his white face, with its ruddy whiskers, seemed suddenly inhuman. A long black column, he stood and awaited her reply" (224). Evidently, Beebe's "interest" is in conflict not only with George's passion for Lucy but also with the projected heterosexual resolution of the novel itself.

The strongest indication of Beebe's homoerotic desire in the published version of the novel, however, occurs at the Sacred Lake, where George and Freddy Honeychurch go to bathe. They are accompanied by Beebe, who initially resists the invitation to bathe and instead takes pleasure in viewing his naked companions from a distance: "[George] . . . followed Freddy into the divine, as indifferent as if he were a statue and the pond a pail of soapsuds. . . . Mr Beebe watched them, and watched the seeds of the willow-herb dance chorically above their heads" (148–49). Through the use of indirect discourse, Beebe's point of view blends with the narrator's, thereby linking Beebe with the erotic and aesthetically infused description of George as "Michelangelesque on the flooded margin" (149). Meyers argues that in this scene, "Beebe's latent homosexuality has been released and he has fallen in love with George."[18] But Forster's revisions to his early drafts conceal most of the evidence of this love, and obscure the motives for Beebe's sudden coldness at the novel's end. Though Forster announces that "Mr Beebe was, from rather profound reasons, somewhat chilly in his attitude towards the other sex" (53–54), the nature of these "profound reasons" is left opaque. To discuss the homoerotic representations in Forster's entire literary output is beyond the scope of this epilogue. My purpose is to trace a specific and crucial conflict in Forster's writing, between a desire for sexual openness and discovery—represented by the sudden self-insight or sexual epiphany between men or between a man and a woman—and the counterreaction of self-censorship. In terms of the dual influences of Carpenter and Wilde on Forster, one might say that the homoerotic—and democratic—utopia of Carpenter's visionary politics was in constant tension with the homophobic—and class-conflicted—catastrophe of Wilde's actual fate. Forster's secret fictions dramatize this cultural conflict perhaps more vividly than any other writing of the period. Indeed, the tension between a Carpenterian optimism and a Wildean panic can be detected in many of Forster's writings; in *Howards End*, for example, the terror of the "abyss," the dread of "panic and emptiness" that afflicts Helen Schlegel—whose own sexual relationship with Leonard Bast suggests a heterosexual version of Forster's cross-class fantasy—might be viewed as Forster's encoded response to the Wilde trials and the hostile atmosphere they had created for expressions of same-sex desire, especially between men of different classes.[19]

The homosexual relationship between a middle-class, Cambridge-educated "normal" man and his working-class gamekeeper-lover also demonstrates the inspiration provided by Carpenter for the plot of *Maurice*. Following Maurice's rejection by his Cambridge lover, Clive Durham, the hero realizes his desire—that includes love of the body—with Clive's gamekeeper, Alec Scudder. Like the passion between George and Lucy, the spark of desire between Maurice and Alec defies the expectations of respectable society (Lucy is originally engaged to the straitlaced Cecil Vyse, while Maurice plays the domestic tyrant over his mother and sisters) as well as their own self-control. To this extent, it represents Forster's literary representation of the liberating, democratic same-sex desire envisioned by Carpenter. Forster's engagement with the obstacles facing same-sex lovers, however, can also be seen at work in this most explicitly homoerotic of his novels and the one that most clearly reveals Wildean and Carpenterian influences. Indeed, attention to this conflict throws some light on one of the most puzzling episodes in Forster's entire fictional oeuvre: the sudden and dramatic "conversion" of Clive Durham to heterosexuality at the center of *Maurice*.

John Fletcher, in an important article on *Maurice*, writes that "Clive's conversion to heterosexuality is an anomaly at the heart of the book that remains inexplicable and unassimilable."[20] In the novel the change is indeed sudden, as abruptly stated by Durham in a letter to Maurice from Greece: "Against my will I have become normal. I cannot help it." Forster is insistent on the inscrutable nature of sexual desire, asserting that "not only in sex, but in all things men have moved blindly" (116). Of Clive's conversion, Forster simply comments that "there had been no warning—just a blind alteration of the life spirit, just an announcement, 'You who loved men, will henceforth love women. Understand it or not, it's the same to me'" (118). There is no indication at this point in Forster's narrative that Clive is deliberately forcing himself to alter his sexuality so as to conform to external social pressures or to his family's expectations.[21] Yet, the novel concludes by stressing Clive's sexual deceit and hypocrisy: when Maurice walks away from Clive's house, having told him about his affair with Alec, Clive "returned to the house, to correct his proofs and to devise some method of concealing the truth from Anne" (246). The practice of textual revision is here associated with "concealing the truth"—a juxtaposition that brings into focus Forster's own strategies of self-censorship.

Earlier in the novel, moreover, Clive has told Maurice's sister Ada that "while in Greece I had to reconstruct my life from the bottom. Not an easy task, but I think I've done it" (125). Forster here suggests—in language that recalls the account of his own sexual "reconstruction" several years earlier—that Clive's renunciation of same-sex desire has been self-conscious and deliberate, perhaps due to fear of the penalties for defying the prevailing sexual morality. The "reconstruction" is undertaken on Clive's part as a determined effort to redirect his desire toward women and explicitly involves his adaptation to the expectations of his family and society. When Clive informs Maurice that "I've changed," Maurice replies incredulously, "Can the leopard change his spots?" But this is precisely what Clive has done in constructing a more effective form of camouflage to avoid the detection and punishment of his "strange desires." Maurice, echoing

Mr. Emerson in *A Room with a View*, tells Clive that "you're in a muddle" and insists on the endurance of his transgressive kinship with Clive, stating that "you and I are outlaws" (127). This "outcast" state is precisely the Wildean tragedy that Clive's "reconstruction" is designed to avoid, however, and as such mirrors Forster's own ambivalence toward an "outlaw" existence.[22] Although Forster fantasized about an escape into what he called the greenwood—a pastoral freedom that included cross-class sexual intimacy—like Clive, "he wanted to . . . flee, but he was civilized, and wanted it feebly" (243). Instead, Forster lived out his life in suburban security and cloistered academic seclusion. Only Maurice—from whom Forster explicitly distances himself in the "terminal note"—has the courage to follow his desire, in the search for a passion "big enough to hang a life on" (245).

The import of what has been described as Clive's sexual conversion in *Maurice* extends beyond the pages of the novel itself to include the scene of its original conception. In a "terminal note" to *Maurice* that was originally written in 1960, Forster states that the novel "was the direct result of a visit to Edward Carpenter at Millthorpe," adding that "Carpenter had a prestige which cannot be understood today. He was a rebel appropriate to his age." Forster's sense of indebtedness to Carpenter is specifically related to his sexual politics, for "finally, he was a believer in the Love of Comrades, whom he sometimes called Uranians. It was this last aspect of him that attracted me in my loneliness" (249). Translating this powerful "attraction" into a new work of fiction, Forster explores a sexual fantasy in which the working-class Alec is, unlike the patrician Clive, able to reciprocate and satisfy Maurice's desire—a sexual impulse the hero is resisting and trying to terminate by means of hypnosis—without anything being said. The scene in which Alec comes to Maurice's room invokes the merging of selves that constituted the heart of Forster's fantasy of sexual union. As Maurice goes to bed, "a little noise sounded, a noise so intimate that it might have arisen inside his own body. He seemed to crackle and burn and saw the ladder's top quivering against the moonlit air. The head and the shoulders of a man rose up, paused, a gun was leant against the window sill very carefully, and someone he scarcely knew moved towards him and knelt beside him and whispered, 'Sir, was you calling out for me? . . . Sir, I know. . . . I know,' and touched him" (192). The passionate relationship between Maurice and Alec strongly reproduces the relationship between Merrill—another George—and Edward Carpenter. Merrill had touched Forster's backside—"gently and just above the buttocks"—during the latter's visit to Millthorpe. Calling the experience "as much psychological as physical," Forster expands the memory into a Carpenterian account of male conception, remembering that the touch "seemed to go straight through the small of my back into my ideas, without involving my thoughts." It was only later that Forster realized that "at that precise moment I had conceived" (249).

Forster's description here recalls the "seed of new conceptions" that Carpenter had received from Whitman. As occurred with Carpenter, the immediate effect of this sexual transmission is a burst of literary inspiration: when Forster returned to Harrogate, he "immediately began to write *Maurice*" and found that the new novel "all rushed into my pen" (250). Having resisted the awakening of his own sexuality for fear of its traumatic effects, Forster chose to embroil Maurice in a similar trial of sexual deferral and painful self-recognition; into his hero's "suburban soul" Forster "dropped an ingredient that puzzles him, wakes him up, torments him and finally saves him" (250–51). Conversely, it is Clive—the representative of Victorian Cambridge, where both Carpenter and Forster had been students—who fails to realize the redemptive power of same-sex passion. Forster uses Clive to demonstrate the limitations of the Cambridge idealism, particularly its stifling prohibition on physical sexuality, against which Carpenter had rebelled but to which Forster himself was irresistibly drawn.[23]

Alec Scudder is, of course, the antithesis of genteel Cambridge: as Forster writes, he is "an emanation from Milthorpe [*sic*], he is the touch on the backside." Carpenter and Forster both idealized the male, working-class lover because he seemed to offer an escape from the sexual inhibitions and insidious respect for conventions that were the legacy of an upper-middle-class English upbringing. Hence, the advocacy of same-sex desire that crossed class boundaries was central to the work of both writers. Forster's journal for 1913 concludes simply, "Edward Carpenter! Edward Carpenter! Edward Carpenter!" and one could hardly ask for a clearer statement of Forster's excited admiration and emulation at the period of writing *Maurice*. Forster recognized that it was the "happy ending" to *Maurice*, rather than the representation of homosexuality itself, that made the novel impossible to publish. This "happy ending," it is now clear, makes the strongest statement of his adherence to Carpenter's values. Forster wrote in his terminal note that "Carpenter believed that Uranians remained loyal to each other for ever": it is this loyalty which Forster covets and which the ending of the novel celebrates.[24] Unlike in *A Room with a View*, however, which also ends happily, we recognize that Forster is able to dispense with the disguise of heterosexual romance in *Maurice*, a literary convention of which he had become "weary."[25] Though both novels represent the formation of a passionate and equal relationship against intense social and psychic opposition, the subversive love story in *Maurice* has been reconstructed in explicitly homosexual terms.

If *Maurice* gestures toward an imaginary "happier year" — a year when, among other things, it would be possible to publish homosexual fiction — it remains, in its inception, bound up with a period of intense sexual misery that was temporarily assuaged by Forster's first visit to Carpenter. At the end of 1913, Forster wrote with mixed exultation and despair in his "Locked Journal": "Maurice born on Sept 13th. He tells the mood that created him. But will he ever be happy. He has become an independent existence — Greenwood feels the same. . . . I woke with desolation and impotence weighing on me, and felt it grotesque to continue Maurice. This goes as soon as I begin — My second visit was not as Sep 13, but it preserved joy."[26] Forster's anxious uncertainty over whether Maurice "will . . . ever be happy" evidently pertains to his own sexual crisis and suggests an identification between author and hero that Forster carefully disavowed in print. However dissatisfied Forster eventually became with *Maurice*, it is important to remember that the novel was "conceived" in a moment of joy inspired by Carpenter and Merrill. *Maurice* represents a breakthrough that dramatizes the central aspects of Carpenter's sexual philosophy, without the previous "disguise" of a heterosexual plot.

Crucially, though, the creative impetus came from George Merrill, who provided the intimate greeting that would "make a profound impression on me and . . . touch a creative spring." The working-class male body serves as a conduit, in Forster's imagination, for forms of erotic expression and physical contact not permissible between middle-class, Cambridge-educated men. Indeed, the novel represents an attempt to recuperate the working-class male body as an object of veneration and desire, following its traumatic inscription as a commodity within the narrative of Wilde's disgrace. Arguably, Forster in *Maurice*—similarly to Carpenter in *My Days and Dreams*—is not merely contesting the homophobic disavowal of same-sex desire, especially that between members of different classes, but also rejecting the exploitation of the working-class body within a system of exchange. This notion of exchange, in terms of which Wilde's relationships with male prostitutes were characterized, is enacted by Alec's futile attempt to threaten Maurice with blackmail following their first sexual encounter. The threat of blackmail—and the terror of an economic and sexual ruin it invokes—is idealistically expelled by the assertion of a spiritual equality between the lovers. Yet the scene also embeds the threat of a Wildean scandal within the idealistic Forsterian text.

Carpenter's relationship with George Merrill demonstrated, for Forster and others, the real possibility of sexual comradeship within the context of a cross-class relationship. As the heir of Carpenter's utopian liberalism and the secret sharer of his desire for working-class men, Forster sought to represent same-sex desire by means of a positive, epiphanic, and at times even humorous aesthetic. As the unwilling recipient of the still-potent cultural anxiety and sexual persecution epitomized by the destruction of Wilde, Forster also struggled with the emotional, social, and legal obstacles to sexual fulfillment and creative freedom. The vision of the future inscribed in a "happier year" enticed Forster with the prospect of renouncing his sexual secrecy and "publishing" his desire. That this epiphanic "year" occurred only posthumously is at once poignant and appropriate: for its tardiness is attributable less to the personal caution of Forster than to the inevitable deferral of sexual disclosure that manifests itself in all the confessional narratives discussed in this book. Forster's work, despite its emphasis on emotional honesty and sexual liberation, ultimately confronts the same aesthetic dilemma that informs the autobiographies of Symonds, Wilde, and Carpenter: secrecy proves to be not simply an obstacle to the disclosure of same-sex desire but also the very condition of its textual representation.

NOTES

INTRODUCTION

1. De Man, "Autobiography," 67–68.

2. Foucault, *Introduction*, 27.

3. Swindells, *Victorian Writing*, 121–22. Among other influential accounts of autobiography that have expanded the definition of the genre to include narratives written by members of "marginal" groups, such as the working classes, women, and homosexuals, see in particular Gagnier, *Subjectivities*; Lejeune, *On Autobiography*; and Vincent, *Bread, Knowledge, and Freedom*.

4. Bakhtin makes an interesting and important distinction between the novel of "trial" and "testing" and the novel of "development" or "bildung." Although the "idea of testing the hero, or testing his discourse, may very well be the most fundamental organizing idea in the novel" (*Dialogic Imagination*, 388), Bakhtin points out the limitations of this form, in terms of individual change: "In several of its forms it knows crisis and rebirth, but it does not know development, becoming, a man's gradual formation. Testing begins with an already formed person and subjects him to a trial in the light of an idea also already formed" (392). By contrast, in the novel of development— what Bakhtin calls the "modern novel"—"life and its events, bathed in the light of becoming, reveal themselves as the hero's experience, as the school or environment that first forms and formulates the hero's character and world view" (393). According to these definitions, it is when the novel takes development, rather than testing, as its theme that it becomes closest to the autobiography, in which individual experience and growth constitute the central theme.

5. Eakin, *Fictions in Autobiography*, 17.

6. Lejeune, *On Autobiography*, 12–13; Lejeune's emphasis.

7. For a reading of Dickens's novel that focuses on the complex relation between author, autobiography, and fiction and explores the representation of same-sex desire in the novel, see Buckton, " 'The Reader Whom I Love.' "

8. Lejeune, *On Autobiography*, 19–20; Lejeune's emphasis.

9. Foucault, *Introduction*, 43.

10. Ibid., 21.

11. Sinfield, *The Wilde Century*, 3, 18.

12. Ibid., 3.

13. Foucault, *Introduction*, 59.

14. Ibid., 42, 43.

15. Tambling, *Confession*, 174. Tambling also finds a link between homosexuality and the confession, arguing that "to some extent the apparently frank and spontaneous 'coming out' declaration with its power to shock initially, has taken the form of confession itself, showing the marks of a prior power exercised upon it, which has, of course, created the 'homosexual' as a category—and made certain types of 'gayness' representable" (178). Implicitly, according to Tambling, other types of gayness are *not* representable under the confessional regime of "coming out"—perhaps those which continue to focus on sexual acts and behavior, rather than the consolidation of those acts into an "identity," or which define themselves in ways that cross other boundaries, of gender, class, and so forth.

16. Dollimore, "Different Desires," 31.

17. De Man, "Autobiography," 67.

18. Olney, "Autobiography and the Cultural Moment," 13.

19. Bruss, "Eye for I," 298 n.

20. Ibid., 298.

21. Sidonie Smith, *Poetics of Women's Autobiography*, 5. For other examples of works that present a challenging poststructuralist account of autobiographical texts as "fictions" and assume a postmodernist model of the subject as culturally constructed and fragmentary, see in particular books by Eakin, *Fictions in Autobiography*; Jay, *Being in the Text*; and Lejeune, *On Autobiography*.

22. Olney, "Autobiography and the Cultural Moment," 23.

23. De Man, "Autobiography," 69.

24. Sidonie Smith, *Poetics of Women's Autobiography*, 6; Smith's emphasis.

25. Olney, "Autobiography and the Cultural Moment," 22.

26. Sidonie Smith, *Poetics of Women's Autobiography*, 16.

27. Ibid., 15.

28. Ibid., 13.

29. Ibid., 17.

30. A shortlist of such works would have to be headed by Dellamora's *Masculine Desire*—the work closest to this book in its exploration of same-sex desire as a rhetorical device or strategy for the construction of transgressive readings of aesthetic texts. The list would also include Bristow, *Sexual Sameness*; Cohen, *Talk on the Wilde Side*; Dollimore, *Sexual Dissidence*; Edelman, *Homographesis*; Sinfield, *The Wilde Century*; Sussman, *Victorian Masculinities*; as well as Adams, "Gentleman, Dandy, Priest"; Cohen, "Writing Gone Wilde"; and Koestenbaum, "Wilde's Hard Labor." The work of each of these

critics, as will be evident, has to a greater or lesser extent influenced the thinking and arguments in the individual chapters that follow.

31. For Sedgwick's argument about "homosexual panic" as a crucial component in the construction of nineteenth-century masculinity, see *Between Men* (esp. chap. 5) and *Epistemology of the Closet* (esp. chap. 4). According to Sedgwick, the fear—or, to use her term, "terror"—experienced by men in confronting (or, rather, avoiding) their own same-sex desire is the corollary of often intense homosocial bonds that are scrupulously, even paranoically, desexualized. The role of women in the homosocial bond is to serve as the figure of displacement or projection for same-sex desire that cannot be acknowledged either as part of individual masculine identity or as a factor informing the relationships between men. To the extent that male writing of the period is misogynistic, therefore, this involves the demonized role of woman as the dual site of an officially sanctioned heterosexuality, and the displacement of inadmissible, panic-inducing, same-sex desire.

32. Sussman, *Victorian Masculinities*, 173. Indeed, his study of the relation between cultural constructions of masculinity and their anticipation of later-Victorian discourses of homosexuality is an important corrective to work that tends to assimilate this linkage into the later years of the century.

33. Ibid.

34. See Morgan, *Victorian Sages*, 1–18. The seminal use of the phrase is John Holloway's. See *The Victorian Sage*.

35. Adams, "Gentleman, Dandy, Priest," 442, 449, 451, 454, 453.

36. Dellamora, *Masculine Desire*, 130.

37. Ibid., 141.

38. Ibid., 146.

39. Koestenbaum, "Wilde's Hard Labor," 178.

40. Wilde, *The Picture of Dorian Gray*, 26.

41. Dellamora, "Textual Politics," 155.

42. McGann, *The Textual Condition*, 9.

43. Dellamora, "Textual Politics," 156–57.

44. Ibid., 163.

45. McGann, *The Textual Condition*, 60–61. McGann argues that "these nonauthorial interventions are important, theoretically, because they expose the problematic character of the concept of final intentions" (61).

46. Dellamora, "Textual Politics," 164.

CHAPTER ONE

1. An entry in Newman's journal for 22 February 1865 contrasts markedly in tone with the despondent note characterizing many of his private reflections in the later years of his life: "In the last year a most wonderful deliverance has been wrought in my favour, by the controversy, of which the upshot was my Apologia. It has been marvellously blest, for, while I have regained, or

rather gained, the favour of Protestants, I have received the approbation, in formal addresses, of good part of the English clerical body . . . thus I am in a totally different position now to what I was in January 1863" (*Autobiographical Writings*, 260–61).

2. Newman, however, had broken his silence on several occasions. In 1862, not long before the controversy with Kingsley, he responded to a rumor that he was on the verge of converting back to the Church of England with a letter of denial that has been described by Robert B. Martin as "a masterpiece of sarcasm about the English Church." Again, in 1863, he wrote to the *Times* to defend *Tract 90* against F. D. Maurice's damaging interpretation. One can see, then, that Newman was tentatively moving back into the public forum that he had abandoned many years earlier, though it was only following Kingsley's attack that Newman "changed from the defensive to the offensive" (Robert B. Martin, *Dust of Combat*, 246).

3. "Mr. Kingsley and Dr. Newman: A Correspondence," 344.

4. The term "muscular Christianity" was first applied to Kingsley in 1858. He "was far from pleased by it, and described it as 'a painful, if not offensive term,' but eventually, and somewhat characteristically, he began to trade on it" (Chitty, *Beast and the Monk*, 196). Robert B. Martin cites a passage from Kingsley's 1864 Christmas sermon at Cambridge that displays his ambivalent attitude to the tag that had helped to make him famous, in terms strikingly relevant to his conflict with Newman: "We have heard much of late about 'Muscular Christianity.' A clever expression, spoken in jest by I know not whom, has been bandied about the world, and supposed by many to represent some new idea of the Christian character. For myself, I do not know what it means. . . . Its first and better meaning may be simply a healthful and manful Christianity; one which does not exalt the feminine virtues to the exclusion of the masculine" (Martin, *Dust of Combat*, 220).

5. "Mr. Kingsley and Dr. Newman: A Correspondence," 343.

6. Ibid., 346.

7. Newman, *Letters and Diaries*, 73.

8. One might invoke here Pickering's distinction between "three levels" of homosexuality: the first "relates to the general preference that individual adult men have to be in the company of other males, whether boys or adults, or both." The second "relates to those who as individuals become strongly attached in an exclusive way to one particular male." The third "involves physical contact between individuals, such as handling, fondling, and kissing, and which may issue in such forms of physical satisfaction as are possible between two males. Since this level involves men who are sexually active, it refers to those who are commonly called practising homosexuals" (Pickering, *Anglo-Catholicism*, 189–90). Insofar as Newman was homosexual, according to this model he presumably belongs at the first and second levels—that is, his preference was for male company and his primary relationship at any given period of his life was with one particular man. These relationships were char-

acterized by intense affectional ties; but there is no evidence of any physical sexuality between Newman and his closest friends. There are obvious drawbacks to this rather systematic model, however: in the first place, Pickering's suggestion that homosexual love offers less opportunity of "physical satisfaction" than does heterosexual love is problematic. The concept of "homosociality" as developed by Sedgwick in *Between Men* (esp. 1–20) would seem more adequate than "homosexuality" as a description of the male camaraderie evoked in Pickering's first level.

9. Dollimore, *Sexual Dissidence*, 120; and C. Kingsley, "What, Then, Does Dr. Newman Mean?," 369.

10. That Newman had sought to reconcile the teachings of the two churches, in *Tract 90* and, at greater length, in his *Essay on the Development of Christian Doctrine* (1845), suggests the context of national loyalty to the invocations of "perversion" in the Newman-Kingsley controversy. Kingsley feared that Catholicism, which he portrayed as a hostile foreign force emanating from papist Rome, might in fact turn out to have been in an "intimate relation" all along with the tradition of Anglicanism that sought to exclude it. Because of the peculiarly close ties between church and state in Victorian England, any assault on the English church could easily be confused with or collapsed into an attack on the nation itself. Thus, Kingsley's slippage between church and nation in his attack on the Catholic priesthood is significant: "If there is (as there is) a strong distrust of certain Catholics, it is restricted to the proselytizing priests among them; and especially to those who, like Dr Newman, have turned round upon their mother-Church (I had almost said mother-country) with contumely and slander" (Kingsley, "What, Then, Does Dr. Newman Mean?," 365). Kingsley went on to suggest that Newman's "perversion" was not restricted to his interpretation of Scripture but was also evinced by his failure to enact norms of national character: "If, whenever he touches on the question of truth and honesty, he will take a perverse pleasure in saying something shocking to plain English notions, he must take the consequences of his own eccentricities" (372).

11. Any list of critical studies of Newman's *Apologia* would obviously have to include Houghton's *Art of Newman's "Apologia"* and the collection of essays edited by Blehl and Connolly (*Newman's "Apologia"*). Houghton's essay "The Issue between Kingsley and Newman" is useful as well. There are also substantial chapters on the literary and rhetorical aspects of the *Apologia* in Harrold, *John Henry Newman*; Jost, *Rhetorical Thought in John Henry Newman*; and Helmling, *Esoteric Comedies of Carlyle, Newman, and Yeats*. Peterson, *Victorian Autobiography*, and Henderson, *The Victorian Self*, discuss the *Apologia* in terms of Newman's use of the traditions of spiritual autobiography and biblical typology, respectively. Loesberg, *Fictions of Consciousness*, is more interested in what he describes as "the philosophic context of Newman's *Apologia*" than in its cultural contexts. Loesberg does address the polemical status of the work as a response to Kingsley's charges, though without

raising the sexual aspects of Kingsley's attack. Fuller treatment of the ideological issues at stake in the controversy between Newman and Kingsley is given in the various biographies of the two protagonists. Volume 2 of Ward's *Life* and Trevor's *Newman: Light in Winter* are important sources of information about the personality clash between Newman and Kingsley. Ker, *John Henry Newman: A Biography*, and Gilley, *Newman and His Age*, offer two of the more recent accounts of the controversy from Newman's perspective. Kingsley has not been short of biographers either. The posthumously published collection of his letters and papers, edited by his wife, Fanny Kingsley (*Charles Kingsley*), is frustratingly vague and evasive in a number of key areas, including the dispute with Newman, but is nonetheless useful for gaining a sense of Kingsley's character. A shortlist of modern biographies would certainly include Pope-Hennessy, *Canon Charles Kingsley*, and Robert B. Martin, *Dust of Combat*. Two more recent biographies deal in greater detail with Kingsley's complex sexuality: Colloms's *Charles Kingsley: The Lion of Eversley* and Chitty's *Beast and the Monk*. Chitty has the distinction of being the first to publish and discuss Kingsley's sadopornographic artwork, featuring himself and his wife Fanny in various erotic poses, which helped transform the critical consensus on Kingsley's sexual persona.

    12. Chadwick, *Spirit of the Oxford Movement*, 126.

    13. See Chapter 2, this volume.

    14. Newman in fact acknowledged as much, by writing letters of gratitude to Hutton for his favorable reviews of the *Apologia* in the *Spectator*. See Trevor, *Newman: Light in Winter*, 324–25.

    15. Newman, *Apologia pro Vita Sua*, ed. Svaglic, 20. Subsequent references to this edition will be cited parenthetically in the text.

    16. Sedgwick, *Epistemology of the Closet*, 73.

    17. Foucault, *Introduction*, 34–35.

    18. "Mr. Kingsley and Dr. Newman: A Correspondence," 344, 341.

    19. Gilley, *Newman and His Age*, 19.

    20. Ibid., 121.

    21. Ibid., 324.

    22. F. Kingsley, *Charles Kingsley*, 2:204.

    23. Svaglic, "Introduction," xxxii.

    24. Chitty, *Beast and the Monk*, 65–66.

    25. Trevor, *Newman: Light in Winter*, 327.

    26. Ibid., 328.

    27. Pope-Hennessy, *Canon Charles Kingsley*, 213; and Robert B. Martin, *Dust of Combat*, 238.

    28. Egner, *Apologia pro Charles Kingsley*, 30. I am grateful to the anonymous reader at *Victorian Studies* who informed me that G. Egner is actually a pseudonym for P. J. Fitzpatrick, a Roman Catholic priest and at the time of publishing his book a lecturer in philosophy at the University of Durham, England.

29. Hilliard, "Unenglish and Unmanly," 188.

30. Robert B. Martin, *Dust of Combat*, 241.

31. C. Kingsley, "Why Should We Fear the Romish Priests?," 469.

32. Chitty, *Beast and the Monk*, 59. This Catholic/monastic "leaning" was, as far as we know, confided only to his wife. By the mid-1860s, Kingsley— at least in the public eye—was (as Newman had long ceased to be) a paragon of establishment respectability. A visible index of Kingsley's increasingly central role in Victorian culture is his position, from 1859, as the chaplain to Queen Victoria and, from the early 1860s, as the private tutor to the Prince of Wales.

33. Newman, *Autobiographical Writings*, 137. Newman goes on, however, to indicate that the married state, while not one that he could ever seriously countenance for himself, nonetheless held powerful attractions for him: "I willingly give up the possession of that sympathy which I feel is not, cannot be granted me. Yet, not the less do I feel the need of it. Who will care to be told such details as I have put down above? Shall I ever have in my old age spiritual children who will take an interest such as a wife does?" (138).

34. Newman, *Loss and Gain*, 135–36, 138, 139.

35. Vance, *Sinews of the Spirit*, 118–19.

36. Ibid., 112–13; Pickering, *Anglo-Catholicism*, 200; Hilliard, "Unenglish and Unmanly," 185.

37. After Froude's death, Newman had in 1838 edited his friend's *Remains*, which contained journals expressing what has sometimes been interpreted as homosexual desire and frustration. The following entries may serve as examples: "January 15. Strengthen me, O Lord my God, that I may dare to look in the face the hideous filthiness of those ways, in which, for the sin that with open eyes, I have acted, Thou has permitted me blindly to stray. January 21. My soul is a troubled and restless thing, haunted by the recollection of past wickedness. Feb 22. I am no longer in the company of those who scorn the appearance of piety, nor dazzled with examples of fascinating vice" (Froude, *Remains*, cited in Faber, *Oxford Apostles*, 220–21). Although these *cris de coeur* have sometimes been attributed to a religious crisis rather than homosexual panic, they can certainly be interpreted as evidence of conflicted sexual desire. In any case, the publication of Froude's *Remains*, with the Roman Catholic sympathies expressed therein, "shocked the ordinary English mind that the very University which was the guardian of the nation's youth was subverting the national religion" (Gilley, *Newman and His Age*, 165).

38. Faber, *Oxford Apostles*, 223.

39. Reade, *Sexual Heretics*, 4.

40. Brendon, *Hurrell Froude*, 113; Gilley, *Newman and His Age*, 20.

41. Kingsley to Fanny Kingsley, cited in Chitty, *Beast and the Monk*, 52. That Kingsley's adoring relation to other men did not die out with his youth is made apparent in a letter written shortly after his first meeting with the royal couple in 1859, where he stated that " 'I know one more strong good

man than I did—and that is the Prince Consort. I have fallen in love with that man'" (Robert B. Martin, *Dust of Combat*, 222).

42. Sinfield, *The Wilde Century*, 59.

43. Gilley, *Newman and His Age*, 325.

44. Despite this resistance on Kingsley's part, some of his contemporaries were not taken in by his carefully cultivated "machismo." Justin McCarthy, for instance, wrote of Kingsley that "despite his rough voice and vigorous manner, he was as feminine in his likes and dislikes, his impulses and prejudices as Harriet Martineau was masculine in her intellect and George Sand in her emotions" (Chitty, *Beast and the Monk*, 52).

45. Pickering, *Anglo-Catholicism*, 205; Hilliard, "Unenglish and Unmanly," 181, 209.

46. Weeks, *Coming Out*, 34.

47. Honey, *Tom Brown's Universe*, 191.

48. Vance, *Sinews of the Spirit*, 149.

49. Hilliard, "Unenglish and Unmanly," 185; Gilley, *Newman and His Age*, 20.

50. "Mr Kingsley and Dr Newman," 149–50.

51. "Kingsley and Newman," 118.

52. Chitty, *Beast and the Monk*, 236; Colloms, *Charles Kingsley: The Lion of Eversley*, 271; Robert B. Martin, *Dust of Combat*, 239, 241; Harrold, *John Henry Newman*, 305.

53. Svaglic, "Introduction," lvii; Ker, *John Henry Newman: A Biography*, viii.

54. Butler, *Gender Trouble*, x.

55. Butler, "Imitation and Gender Insubordination," 24; Butler's emphasis.

56. Epstein and Straub, *Body Guards*, 3.

57. Sedgwick, *Epistemology of the Closet*, 31, 32.

58. Robert B. Martin, *Dust of Combat*, 239.

59. Dellamora, *Masculine Desire*, 199.

60. Hilliard, "Unenglish and Unmanly," 188.

61. Sinfield, *The Wilde Century*, 26; Dowling, *Hellenism and Homosexuality*, 46.

62. F. Kingsley, *Charles Kingsley*, 1:249.

63. C. Kingsley, "What, Then, Does Dr. Newman Mean?," 362–63.

64. Cited in Gilley, *Newman and His Age*, 126.

65. Chitty, *Beast and the Monk*, 231.

66. "Mr. Kingsley and Dr. Newman: A Correspondence," 342. The *Westminster Review* observed at the time of the controversy, "To any impartial reader of the incriminated sermon on 'Wisdom and Innocence,' it is simply bewildering how Mr Kingsley could have deduced from it the conclusions he did" ("Dr Newman, Mr Kingsley," 138).

67. "Mr. Kingsley and Dr. Newman: A Correspondence," 339.

68. Douglas, *Purity and Danger*, 113.

69. Ibid., 36.

70. In his remarkable "Autobiographical Memoir," written entirely in the third person, Newman gave the following account of his unusually close connection with his group of "special pupils": "With such youths he cultivated relations, not only of intimacy, but of friendship, and almost of equality, putting off, as much as might be, the martinet manner then in fashion with College Tutors, and seeking their society in outdoor exercise, on evenings, and in Vacation. And, when he became Vicar of St Mary's in 1828, the hold he had acquired over them led to their following him on to sacred ground, and receiving directly religious instruction from his sermons; but from the first, independently of St Mary's he had set before himself in his Tutorial work the aims of gaining souls to God" (Newman, *Autobiographical Writings*, 90).

71. Newman, *Letters and Diaries*, 90.

72. In response to one critic's accusation that he had been a "concealed Romanist" while "officially" still an Anglican, Newman wrote: "By a 'concealed Romanist' I understand him to mean one, who, professing to belong to the Church of England, in his heart and will intends to benefit the Church of Rome, at the expense of the Church of England. He cannot mean by the expression merely a person who in fact is benefiting the Church of Rome, while he is intending to benefit the Church of England, for that is no discredit to him morally" (*Apologia*, ed. Svaglic, 169). Ironically, Newman here comes perilously close to the casuistry that had been interpreted by Kingsley as a key indication of his oversubtle and dishonest intellectualizing. Such subtle distinctions are, however, relatively rare in the *Apologia*. His blanket assertion that "I never could understand how a man could be of two religions at once" (194) is more typical and more useful for his purpose, asserting as it does the "masculine" unity of his religious position.

73. C. Kingsley, "What, Then, Does Dr. Newman Mean?," 362.

74. Ibid., 363.

75. Coincidences abound in the controversy between Newman and Kingsley: J. A. Froude, besides being the author of the work that Kingsley was reviewing when he made his attack on Newman, was also the younger brother of Newman's closest friend at Oxford. Newman's fateful trip to Europe following his dismissal as tutor at Oriel was made in the company of Hurrell Froude; Kingsley was accompanied on his travels during the period of the publication of the *Apologia* by J. A. Froude, at that time his brother-in-law.

76. Susan Chitty writes of Henry Kingsley, who, like his brother, was a novelist: "He left Oxford without a degree and there is a strong suspicion that he was sent down for homosexual practices. Certain aspects of his behaviour at the University would lead one to imagine this, for he was a founder of the Fez Club, members of which were vowed to celibacy and who met monthly (suitably fezzed) to denounce womankind in all its forms. There were also overtly homosexual references in several of his books" (*Beast and the Monk*, 187).

77. Gilley, *Newman and His Age*, 325.

78. Robert B. Martin, *Dust of Combat*, 242.

79. Ward, *Life*, 2:15.

80. "Mr. Kingsley and Dr. Newman: A Correspondence," 345; Newman's emphasis.

81. Ibid., 346, 349; C. Kingsley, "What, Then, Does Dr. Newman Mean?," 368.

82. "Dr Newman's Religious Autobiography," 785.

83. Virgil, *Aeneid*, 33.

84. Gilley, *Newman and His Age*, 333.

85. Trevor, *Newman: Light in Winter*, 344.

86. "Rev. Charles Kingsley and Dr Newman," 294.

87. Hutton, "Dr Newman's Apology," 655.

88. "Apologia pro Vita Sua," *Times*, 12.

89. Ward, *Life*, 2:31.

90. Svaglic, "Introduction," xliii–xliv.

91. "John Henry Newman," 11, 14–15.

92. "Authority and Free Thought," 311.

93. "Apologia pro Vita Sua," *Christian Remembrancer*, 172–73.

94. "Whately, Newman," 291.

95. "Dr Newman's 'Apologia,' " *Fraser's*, 278.

96. "Whately, Newman," 291.

97. Newman justified his management of the publication of his autobiographical narrative and his inclusion of "Letters of Approbation and Encouragement" in the "Supplemental Matter" of editions from 1865 onward (*Apologia*, ed. Svaglic, 316–25) by appealing to the injustice with which his Catholic status was commonly viewed: "The belief obtains extensively in the country at large, that Catholics, and especially the Priesthood, disavow the mode and form, in which I am accustomed to teach the Catholic faith, as if they were not generally recognized, but something special and peculiar to myself. . . . Such testimonials, then, as now follow from as many as 558 priests . . . scatter to the winds a suspicion, which it is not less painful, I am persuaded, to numbers of those Protestants who entertain it, than it is injurious to me who have to bear it" (319).

98. Chadwick, *Spirit of the Oxford Movement*, 129.

99. Dellamora, *Masculine Desire*, 193.

100. Mosse, *Nationalism and Sexuality*, 23.

101. Hyam, *Empire and Sexuality*, 72.

102. Ibid., 72–73.

CHAPTER TWO

1. Symonds's translation of *The Life of Benvenuto Cellini* was published in 1888. His translation of *The Memoirs of Count Carlo Gozzi* followed in 1890.

In both works, Symonds described the sexual exploits of the autobiographers with what might be characterized as typical Victorian caution and reticence.

2. Symonds, *Letters*, 3:364.

3. "Scribbling" was a term often associated, in a trivializing sense, with female writers. For example, Florence Hardy, the second wife of Thomas Hardy, wrote to a friend in 1914 that her husband "rather dislikes my being a scribbling woman" (Seymour-Smith, *Hardy*, 800).

4. Symonds's motive for approaching Ellis, Wayne Koestenbaum argues, was that he "knew that a medical man could help him evade the injunction that homosexuals must not speak" (*Double Talk*, 46). It would be more accurate to say that Ellis's status would help to legitimize Symonds's discourse on homosexuality. For an excellent discussion of the influence of Greek pederasty on Victorian and modern constructions of homosexual identity, see Halperin, *One Hundred Years of Homosexuality*.

5. Symonds, *Letters*, 3:364.

6. Ibid., 1:446. Symonds's interest in autobiography also appears in a letter he wrote in October 1873 to Dakyns, in praise of John Stuart Mill's posthumously published *Autobiography*: "I am getting a profound impression from Mill. It is as good as a tonic to come so closely into contact with such a pure & high-strung spirit, although his mode of evolution is utterly beyond my experience & only dimly discerned by my imagination" (*Letters*, 2:316). Particularly interesting is Symonds's response to Mill's theory of desire, which Symonds interprets as meaning "that freedom of the will consists in desire (as an independent force)." Symonds counters by asking, "Is not desire itself a circumstance — conditioned, that is, by an inevitable concurrence of predisposing causes, hereditary & other; so that a habit, even if formed by conscious acts of volition, is the product of two necessities, external . . . & internal?" (*Letters*, 2:316-17). In this passage, one can see Symonds working through his own thinking on the origins and causes of his homosexuality, trying to discover the extent to which it was determined by his background and childhood experiences. These are, of course, precisely the questions that his own autobiography explores.

7. Koestenbaum, *Double Talk*, 49. For useful discussions of the legislation used to incriminate Wilde, see F. B. Smith, "Labouchère's Amendment," and Weeks, *Coming Out*, 14-20.

8. Symonds's book came several years after Arnold's and was based on a course of lectures he had given at Clifton College in Bristol; the first series of the *Studies* (1873) was one of Symonds's earliest published works. It was the conclusion of the second series, however, published in 1876, to which Tyrwhitt most strongly objected. The two series were subsequently published as a single volume, under the collective title *Studies of the Greek Poets*.

9. Tyrwhitt, "The Greek Spirit," 557.

10. Ibid., 565.

11. Symonds, *Studies of the Greek Poets*, 570.

12. Symonds, *Memoirs*, 29–30. All further references to this edition will be cited parenthetically in the text.

13. De Man, "Autobiography," 70, 72, 69.

14. Ibid., 81.

15. Koestenbaum, *Double Talk*, 58.

16. Ibid., 57.

17. Ibid., 50.

18. Ibid., 58.

19. See Chapter 3 for an elaboration of the significance of the mask in Wilde's work.

20. Koestenbaum, *Double Talk*, 57.

21. Ibid., 57, 59.

22. This observation is based on my study of the complete manuscript of Symonds's *Memoirs*, held in the London Library.

23. Koestenbaum, *Double Talk*, 59. "Uranian" was Carpenter's word for homosexual, based on the German *Urning* coined by Ulrichs. However, the "Uranians" also referred to a group of poets in the 1880s and 1890s who depicted same-sex desire.

24. Symonds suggested the collaboration on *Sexual Inversion* in a letter to Ellis in 1892, but he did not complete his memoirs until 1893, when he wrote the preface.

25. Koestenbaum, *Double Talk*, 51.

26. Ibid., 60. An example is when he states that "Symonds saw collaboration with Ellis as a method of becoming intimate again with language, of regaining writerly pluck" (61).

27. Ibid., 62.

28. For the fullest account of the evolution of homosexuality as a "stigma," see Plummer, *Sexual Stigma*. For the pathbreaking discussion of homosexuality as an identity that is socially constructed, see McIntosh, "The Homosexual Role." Plummer's collection *The Making of the Modern Homosexual* also contains useful constructionist accounts of homosexual identity.

29. For example, an entry in E. M. Forster's *Commonplace Book* describes Forster's responses to reading the manuscript of the *Memoirs* in the London Library. The entry begins with a summary of the Vaughan episode discussed here (Forster, *Commonplace Book*, 227). My thanks to Joseph Bristow for drawing my attention to this reference.

30. See, for example, Honey, *Tom Brown's Universe*, 169.

31. Symonds had also arrived in Davos in hope of a cure for tuberculosis, and their shared illness was one cause of the friendship that developed between the two writers, who died within a year of each other. McLynn, *Robert Louis Stevenson*, 188–89, 204–5.

32. Stevenson, "Dr Jekyll and Mr Hyde," 81.

33. Symonds, *Letters*, 3:120.

34. Stevenson, "Dr Jekyll and Mr Hyde," 83.

35. Symonds would subsequently lament the fact that, in the eyes of the public and the law, the "depraved debauchee who abuses boys receives the same treatment as the young man who loves a comrade" (Symonds, *A Problem in Modern Ethics*, 15).

36. It is interesting to compare Symonds's description of his reading of Plato with section 14 in case 17 of Symonds and Havelock Ellis's *Sexual Inversion* (1897), included by Grosskurth as an appendix to the *Memoirs*. "It was in his 18th year that an event which A. regards as decisive in his development occurred. He read the *Phaedrus* and *Symposium* of Plato. A new world opened, and he felt that his own nature had been revealed" (Symonds, *Memoirs*, 286). The individual referred to as "A." (the subject of case 17) is, of course, Symonds himself. Yet the subjective detail of the moment is abandoned in the quasi-scientific summary that Symonds provided for his collaboration with Ellis.

37. Augustine, *Confessions*, 177.

38. Ibid., 178.

39. Newman, *Apologia pro Vita Sua*, ed. Svaglic, 110–11. Newman emphasizes the significance of Augustine's words as a culmination of the process of change, which is at once historical and personal: the "long and varied course of ecclesiastical history" mirrors Newman's own religious "development," whereas the destruction of the Via Media prepares the ground for his conversion to a new faith. David J. DeLaura translates Augustine's sentence as follows: "The world judges with assurance that they are not good men who, in whatever part of the world, separate themselves from the rest of the world" (Newman, *Apologia*, ed. DeLaura, 98 n).

40. Dowling, *Language and Decadence*, 164–65.

41. Symonds, *A Problem in Greek Ethics*, 121.

42. Sanders, *Private Lives of Victorian Women*, 100.

43. Grosskurth, "Where Was Rousseau?," 26–38. The very qualities of intimate self-disclosure that characterized Rousseau's *Confessions* made the work an obvious model for Symonds, who had things to say that could not be easily accommodated by the more puritanical approach to autobiography that had become dominant in his native country.

44. Horatio Brown, *John Addington Symonds*, vii, viii.

45. It is unclear which, if any, of Symonds's friends were allowed access to the manuscript of the memoirs during Symonds's lifetime. He refers, in various letters to his close friends, to the fact that he was writing an autobiography, hinting darkly at the reasons why it would never be published. But there is no clear evidence that any of his friends, even those who knew he was homosexual, ever actually read the memoirs in their entirety.

46. Lejeune, *On Autobiography*, 192.

47. Peterson, *Victorian Autobiography*, 2.

48. Although Honey argues that "it is too easy to trace this attitude of what is now popularly known as 'Platonic Love' to the Victorians' study of

ancient Greek culture" (*Tom Brown's Universe*, 188), Symonds's case would suggest that the two were in fact closely connected.

49. An early reference to Conington occurs in a letter of February 1859 from Symonds to his sister Charlotte: "I am in such a hurry that my scrawl can only be a short one, for I am expecting Mr Conington to take tea in my rooms. I see a great deal of him, & like him even better than I did at first. Though pompous rather & conceited (I fancy) a good deal, he is yet very kind; & of course it is an immense advantage for me to see so much of such a man. I suppose you have not any of you read some poems called Ionica: they are making a stir in Oxford, both on account of their true poetry & the curious personal history involved. The author is an Eton Master, & I had all the enigmatical facts expounded to me" (Symonds, *Letters*, 1:178). The juxtaposition of this somewhat ambivalent praise of his tutor and his reference to *Jonica* was not, it will become apparent, coincidental.

50. Honey, *Tom Brown's Universe*, 190. It is ironic that the work that indirectly led to Vaughan's downfall should have been written by another schoolteacher who was disgraced in a homosexual scandal.

51. Unfortunately, this correspondence is not included in Schueller and Peters's three-volume edition of Symonds's *Letters*. In some ways, this correspondence anticipates that between Symonds and Whitman in the 1880s and 1890s, when Symonds would again write a letter "exposing the state of my feelings" in enraptured response to a book of poetry. Whitman's reply, however, was much less forthcoming and affirmative than Johnson's (see Kaplan, *Walt Whitman*, 45–47).

52. A striking example of such an exchange occurs in E. M. Forster's *Maurice*, in which Clive Durham, in an effort to communicate his love for Maurice, asks him to read Plato's *Symposium* during the vacation. Maurice does so, and when they return to Cambridge, Clive assumes that Maurice will "understand—without me saying more" (58).

53. Dowling, *Language and Decadence*, 164.

54. The nationalistic resonance of the last part of this comment can better be understood by juxtaposing it with a passage from Thomas Hughes's *Tom Brown's Schooldays* that describes Doctor Arnold's influence at Rugby School: " 'What a sight it is,' broke in the master, 'the Doctor as a ruler. Perhaps ours is the only little corner of the British Empire which is thoroughly wisely and strongly ruled just now' " (272). The headmaster in both instances is a surrogate for a national, or imperial, leader.

55. I have no evidence to suggest that Conington was under suspicion at Oxford at the time of being a homosexual. The fates of Vaughan and Johnson, however, reveal how suddenly an apparently secure position in the elite educational establishment could be undermined by sexual scandal. In the case of Symonds, such a scandal did indeed erupt shortly afterward, when his involvement in the Vaughan affair was—or appeared to be—at an end.

56. Symonds left instructions to omit these three sentences from the original manuscript.

57. The emergence of a "dual self" in the context of—arguably as the result of—a secret is a feature of other autobiographies of the period. Edmund Gosse, for instance, writes in *Father and Son* of the emergence of his "other self" as a result of his father's failure to discover a minor act of vandalism: "I had found a companion and a confidant in myself. There was a secret in this world and it belonged to me and to a somebody who lived in the same body with me. There were two of us, and we could talk with one another. It is difficult to define impressions so rudimentary, but it is certain that it was in this dual form that the sense of my individuality now suddenly descended upon me" (35).

58. Pretor eventually became a classical tutor at St. Catherine's College, Cambridge, and a friend of Thomas Hardy and his first wife, Emma. Ironically, Hardy was also friendly toward Symonds, "whom he respected as an emancipated spirit" (Seymour-Smith, *Hardy*, 450). Seymour-Smith speculates about how much Hardy knew of the schoolboy involvement of his two friends: "A 'sensational scandal' in his schooldays . . . is exactly what he [Pretor] *had not* been involved in: the whole matter had been hushed up, and the only threat to the cover-up had been Pretor himself, with his 'incredible levity and imprudence.' If Tom [Hardy] did know about it, then he would have heard if from that connoisseur of such matters, [Edmund] Gosse. How Pretor would have reacted, had Tom brought up the subject of his friend the classicist John Addington Symonds, is quite a question. Pretor and he had not seen each other since 1859. They would have had a lot to talk about" (560).

59. One of the ironies of a text that is structured around ironies and coincidences is that Symonds should have been staying with Rutson during this crisis. It was Rutson, of course, to whom Symonds had written of his desire to author his "confessions." A close friend of Symonds, Rutson eventually asked for his sister's hand in marriage. When his proposal was rejected by Dr. Symonds on the grounds of hereditary insanity in his family, Rutson declared that he had actually been in love with Catherine North (by this time Symonds's wife) but had not pursued her for Symonds's sake. His insistence on holding long arguments on the subject in Hyde Park during the midwinter precipitated the collapse of Symonds's left lung, eventually resulting in Symonds's permanent departure from England.

60. This embarrassing scandal in academe undoubtedly contributed to his desire to win the post of professor of poetry, for which he was in competition with Walter Pater, F. T. Palgrave, and J. C. Shairp (who eventually won it). As Dellamora writes of the Shorting affair, "Against this background of early defeat, one may better understand the obsessive interest that he took in the election for Professor of Poetry in 1877" (*Masculine Desire*, 160).

61. Horatio Brown, *John Addington Symonds*, 152.

62. In *A Problem in Greek Ethics*, Symonds bitterly lamented the prevalence of blackmail as a direct consequence of the lack of social tolerance of male homosexuality.

63. A diary entry of 18 June 1869, however, finds Symonds complaining that "I am not even allowed to exercise my paedagogic faculty for his [Norman's] good in any definite way" (*Memoirs*, 207).

64. Symonds, *Letters*, 1:829. With this phrase, Symonds referred to the homosexual poem "John Mordan" that was named after a London newspaper vendor who had caught his eye.

65. The first of these poems was inspired by a performance of Mozart's *The Marriage of Figaro* in 1866. The second is described by Symonds—innocuously enough—as the story of a "Greek boy who responds to his lover and lives a noble life with him" (195). Phyllis Grosskurth comments that "these poems seem to have disappeared" (Symonds, *Memoirs*, 307 n. 6).

66. Koestenbaum, *Double Talk*, 48.

67. Symonds, *Letters*, 3:691.

68. Ibid., 2:34.

69. Ibid., 47.

70. Ibid., 118.

71. We find his initial enthrallment with Moor's charms and his desire to spend time alone with him first alternating with and then gradually giving way to disillusionment and even disgust. As early as April 1869, Symonds began to retract his previous words of affection, asking Moor's apology for "the strong language of attachment I have used" (*Letters*, 2:57). Yet one month later he was writing ecstatically to Dakyns of a week he and Moor had spent together in London, identifying his relationship with Moor as the realization of his poetic fantasy: "He had never been in London before. We saw sights & went to operas & plays. His sister was in town & we 3 were together twice. I do not feel up to writing about these things. But I am satisfied. I think that my poems were not all untrue to life, not all too grob [coarse], but that Ichabod [the hero of one of his homosexual poems, later changed to Gabriel] at least was fact" (65). Symonds was profoundly reassured to find his poetic ideal borne out by "real life" in a way that had not been hitherto possible. Increasingly, however, Moor becomes a source of anxiety and distress rather than inspiration and pleasure for Symonds, who begins to suspect that his love is unrequited. He laments in a letter to Dakyns that "my novelty has worn off; & there are little signs wh[ich]—after due allowance for suspiciousness & over caution—make me pretty nearly certain that he has found me not so delightful as he once thought I might prove" (72). Moor's novelty wears off for Symonds as well: "Norman lives an odd fungoid life on some decaying branch of my Soul" (74), he wrote to Dakyns in May 1869. A visit they made together to Europe apparently proved far less successful than their liaison in London, and Symonds concluded a letter to Dakyns on 16 August 1869 with

words that effectively signaled the end of his obsession: "Norman has not in him the tracts of undiscovered country I imagined. I have done him no good. I ought to have remained selfinvolved & not to have gone out toward this object" (78–79).

72. This letter is transcribed by Grosskurth in an appendix to her edition of the *Memoirs* (295–97).

73. The *OED* defines the verb "spoon" as "to make love, esp. in a sentimental or silly fashion."

74. Symonds, *Letters*, 3:705.

75. Ibid., 642.

76. Ibid., 642–43.

77. Horatio Brown, *John Addington Symonds*, x–xi.

78. Seymour-Smith, *Hardy*, 834.

79. Koestenbaum, *Double Talk*, 63.

80. Scholars were allowed, with special permission, to study the manuscript from the 1950s on, but not to quote from it. Hence those scholars who wished to use the memoirs as a source, such as Phyllis Grosskurth, whose biography of Symonds, *The Woeful Victorian*, appeared in 1964, were restricted to Brown's biography for their quotations.

81. The manuscript of the *Memoirs* was bequeathed to the London Library enclosed in what Brown described as "a green card-board box, tied with strings, measuring at most 6 inches by 12 inches by 18 inches and labelled 'J. A. Symonds's Papers' " (H. Brown, cited in Grosskurth, "Foreword," 10).

82. Unfortunately, Grosskurth omits "roughly one fifth of the text—not to the detriment of the original, I believe. The omitted passages are confined mainly to Symonds's execrable poetry and to self-conscious nature descriptions quoted from his own letters" (Symonds, *Memoirs*, 11). Having studied the original manuscript in the London Library, I must disagree with Grosskurth's verdict. The poetry and travel writing she omits are, despite their occasional verbosity, extremely revealing of Symonds's personality and are also of considerable historical interest. Grosskurth has done much to bring the work of Symonds to public attention—both with her edition of the *Memoirs* and her earlier biography of Symonds, *The Woeful Victorian*. Yet the latter work also demonstrates a tendency to pathologize its subject's homosexuality by referring to it throughout as "the problem." A truly complete edition of the *Memoirs* and a new biography of Symonds are both overdue.

CHAPTER THREE

1. For recent examples of criticism of these writings that focuses on Wilde's sexuality, see Cohen, "Writing Gone Wilde" and *Talk on the Wilde Side*; Craft, "Alias Bunbury"; Dellamora, *Masculine Desire*, esp. chap. 10; Dollimore, "Different Desires"; Edelman, *Homographesis*, chap. 1; and Koestenbaum,

"Wilde's Hard Labor." Though I group this critical work together here, it is part of my argument that each critic adopts a different approach to "deciphering" the textual encodings of Wilde's sexuality, some of which are significantly more successful than others.

2. In his important essay on "Dorianism," for example, Dellamora reads *The Picture of Dorian Gray* in the context of the nineteenth-century aesthetic project of associating same-sex desire with what he terms "the salvation of the state." Examining the role of Walter Pater, Wilde's mentor at Oxford, in this project of cultural legitimation, Dellamora shows how Wilde's novel subverts many of the assumptions of his peers and "dissociates masculine desire and the art it prompts from hope for social transformation" (*Apocalyptic Overtures*, 63, 59).

3. Dollimore, *Sexual Dissidence*, 11.

4. Ellmann, *Oscar Wilde*, 589.

5. Dollimore, *Sexual Dissidence*, 14.

6. For my use of metaphor and metonymy in the context of sexual desire and identity, I am indebted to Lee Edelman, whose essay "Homographesis" I discuss at greater length below.

7. See Cohen, *Talk on the Wilde Side*, esp. chap. 5, and Edelman, *Homographesis*, chap. 1.

8. De Man, "Autobiography," 69. Richard Dellamora reminds us that "the leap from expertise about textual truth to knowledge of the consciousness of the author is an assumption basic to the discipline of romantic philology, from which modern textual scholarship derives" ("Textual Politics," 156).

9. De Man, "Wordsworth," 91, 92. Lee Edelman, in a discussion of the specific homosexual significance of de Man's conceptualizing of the "face," writes that " 'the homosexual' enters historical view *as a 'homosexual'* only through a rhetorical operation that essentializes as a metaphoric designation, a totalized identity, what had been understood before this tropological shift as a contingent aspect of self. The 'homosexual,' that is, acquires a 'face' only through the rhetorical redistribution of 'meanings' at a specific moment in the history of the West" (*Homographesis*, 196; Edelman's emphasis).

10. Wilde, *The Picture of Dorian Gray*, 34, 33.

11. Wilde, *The Artist as Critic*, 342.

12. Ibid., 341. Gilbert's criticism of biographers is characteristically outspoken: "They are the pest of the age, nothing more and nothing less. Every great man nowadays has his disciples, and it is always Judas who writes the biography" (342).

13. Wilde, *The Picture of Dorian Gray*, 24.

14. Ibid., 27.

15. White, *Uses of Obscurity*, 8.

16. *Letters of Oscar Wilde*, 352.

17. Ed Cohen's book is especially illuminating in this context, showing how the visual images of Wilde popularized during the trials were grotesque

caricatures, rather than realistic (or photographic) representations of his appearance. See *Talk on the Wilde Side*, esp. 140–41.

18. Hyde, *Trials of Oscar Wilde*, 110, 111.

19. Ibid., 196.

20. Foucault, *Introduction*, 43.

21. Wilde, *The Picture of Dorian Gray*, 182–83. What emerges from this juxtaposition of writings on the ineluctable visibility—the involuntary confession—of the "secret," oddly, is a certain asymmetry between them: Foucault does not state what features, exactly, are "written immodestly" on the homosexual's "face and body," only that this somatic legibility constituted a form of homosexual "confession." Basil Hallward, by contrast, goes into considerably more detail about the specific symptoms "written" on the face of the "sinner"—the lines of his mouth, the droop of his eyelids, and so forth—but is subsequently vague about the specific origin of those symptoms. Although the physical traces of "sin" are vividly described, the activity they indicate is left unspecified. What this suggests is that the evacuation of a specific desire, in one case, and the erasure of specific signs of that desire, in the other, means that neither the "face" described by Foucault nor that invoked by Hallward/Wilde can be "read" as indicative of homosexuality. Only if one were to conflate the two accounts might one extrapolate Hallward's "sin" as a specifically (homo)sexual one. But this, it hardly needs pointing out, is an anachronistic photofit rather than a textual representation of homosexual desire. The recognizable "face" of the homosexual, in other words, is derived from the totalizing composite of discrete textual sources.

22. Edelman, *Homographesis*, 9–10.

23. Ibid., 10.

24. Ibid., 197.

25. For a telling critique of this theoretical crux, see Dellamora, "Textual Politics."

26. Edelman, *Homographesis*, 15.

27. Wilde, *The Picture of Dorian Gray*, 48.

28. Edelman, *Homographesis*, 17.

29. Wilde, *The Picture of Dorian Gray*, 48–49; emphasis added. Compare Edelman, *Homographesis*, 15.

30. De Man, "Autobiography," 70. For de Man, "This specular structure is interiorized in a text in which the author declares himself the subject of his own understanding" (70), hence its autobiographical significance.

31. Wilde, *The Picture of Dorian Gray*, 187.

32. Ibid., 27.

33. *Letters of Oscar Wilde*, 266.

34. Edelman, *Homographesis*, 18.

35. Carson, cited in ibid., 17.

36. Ibid., 11. The phrase "For Oscar Wilde, posing as a somdomite [*sic*]" was written by Queensberry on a card left for Wilde at his club.

37. Cohen, *Talk on the Wilde Side*, 127.

38. Ibid., 143.

39. Craft, "Alias Bunbury," 41.

40. On this occasion Queensberry was forestalled by the sharp thinking of Wilde, George Alexander (actor-manager of the St. James's Theatre), and the business manager of the St. James's, whose combined efforts managed to keep him out of the theater (Ellmann, *Oscar Wilde*, 430).

41. The only strong dissenting voice was that of Shaw, who, having greatly admired *An Ideal Husband*, found that *Earnest* failed to move him. See Beckson, *Oscar Wilde: The Critical Heritage*. Wilde's friend Max Beerbohm, by contrast, pronounced the play "a masterpiece" (Ellmann, *Oscar Wilde*, 430).

42. Craft, "Alias Bunbury," 20.

43. Ellmann, *Oscar Wilde*, 430.

44. The nearest approach to an infringement of this rule occurs in a key episode that was deleted from the produced and subsequently published three-act version of the play. In the so-called Gribsby episode from the original four-act version of *Earnest*, a debt collector arrives to arrest "Ernest Worthing" for debt, and Jack is on the point of forcing Algy—who has taken on the role of Ernest—into prison for his own unpaid bills.

45. Wilde, *The Importance of Being Earnest*, 256.

46. Ibid., 258.

47. Hyde, *Trials of Oscar Wilde*, 149.

48. Wilde, *The Importance of Being Earnest*, 258.

49. I am indebted to Craft's insightful reading of the sexual significance of the cigarette case in *Earnest* and the crucial recurrence of this object during Wilde's trials ("Alias Bunbury," 29–30). Aside from its status as "the most durable material trace of Wilde's illegal sexual practice" (29), the cigarette case, Craft argues, is not only an index of the class crossing of Wilde's sexual relations—the "gift" of the silver case clearly inscribing Wilde's social and economic superiority to his sexual partners—but also a reminder of "the orality that was both Wilde's sexual preference and *Earnest*'s primary trope of displacement" (30). Though I disagree with Craft's precise identification of orality as a form of sexual displacement in the play, his tracing of the "prop" through its various discursive appearances is exemplary. The "secret" of Bunburyism that Algy derives from the inscription on the case is read by Craft as, among other things, a code for sodomy—the desire to "bury in the bun." This ascription of a specific sexual meaning to the "secret" of the play, however, does not affect my argument about the key difference between the scene in the play and the scene in court. The crucial difference is one of *context*: the legal system is using the evidence of the cigarette case to isolate and incriminate Wilde as an aberrant and corrupt sexual being; Algy is using it to identify a fellow Bunburyist as a member of a select, clandestine group to which he himself belongs. Whether "Bunburyism" is a signifier for homosexuality or for something else is less important than the fact that Algy *shares*

Jack's "secret" and is in this sense a coconspirator. That Algy requests an "improbable" explanation indicates that no explanation is in fact necessary, for the key instance of recognition has already occurred.

50. Ellmann, *Oscar Wilde*, 431.

51. Cited in Pearson, *Life of Oscar Wilde*, 257. Ellmann recounts the anecdote slightly differently (though citing the same source): "Wilde came to a rehearsal and said, 'Yes, it is quite a good play. I remember I wrote one very like it myself, but it was even more brilliant than this' " (*Oscar Wilde*, 430).

52. The original version can be reconstructed from the original manuscript, acts 1 and 2 of which are in the New York Public Library and acts 3 and 4 of which are in the British Library. Three editions of the four-act version have also been published: one by the New York Public Library in 1956 (which is the edition cited in this chapter), edited by Sarah Dickson; a second one in 1957 by Methuen, under the editorship of Vyvyan Holland, Wilde's son; and a 1987 edition that claims to be the "definitive" one, published by Vanguard Press, New York, and edited by Ruth Berggren.

53. I am indebted to Glavin, who carefully mapped the variants between the three- and four-act versions, arguing that the latter is closer to what Wilde intended. Glavin points out that because the play was further revised by Wilde prior to its publication by Leonard Smithers in 1899, the version that is used today for performances and texts is neither the play Wilde originally wrote nor the one Alexander produced but something significantly different from either. According to Glavin, Wilde's original version vindicates Jack's distrust of disguise and deception, indicating his determination to renounce his fictional persona, whereas Algy's insistence on the necessity of "Bunburying" is ultimately shown to be futile and self-defeating. In Alexander's three-act version, the roles are reversed, with Algy coming off as a largely successful trickster, whereas Jack is a paternal and impotent Victorian prude. Lady Bracknell, who dominates the third act of Alexander's version, is forced to concede to Jack's vision of community in Wilde's four-act play. See Glavin, "Deadly Earnest," 13–24.

54. *Letters of Oscar Wilde*, 452. All further references to this edition of the letter known as *De Profundis* will be cited parenthetically in the text.

55. Ibid., 263.

56. Raby, *Wilde*, 121.

57. Barber, *Shakespeare's Festive Comedy*, 37.

58. Wilde, *The Importance of Being Earnest in Four Acts*, 77.

59. Ibid., 79.

60. Ellmann, *Oscar Wilde*, 422.

61. Compare Craft, "Alias Bunbury," 43 n.

62. As Andrew Miller writes of another literary instance of muffin eating, this one from Thackeray, "Everyone continues to want muffins in one form or another, though the grease butters their chins. The ability to consume, whether comestibles or more lasting commodities, is without limit and,

finally, repellant; when objects of use enter into a system of exchange, need is lost amid the pulsations of desire" (Miller, *Novels behind Glass*, 25). Miller's is among the best of more recent accounts of the power of commodities in Victorian culture to shape subjectivity, tracing the associations of extravagant consumption with economic ruin and death. See especially the introduction and chap. 1.

63. Craft, "Alias Bunbury," 28.

64. Ellmann, *Oscar Wilde*, 422.

65. For example, Craft argues that Algy's reference to muffins and butter is a "fastidious allusion to Wilde's sexual practice" by which "Wilde adopts a polite decorum (no danger to Algy's cuffs) in order to display and displace a desire to bury in the bun" ("Alias Bunbury," 29). How this implicitly sodomitical desire relates to Wilde's preference for oral sex is not fully explained by Craft.

66. Ibid., 32.

67. Raby, "Making of *The Importance of Being Earnest*," 13.

68. In this context, it is worth remembering that *Salomé*, Wilde's most explicitly perverse and erotic play, was banned by the Lord Chamberlain before it could be performed in London, and was not produced in England until years after Wilde's death.

69. Wilde, *The Importance of Being Earnest in Four Acts*, 35–36.

70. Wilde, *The Picture of Dorian Gray*, 26.

71. Wilde, *The Importance of Being Earnest*, 263.

72. For an interesting and influential account of Wilde's practice of inversion—its transgressive purpose and limitations—see Dollimore, "Different Desires," esp. 31–33.

73. Wilde, *The Importance of Being Earnest*, 243, 244.

74. Hyde traces the history of the letter in terms of the rivalry between Ross and Douglas for the affection of Wilde during his lifetime and for the association with his name after his death. In this light, Ross's attempt to "appropriate" Douglas's letter for himself—both by retaining the original manuscript and by implying that he had been the intended recipient—becomes meaningful as another instance of Ross's loyalty to and desire for Wilde being displaced onto the letter itself. See Hyde, "Riddle of *De Profundis*," esp. 111–19.

75. In 1909, Ross deposited the manuscript with the British Library, with a fifty-year embargo on the publication of its full contents. The full text of the letter might have remained a closely guarded secret were it not for a libel suit issued by Douglas against Arthur Ransome in 1912. Ransome, a friend of Ross's, had been allowed access to one of the typescripts of the letter while writing his critical study of Wilde, which was the first full-length study to be published in English. In his book Ransome referred to Wilde's prison letter, stating that it contained a bitter attack on Douglas that had not been published in the 1905 edition. Douglas, claiming he had no knowledge of a letter written to him by Wilde from Reading Gaol, sued Ransome for libel, and the

manuscript of the letter was retrieved from the British Library to be used as evidence in the court case. Douglas not only lost the case but also became a notorious figure when previously unpublished extracts from the letter, which had been read out in court, were published in the *Times* as part of its report from the trial. Much of the public animus that had been directed at Wilde was now deflected to Douglas, where it has remained.

76. Beckson, *Oscar Wilde: The Critical Heritage*, 257–58.

77. Shaw, cited in ibid., 244.

78. Lucas, cited in ibid., 245; Stead, cited in ibid., 242.

79. Street, cited in ibid., 253.

80. Wilde, *The Artist as Critic*, 305.

81. Dollimore, "Different Desires," 33–34.

82. Gagnier, *Idylls of the Marketplace*, 180. It should be noted that Gagnier is referring to "audience" in the sense of a "market" for his work, as might be expected in a book that focuses on Wilde's commodification as an artist throughout his career. I am using the "audience" somewhat differently, to denote an imaginary construct, a (perhaps fictional) sense of a reader, in the present or the future, that would shape the address and the voice of the speaker. Though Douglas was the explicit addressee of the letter, it seems probable that Wilde was imagining other readers for his work.

83. I am uncomfortable with Wayne Koestenbaum's hasty move "to generalize from Bosie's position to the stance of post-Wilde gay readers," not because I believe that Wilde attempts to exclude other readers, but because the specific series of displacements I trace depends on his construction of "Bosie" as his alter ego. Hence "Bosie's position" is not simply that of the reader but also the central preoccupation of the letter as an autobiographical narrative. See Koestenbaum, "Wilde's Hard Labor," 178.

84. Wordsworth, *Prelude* (1805–6), 475, lines 186–87, 190–94. The 1971 edition contains both the 1805–6 and 1850 versions of *The Prelude*. In the 1850 version of the poem, Wordsworth modifies the tone slightly by omitting the line containing "greedy in the chase."

85. Gill, *Wordsworth*, 133–34.

86. Wilde, *The Importance of Being Earnest in Four Acts*, 77.

87. Wilde's emphasis. Wordsworth had written his sonnet on his return to England following a brief visit to his former mistress, Annette Vallon, and their illegitimate daughter, Caroline, in Paris. On returning to England, as he wrote in a note to the poem, "I could not but be struck, as here described, with the vanity and parade of our own country, especially in great towns and cities, as contrasted with the quiet, and I may say the desolation, that the revolution had produced in France" (Gill, *Wordsworth*, 710). In the sonnet, Wordsworth attacks the "rapine, avarice, expence" of his countrymen, contrasting it with the "plain living and high thinking" of the past generations (ibid., 285). In another sonnet written in the same period, Wordsworth identifies these latter, homely virtues with Milton.

88. Dollimore, "Different Desires," 28, 31.

89. Ibid., 40 n. 59. I have quoted Dollimore at length here because his argument represents, in its most theoretically incisive form, the common view that Wilde's prison letter is a form of (culturally enforced) self-betrayal, not a development (and, I would argue, the culmination) of his relentless assault on the integrity of the confessional subject.

90. Jerome Buckley argues that Wilde "had his own special insights, his 'spots of time,' and he even borrowed directly from Wordsworth when he discussed the problem of sustaining such vision. . . . But he dreaded revealing the long dull stretches of commonplace routine, the emptiness of the 'ordinary' Wordsworthian perception" ("Towards Early-Modern Autobiography," 4–5). Buckley seems to me incorrect in this final assertion; there are, in the prison letter, numerous examples of what Wordsworth describes, in the "Spots of Time" passage from the *Prelude*, as an "ordinary sight" being transformed by the imagination into "visionary dreariness" (254–56). See, for example, the description in the prison letter of the "interminable visits paid by me to the solicitor Humphreys in your company, when in the ghastly glare of a bleak room you and I would sit with serious faces telling serious lies to a bald man" (493). The chief instance of this stylistic feature, discussed later in the chapter, is Wilde's account of his humiliation on the platform of Clapham Junction.

91. Gagnier, "*De Profundis* as *Epistola*," 335. Gagnier's "materialist reading" of Wilde's letter succeeds in reminding us of the actual conditions of his imprisonment, and exploring their effect on the composition of his letter. More specifically, Gagnier argues that Wilde's letter "was an indirect response to the uselessness of prison labor" (338).

92. Ibid., 342.

93. Ibid., 345.

94. Hence, points in the narrative that Gagnier describes as "hopelessly confused," such as Wilde's statement that "I blame myself for the entire ethical degradation I allowed you to bring on me" (429), become legible as part of Wilde's subversion of the confessional mode. Gagnier finds in this sentence a "crazy syntactical subordination of subject and object" ("*De Profundis* as *Epistola*," 342), but the subordination is really far from crazy. Wilde invokes the conventional "mea culpa" of confessional discourse, only immediately to subvert it by displacing the cause of his "ethical degradation" onto Bosie himself. If Wilde suggests that his fatal flaw was his passivity—a failing syntactically embodied in this sentence—he makes of this passivity a redemptive, Christlike virtue, a humility that prevents him from defending himself against the villainy of others. Gagnier has explored at greater length Wilde's brilliant manipulation of the media and other organs of publicity to promote his image, along with the revengeful backlash against him of the same machinery of publicity during his trials. My argument—related, but distinct—is that Bosie is used by Wilde to represent the rampant consumerism which he, in his

newly discovered spiritual mask, wishes to repudiate. See also Gagnier's *Idylls of the Marketplace*, 19–47, 179–95.

95. Shaw, " 'To Tell the Truth of Sex,' " 95–96.

96. Cited in Buckley, "Towards Early-Modern Autobiography," 5.

97. Compare the attack on Wilde after his conviction, cited by Dollimore, for having "tried to subvert the 'wholesome, manly, simple ideals of English life.' " As Dollimore points out, from this viewpoint "sexual deviation is symptomatic of a much wider cultural deterioration and/or subversion" ("Different Desires," 34).

98. Buckley, "Towards Early-Modern Autobiography," 5.

99. De Man, "Autobiography," 75–76.

100. Koestenbaum, "Wilde's Hard Labor," 179.

101. Gagnier, "*De Profundis* as *Epistola*," 342.

102. According to the *OED*, the rhetorical meaning of an "apostrophe" is "a figure of speech, by which a speaker or writer suddenly stops in his discourse, and turns to address pointedly some person or thing, either present or absent." This, of course, is the gesture Wilde performs in his letter to Douglas: he turns away from the audience with which he had established a relationship as an author and playwright, to address the single reader whose physical absence and failure of response had caused him so much anguish.

103. De Man, "Autobiography," 70.

104. Ibid., 72.

105. The suspicion that the absence of Douglas from the trials was part of a conspiracy to protect a member of the aristocracy was widespread even at the time. Douglas responded to accusations that he was a coward not to appear in court by writing a letter claiming that "Mr Wilde's own counsel absolutely declined to call me as a witness, fearing the harm I might do him in cross-examination, so that had I been called as a witness at all, it would have only been under a subpoena from the prosecution" (*Letters of Oscar Wilde*, 450 n). On the final day of the trial, the foreman of the jury asked whether a warrant had ever been issued for the arrest of Douglas. On being answered in the negative, the foreman pointed out that "if we are to consider these letters as evidence of guilt . . . it applies as much to Lord Alfred Douglas as to the defendant." This comment prompted a remarkable (though probably unintentional) play on words by Justice Wills: "There is a natural disposition to ask, 'Why should this man stand in the dock and not Lord Alfred Douglas?' But the supposition that Lord Alfred Douglas will be spared because he is Lord Alfred Douglas is one of the *wildest injustice*" (498–99 n; emphasis added).

106. Interestingly, Wilde wrote in his preface to *The Picture of Dorian Gray* that "the nineteenth-century dislike of Realism is the rage of Caliban seeing his own face in a glass" (21).

107. Koestenbaum, "Wilde's Hard Labor," 178.

108. Does Wilde imagine himself here as the victim of what Lady Brack-

nell describes as a "revolutionary outrage"? Certainly, the image of being beheaded might conjure up "the worst excesses of the French Revolution" (Wilde, *The Importance of Being Earnest*, 268). And, of course, the "execution" occurs at the point where Wilde's secret life, like that of Algy's Bunbury, has just been "exploded."

109. Ibid., 268.

110. De Man, "Autobiography," 74.

111. Wilde would publish "The Ballad of Reading Gaol," his other major work of prison literature, under the "name" of this very "letter," C.3.3, which is his cell number at Reading.

CHAPTER FOUR

1. Carpenter, *Sex*, ed. Greig, 297 n.

2. Though Dollimore does not discuss him in his book *Sexual Dissidence*, Carpenter represents a clear example of one who integrated a transgressive sexuality into his lifestyle and combined it with a specifically political agenda. Hence, the political implications of sexual transgression contained in Dollimore's thesis are certainly realized by Carpenter — perhaps more so than by the other writers I discuss in this book.

3. Carpenter, *My Days and Dreams*, 71. Subsequent references to this edition will be cited parenthetically in the text.

4. See Rowbotham and Weeks, *Socialism and the New Life*, and Weeks, *Coming Out*.

5. See Brown, *Edward Carpenter*.

6. Sedgwick, *Between Men*, 201–17.

7. In addition to the drafts, notes, and fragments contained in the Carpenter Collection, there are versions of the entire manuscript in the collection of the John Rylands Library, University of Manchester, England.

8. Dellamora, *Apocalyptic Overtures*, 44.

9. Carpenter, *Love's Coming-of-Age*, 140.

10. Ibid., 132–33.

11. Ibid., 134.

12. Ibid., 133, 135.

13. Ibid., 129, 124, 123.

14. Ibid., 129.

15. Ibid., 126.

16. Carpenter, *Sex*, 289; emphasis added.

17. Ibid.

18. Thiele, "Coming-of-Age," 106.

19. Carpenter, *Love's Coming-of-Age*, 7.

20. Carpenter, *Sex*, 290.

21. Ibid.

22. Ibid.

23. The best account of Whitman's reception by English gay readers — specifically, Symonds and Carpenter — is that of Sedgwick, to whom I am grateful for having helped to bring renewed critical attention to Carpenter (Sedgwick, *Between Men*, 201–17). Both Symonds and Carpenter published early studies of Whitman (Carpenter's, entitled *Days with Walt Whitman*, appeared in 1906) that were influential in bringing attention in England to his poetry and philosophy.

24. It is interesting, with respect to the continuation and exploration of Carpenter's ideas in the work of E. M. Forster, to note Forster's early appreciation of Whitman. His notebook journal for 16 June 1908 — the year that saw the publication of *A Room with a View* and the earliest ideas for *Howards End* — offers the following response: "I opened Walt Whitman for a quotation, & he started speaking to me. That the unseen is justified by the seen: which in its turn becomes unseen and is justified by the other. — He is not a book but an acquaintance, and if I may believe him, he's more. Others whose work attracts me remain memories, more or less vivid: he as something objective, convincing me that he knows me personally" (Forster Archive, King's College, Cambridge). The literary influence of Whitman on Forster is supported by the fact that the title of Forster's most famous novel, *A Passage to India*, was taken from a poem of the same name by Whitman.

25. Hynes, *The Edwardian Turn of Mind*, 263.

26. Symonds, *Letters*, 3:808.

27. I am indebted to Richard Dellamora, who has carefully explored the subtext of same-sex desire at work in much Victorian writing about aesthetics, in particular, Greek art. See his *Masculine Desire* and *Apocalyptic Overtures* (esp. chap. 2, "Dorianism," 43–64).

28. The transforming influence of Europe experienced by the provincial Cambridge don again anticipates the work of Forster. In Forster's novels — especially *Where Angels Fear to Tread* and *A Room with a View* — Italy represents all that is passionate, liberating, erotically stimulating, and opposed to restricted suburban life in England. Trips to Italy for Forster's protagonists are at once liberating and dangerous — they shatter values, alter perceptions, and make a return to the "normal" way of life unthinkable. Here, as elsewhere, Forster's novels dramatize and fictionalize the ideas of Carpenter.

29. Koestenbaum, *Double Talk*, 43.

30. The English disciples of Whitman typically sought a more explicit affirmation of their desire than Whitman wished to provide. Though Whitman's poetry was inspirational for both Symonds and Carpenter, the American poet was cryptic in his private utterances. Few critics today would deny that Whitman's verse contains, at the very least, a homoerotic subtext, but it helps us to understand the predicament of Symonds and Carpenter when we remember that Whitman self-protectively described such sexual interpre-

tations of his poetry as "undreamed & unrecked possibility of morbid infer-ences—wh[ich] are disavowed by me & seem damnable" (Whitman, quoted in Symonds, *Letters*, 3:818). Symonds went on in this letter to Carpenter to quote Whitman's claim that "though unmarried I have had six children," about which Symonds shrewdly commented, "It struck me when I first read this p.s. that W.W. wanted to obviate 'damnable inferences' about himself by asserting his paternity" (819).

31. Carpenter describes his cohabitation with Albert Fernehough and Charles Fox, two working-class men from the Sheffield area, as providing the needed stimulus for his literary creativity, as the change of lifestyle "seemed to liberate the pent-up emotionality of years. . . . All the feelings which had sought, in suffering and in distress, their stifled expression within me during the last seven or eight years, gathered themselves together to a new and more joyous utterance" (*My Days and Dreams*, 105).

32. Carpenter, *Towards Democracy*, 18.

33. Ibid., 19–20.

34. Ibid., 34, 38.

35. Ibid., 39.

36. Ibid., 67–68.

37. Ibid., 69, 73.

38. Ibid., 94.

39. Ellis, cited in Tsuzuki, *Edward Carpenter*, 61.

40. Havelock Ellis to Edward Carpenter, 1885, Carpenter Collection, MSS 356-2.

41. Rowbotham and Weeks, *Socialism and the New Life*, 94.

42. Thiele, "Coming-of-Age," 109, 108.

43. Carpenter, "Note on *Towards Democracy*," 518.

44. Ibid., 518, 519.

45. Ibid., 517, 518.

46. Ibid., 518.

47. The next few years were spent settling into his new home at Millthorpe, but Carpenter nonetheless undertook a series of lecturing engagements on socialist topics, leading to the publication of two collections of essays based on his political lectures: *England's Ideal* (1887) and *Civilization: Its Cause and Cure* (1889).

48. The illustration appears opposite page 131 of Carpenter's autobiogra-phy. The only other Sheffield friends of Carpenter whose portraits appear in *My Days and Dreams* are George Merrill, his longtime lover, and Albert Fernehough (with whom Carpenter resided at Bradway).

49. Carpenter's correspondence has not yet been published in any com-plete edition. I am drawing on my study of original manuscripts held in the Carpenter Collection at the Sheffield City Archives, Sheffield, England.

50. Hukin to Carpenter, 8 July 1886, Carpenter Collection, MSS 362-1.

51. Hukin to Carpenter, 28 October 1886, Carpenter Collection, MSS 362-5.

52. Hukin to Carpenter, 21 November 1887, Carpenter Collection, MSS 362-16.

53. Hukin to Carpenter, 11 July 1890, Carpenter Collection, MSS 362-35.

54. Tsuzuki, *Edward Carpenter*, 15. For a fuller account of the Socialist revival of the 1880s and 1890s, including Carpenter's role in the movement, see Thompson, *William Morris*.

55. G. B. Shaw to Louis Wilkinson, letter of 20 December 1909, cited in Tsuzuki, *Edward Carpenter*, 143.

56. Rowbotham and Weeks, *Socialism and the New Life*, 116.

57. It is evident, in hindsight, that it was possible to write on the subject of homosexuality in this period without it being assumed that the writer was himself homosexual—providing the subject was treated in a clearly "objective" (that is, scientific, historical, analytical, and so forth) manner. As with Symonds's writings on inversion that led to the *Memoirs*, the transition from historical or scientific studies to a homosexual autobiography would have seemed a dangerous leap that would leave the author vulnerable to public attack.

58. Hukin died in March 1917, a year after the publication of *My Days and Dreams*. Carpenter received a letter of condolence from E. M. Forster in April: "Dearest Edward, I was about to write to you when your letter of April 2nd arrived. I saw GEH[ukin] when I was last at Milthorpe [*sic*]—from the photograph it must have been he. He was walking out of the house just as I came in. We did not speak. I am very glad you cared to tell me such a thing. I know what he is to you both. I am very very sorry." Forster Archive, King's College, Cambridge.

59. My account of the O'Brien episode is based on the correspondence and papers in the Carpenter Collection, MSS 362-98-99, 361-51; on the version given by Rowbotham and Weeks, *Socialism and the New Life*, 88-91; and on the account by Tsuzuki in *Edward Carpenter*, 145.

60. M. D. O'Brien, "Usefulness of Competition," Carpenter Collection, MSS 362-98.

61. Rowbotham and Weeks, *Socialism and the New Life*, 88.

62. The title of O'Brien's pamphlet echoed Carpenter's first published work on homosexuality, *Homogenic Love*. According to his biographer, "A second edition of O'Brien's *Infamy* pamphlet came out, containing quotations from Carpenter's original *Homogenic Love*. Carpenter wrote to [Bruce] Glasier, now editor of the *Labour Leader*, asking him to publish in his paper a brief notice to encourage the readers to read his own book. Glasier received O'Brien's pamphlet from South Wales where it was being circulated, with an alarmed appeal that he should reply to it. Glasier was dismayed, and thought the pamphlet 'villainous,' for it sounded as if Carpenter had justi-

fied sodomy. . . . He even wrote to Carpenter, asking if he would repudiate physical intercourse. It does not appear that Carpenter answered in the affirmative" (Tsuzuki, *Edward Carpenter*, 145).

63. Rowbotham and Weeks, *Socialism and the New Life*, 89–90.

64. Sedgwick, *Between Men*, 212.

65. Hukin to Carpenter, 26 March 1909, Carpenter Collection, MSS 362-99.

66. Carpenter to Hukin, 30 March 1909, Carpenter Collection, MSS 361-51.

67. Sime, *Edward Carpenter: His Ideas and Ideals*, 74.

68. It is interesting to note, however, the discrepancy between Rowbotham and Weeks's account of his removal from the parish council, apparently based on evidence in the Carpenter Collection, and Carpenter's own version, in *My Days and Dreams*, in which he writes: "At one time, as I think I have already mentioned, I was a member of the Parish Council, but the hopelessness of getting any result therefrom, combined with the waste of time connected with it, caused me after a few years to abandon the position" (291). Carpenter goes on to relate, in exhaustive detail, an episode involving his efforts to retain the local award book—"which records the enclosure, early last century, of the Common Lands of Holmesfield Parish" (291)—for the use of his parish. Although his efforts were ultimately successful, he writes, "Exhausted by the labours connected with the affair, and hopeless of ever getting any useful activity out of the P[arish] C[ouncil], I shortly afterwards retired from it" (293). It is extremely interesting that the two versions should diverge in this way and that what, for Rowbotham and Weeks, is attributed to the aftermath of the O'Brien affair is claimed by Carpenter as an act of his own volition (see Rowbotham and Weeks, *Socialism and the New Life*, 91).

69. Rowbotham and Weeks, *Socialism and the New Life*, 91.

70. An interesting view of Carpenter's influence on pacifism and conscientious objectors appears in a 1993 historical novel about the First World War. Sent to a psychiatric hospital following his public statement against the war, the poet (also a homosexual) Siegfried Sassoon is asked by his psychologist, Rivers, whether the ideas of Bertrand Russell were his first exposure to pacifism:

"No. Edward Carpenter before the war."
"You read him?"
"Read him. Wrote to him." He smiled slightly. "I even made the Great Pilgrimage to Chesterfield." [Barker, *Regeneration*, 53]

71. Hukin to Carpenter, cited in Tsuzuki, *Edward Carpenter*, 145.

72. Sedgwick, *Between Men*, 213.

73. Carpenter, "George Merrill: A True History & Study in Psychology," 5 March 1913, Carpenter Collection, MSS 363-17.

74. Thiele, "Coming-of-Age," 107.

75. Carpenter, "George Merrill."

76. Sedgwick, *Between Men*, 213.

77. This inequality is unfortunately reproduced by the most recent biography of E. M. Forster, which refers to Carpenter's "domestic and loving relationship with a working-class boy named George Merrill" (Beauman, *Morgan*, 208). The tendency to diminish Merrill's adulthood has, it appears, stood the test of time.

78. Carpenter, "George Merrill."

79. Ibid.

80. Rowbotham and Weeks, *Socialism and the New Life*, 90.

81. Later in *My Days and Dreams*, Carpenter curiously refers to himself as "a lone bachelor" (175), despite the continued references to Merrill's presence.

82. Tsuzuki comments that "we . . . hear very little about George Merrill from Carpenter, probably as little as we hear about a housewife from the husband, except perhaps that he helped his master to write a sketch of the life of the fowl they kept in the garden. Carpenter kept discreet silence about his relations with him" (*Edward Carpenter* 146).

83. Forster, *Maurice*, 250.

EPILOGUE

1. Beauman, *Morgan*, 208.

2. Dellamora, *Apocalyptic Overtures*, 97.

3. Ibid.

4. Beauman has suggested that Forster's mother took him abroad in the spring of 1895, when Morgan was sixteen, specifically to avoid the publicity surrounding the prosecution of Wilde. Unfortunately, the pair returned just in time for Wilde's conviction, and Beauman speculates that the resulting "atmosphere of sexual repression during Morgan's second summer at Tonbridge [school] must have been appalling" (*Morgan*, 69–70). Beauman's claim is based on the premise that Forster's father had secretly engaged in homosexual practices with a man named Ted Streatfield and that Forster's mother feared that Morgan would also be influenced toward homosexuality.

5. Forster, *Maurice*, 159. All subsequent references to this volume will be cited parenthetically in the text.

6. See Robert K. Martin, "Edward Carpenter."

7. Beauman, *Morgan*, 207; Stallybrass, "Introduction," 7.

8. Forster, *A Room with a View*, 60. All subsequent references to this volume will be cited parenthetically in the text.

9. Beauman, *Morgan*, 209.

10. Lago, *E. M. Forster*, 26.

11. Beauman, *Morgan*, 210.

12. Forster, cited in Heine, "Introduction," xxvi.

13. Dellamora, *Apocalyptic Overtures*, 87.

14. Cited in Beauman, *Morgan*, 245.

15. Heine, "Introduction," xviii–xix.

16. Meyers, "Vacant Heart," 181, 188.

17. Forster, *The Lucy Novels*, 108, 110, 111.

18. Meyers, "Vacant Heart," 184.

19. This is not to attribute the "panic" to Wilde himself but to the legal and cultural forces that combined to produce his downfall and to many of the subsequent reactions, both public and private, to that crisis.

20. Fletcher, "Forster's Self-Erasure," 83.

21. This contrasts markedly with the film version of the novel (directed by James Ivory, 1987), which adds scenes featuring the entrapment and conviction of Lord Risley for homosexual offenses in order to provide an "explanation" for Clive's sudden change to heterosexuality.

22. Stephen Wonham, in *The Longest Journey*, is perhaps the most ambivalent of Forster's "outlaws": he exists outside respectable society, even to his illegitimacy, and Forster's reaction to his character's coarseness and brutality is at once affectionate, excited, and disapproving.

23. Following the loss of West Hackshurst with his mother's death in 1946, Forster returned to King's College, Cambridge, as an honorary fellow. He resided at King's until his death in 1970.

24. Some of Forster's readers were vociferously skeptical about the plausibility of Forster's happy ending; Lytton Strachey, for example, "wrote me a delightful and disquieting letter and said that the relationship of the two [Maurice and Alec] rested upon curiosity and lust and would only last six weeks" (Forster, *Maurice*, 252). Forster himself wrote and then deleted an epilogue to the novel in which Maurice and Alec were discovered by Maurice's sister Kitty as woodcutters in the "greenwood," which offered their only refuge from society. This epilogue, which had the merit of providing a specific future for the couple, was rejected because it was too definite and limiting for Forster's vision of a "happier year" and also raised the aesthetic problems of realistically placing the action during the First World War.

25. Forster originally envisaged a tragic ending to the novel, with George being killed by a falling tree (itself ironic, given Forster's association of the woods with utopian escape and sexual freedom) following Lucy's Beebe-induced refusal to elope with him. He did, however, eventually write a postscript to *A Room with a View*—called "A View without a Room"—in which he imagines some of the difficulties encountered by George and Lucy following their marriage (Forster, *A Room with a View*, 231–33).

26. Forster, MS of "Locked Journal," 31 December 1913, in the Forster Archive, King's College, Cambridge.

WORKS CITED

Adams, James Eli. "Gentleman, Dandy, Priest: Manliness and Social
Authority in Pater's Aestheticism." *ELH* 59 (1992): 441–66.

"Apologia pro Vita Sua." *Times* (London), 16 June 1864, 12.

"'Apologia pro Vita Sua.' By John Henry Newman, D.D." *Christian
Remembrancer* 47 (1864): 162–93.

St. Augustine. *Confessions.* Translated by R. S. Pine-Coffin. Harmondsworth:
Penguin, 1961.

"Authority and Free Thought: Dr Newman's Apology." *Theological Review* 1
(1864): 306–34.

Bakhtin, M. M. *The Dialogic Imagination: Four Essays.* Edited by Michael
Holquist. Translated by Caryl Emerson and Michael Holquist. Austin:
University of Texas Press, 1981.

Barber, C. L. *Shakespeare's Festive Comedy: A Study of Dramatic Form and Its
Relation to Social Custom.* Princeton: Princeton University Press, 1959.

Barker, Pat. *Regeneration.* New York: Plume, 1993.

Beauman, Nicola. *Morgan: A Biography of E. M. Forster.* London: Hodder,
1993.

Beckson, Karl, ed. *Oscar Wilde: The Critical Heritage.* London: Methuen,
1974.

Blehl, V. F., and F. X. Connolly, eds. *Newman's "Apologia": A Classic
Reconsidered.* New York: Harcourt, 1964.

Brendon, Piers. *Hurrell Froude and the Oxford Movement.* London: Paul Elek,
1974.

Bristow, Joseph, ed. *Sexual Sameness: Textual Differences in Lesbian and Gay
Writing.* London: Routledge, 1992.

Brown, Horatio F. *John Addington Symonds: A Biography Compiled from His
Papers and Correspondence.* 2d ed. New York: Scribner's, 1903.

Brown, Tony, ed. *Edward Carpenter and Late Victorian Radicalism.* London:
Cass, 1990.

Bruss, Elizabeth W. "Eye for I: Making and Unmaking Autobiography in

Film." In *Autobiography: Essays Theoretical and Critical*, edited by James Olney, 296–320. Princeton: Princeton University Press, 1980.

Buckley, Jerome H. "Towards Early-Modern Autobiography: The Roles of Oscar Wilde, George Moore, Edmund Gosse, and Henry Adams." In *Modernism Reconsidered*, edited by Robert Kiely and John Hildebidle, 1–15. Harvard English Studies, 11. Cambridge: Harvard University Press, 1983.

Buckton, Oliver S. " 'The Reader Whom I Love': Homoerotic Secrets in *David Copperfield*." *ELH* 64 (1997): 189–222.

Butler, Judith. *Gender Trouble: Feminism and the Subversion of Identity*. New York: Routledge, 1990.

———. "Imitation and Gender Insubordination." In *Inside/Out: Lesbian Theories, Gay Theories*, edited by Diana Fuss, 13–31. New York: Routledge, 1991.

Carpenter, Edward. The Carpenter Collection: A Collection of Papers and Correspondence. Sheffield City Archives, Sheffield, England.

———. *Love's Coming-of-Age*. New York: Modern Library, 1911.

———. *My Days and Dreams: Being Autobiographical Notes*. London: Allen and Unwin, 1916.

———. "Note on *Towards Democracy*." In *Towards Democracy*, 511–19. London: George Allen, 1913.

———. *Sex*, edited by Noel Greig. Vol. 1 of *Selected Writings*. London: Gay Men's Press, 1984.

———. *Towards Democracy: Complete Edition in Four Parts*. 1883–1902. London: George Allen, 1913.

Chadwick, Owen. *The Spirit of the Oxford Movement: Tractarian Essays*. Cambridge: Cambridge University Press, 1990.

Chitty, Susan. *The Beast and the Monk: A Life of Charles Kingsley*. London: Hodder and Stoughton, 1975.

Cohen, Ed. *Talk on the Wilde Side: Toward a Genealogy of a Discourse on Male Sexualities*. New York: Routledge, 1993.

———. "Writing Gone Wilde: Homoerotic Desire in the Closet of Representation." *PMLA* 102 (1987): 801–13.

Colloms, Brenda. *Charles Kingsley: The Lion of Eversley*. London: Constable, 1975.

Craft, Christopher. "Alias Bunbury: Desire and Termination in *The Importance of Being Earnest*." *Representations* 31 (Summer 1990): 19–46.

Dellamora, Richard. *Apocalyptic Overtures: Sexual Politics and the Sense of an Ending*. New Brunswick: Rutgers University Press, 1994.

———. *Masculine Desire: The Sexual Politics of Victorian Aestheticism*. Chapel Hill: University of North Carolina Press, 1990.

———. "Textual Politics/Sexual Politics." *Modern Language Quarterly* 54, no. 1 (1993): 155–64.

De Man, Paul. "Autobiography as De-Facement." In *The Rhetoric of Romanticism*, 67–81. New York: Columbia University Press, 1985.

———. "Wordsworth and the Victorians." In *The Rhetoric of Romanticism*, 82–92. New York: Columbia University Press, 1985.

"Dr Newman, Mr Kingsley." *Westminster Review* 26 (1864): 137–52.

"Dr Newman's 'Apologia.'" *Fraser's Magazine* 70 (1864): 265–303.

"Dr Newman's Religious Autobiography." *Saturday Review*, 25 June 1864, 785.

Dollimore, Jonathan. "Different Desires: Subjectivity and Transgression in Wilde and Gide." *Genders* 2 (Summer 1988): 24–41.

———. *Sexual Dissidence: Augustine to Wilde, Freud to Foucault*. Oxford: Clarendon, 1991.

Douglas, Mary. *Purity and Danger: An Analysis of Concepts of Pollution and Taboo*. New York: Frederick Praeger, 1966.

Dowling, Linda. *Hellenism and Homosexuality in Victorian Oxford*. Ithaca: Cornell University Press, 1994.

———. *Language and Decadence in the Victorian Fin de Siècle*. Princeton: Princeton University Press, 1986.

Eakin, Paul John. *Fictions in Autobiography: Studies in the Art of Self-Invention*. Princeton: Princeton University Press, 1985.

Edelman, Lee. *Homographesis: Essays in Gay Literary and Cultural Theory*. New York: Routledge, 1994.

Egner, G. *Apologia pro Charles Kingsley*. London: Sheed and Ward, 1969.

Ellmann, Richard. *Oscar Wilde*. New York: Knopf, 1988.

Epstein, Julia, and Kristina Straub, eds. *Body Guards: The Cultural Politics of Gender Ambiguity*. New York: Routledge, 1991.

Faber, Geoffrey. *Oxford Apostles: A Character Study of the Oxford Movement*. New York: Scribner's, 1934.

Fletcher, John. "Forster's Self-Erasure: *Maurice* and the Scene of Masculine Love." In *Sexual Sameness*, edited by Joseph Bristow, 64–90. London: Routledge, 1992.

Forster, E. M. *Commonplace Book*. Stanford: Stanford University Press, 1987.

———. *The Longest Journey*. Harmondsworth: Penguin, 1988.

———. *The Lucy Novels: Early Sketches for "A Room with a View."* The Abinger Edition of E. M. Forster, Vol. 3a. Edited by Oliver Stallybrass. London: Edward Arnold, 1977.

———. *Maurice*. New York: Norton, 1987.

———. MSS of *Locked Journal* and *Notebook Journal*. Forster Archive, King's College, Cambridge.

———. *A Room with a View*. With an introduction by Oliver Stallybrass. Harmondsworth: Penguin, 1978.

Foucault, Michel. *An Introduction*. Vol. 1 of *The History of Sexuality*. Translated by Robert Hurley. New York: Random House, Vintage, 1980.

Gagnier, Regenia. "*De Profundis* as *Epistola: In Carcere et Vinculis*:

A Materialist Reading of Oscar Wilde's Autobiography." *Criticism* 26, no. 4 (Fall 1984): 335–54.

———. *Idylls of the Marketplace: Oscar Wilde and the Victorian Reading Public.* Stanford: Stanford University Press, 1987.

———. *Subjectivities: A History of Self-Representation in Britain, 1832–1920.* New York: Oxford University Press, 1991.

Gill, Stephen, ed. *William Wordsworth.* New York: Oxford University Press, 1984.

Gilley, Sheridan. *Newman and His Age.* London: Darton, Longman, and Todd, 1990.

Glavin, John. "Deadly Earnest and Earnest Revised: Oscar Wilde's Four-Act Play." *Nineteenth Century Studies* 1 (1987): 13–24.

Gosse, Edmund. *Father and Son: A Study of Two Temperaments.* New York: Norton, 1963.

Grosskurth, Phyllis. Foreword to *The Memoirs of John Addington Symonds*, 9–12. Chicago: University of Chicago Press, 1984.

———. "Where Was Rousseau?" In *Approaches to Victorian Autobiography*, edited by George P. Landow, 26–38. Athens: Ohio State University Press, 1979.

———. *The Woeful Victorian: A Biography of John Addington Symonds.* New York: Holt, Winston and Rinehart, 1965.

Halperin, David M. *"One Hundred Years of Homosexuality" and Other Essays on Greek Love.* New York: Routledge, 1990.

Harrold, Charles F. *John Henry Newman: An Expository and Critical Study of His Mind, Thought, and Art.* London: Longman's, 1945.

Heine, Elizabeth. Introduction to *The Longest Journey*, by E. M. Forster, vii–lxv. Harmondsworth: Penguin, 1989.

Helmling, Steven. *The Esoteric Comedies of Carlyle, Newman, and Yeats.* Cambridge: Cambridge University Press, 1988.

Henderson, Heather. *The Victorian Self: Autobiography and Biblical Narrative.* Ithaca: Cornell University Press, 1989.

Hilliard, David. "Unenglish and Unmanly: Anglo-Catholicism and Homosexuality." *Victorian Studies* 25 (1982): 181–210.

Holloway, John. *The Victorian Sage: Studies in Argument.* New York: Norton, 1965.

Honey, J. R. de S. *Tom Brown's Universe: The Development of the English Public School in the Nineteenth Century.* New York: Quadrangle–New York Times, 1977.

Houghton, Walter. *The Art of Newman's "Apologia."* New Haven: Yale University Press, 1945.

———. "The Issue between Kingsley and Newman." *Theology Today* 6 (April 1947): 81–101. Reprinted in John Henry Newman, *Apologia pro Vita Sua*, edited by David J. DeLaura, 390–409. New York: Norton, 1968.

Hughes, Thomas. *Tom Brown's Schooldays*. Harmondsworth: Penguin, 1971.

Hutton, R. H. "Dr Newman's Apology." *Spectator* 37 (1864): 654–56, 681–83.

Hyam, Ronald. *Empire and Sexuality: The British Experience*. Manchester: Manchester University Press, 1990.

Hyde, H. Montgomery. "The Riddle of *De Profundis*: Who Owns the Manuscript." *Antigonish Review* 54 (Summer 1983): 107–27.

———. *The Trials of Oscar Wilde*. New York: Dover, 1973.

Hynes, Samuel. *The Edwardian Turn of Mind*. Princeton: Princeton University Press, 1968.

Jay, Paul. *Being in the Text: Self-Representation from Wordsworth to Roland Barthes*. Ithaca: Cornell University Press, 1984.

"John Henry Newman." *American Quarterly Church Review* 17 (1865): 1–38.

Jost, Walter. *Rhetorical Thought in John Henry Newman*. Columbia: University of South Carolina Press, 1989.

Kaplan, Justin. *Walt Whitman: A Life*. New York: Simon and Schuster, 1980.

Ker, Ian. *John Henry Newman: A Biography*. Oxford: Clarendon, 1988.

Kingsley, Charles. "What, Then, Does Dr. Newman Mean?" (1864). Reprinted in John Henry Newman, *Apologia pro Vita Sua: Being a History of His Religious Opinions*, edited by Martin J. Svaglic, 356–84. Oxford: Clarendon, 1967.

———. "Why Should We Fear the Romish Priests?" *Fraser's Magazine* 37 (1848): 467–74.

Kingsley, Fanny, ed. *Charles Kingsley: His Letters and Memories of His Life*. 2 vols. London: Henry S. King, 1877.

"Kingsley and Newman: Romanism in England." *British Quarterly Review* 40 (1864): 102–26.

Koestenbaum, Wayne. *Double Talk: The Erotics of Male Literary Collaboration*. New York: Routledge, 1989.

———. "Wilde's Hard Labor and the Birth of Gay Reading." In *Engendering Men: The Question of Male Feminist Criticism*, edited by Joseph A. Boone and Michael Cadden, 176–89. New York: Routledge, 1990.

Lago, Mary. *E. M. Forster: A Literary Life*. London: Macmillan, 1995.

Lejeune, Philippe. *On Autobiography*. Translated by Katherine Leary. Minneapolis: University of Minnesota Press, 1989.

Loesberg, Jonathan. *Fictions of Consciousness: Mill, Newman, and the Reading of Victorian Prose*. New Brunswick: Rutgers University Press, 1986.

McGann, Jerome M. *The Textual Condition*. Princeton: Princeton University Press, 1991.

McIntosh, Mary. "The Homosexual Role." *Social Problems* 16 (Fall 1968): 182–92.

McLynn, Frank. *Robert Louis Stevenson: A Biography*. London: Pimlico, 1994.

Martin, Robert Bernard. *The Dust of Combat: A Life of Charles Kingsley*. London: Faber, 1959.

{ *Works Cited* }   255

Martin, Robert K. "Edward Carpenter and the Double Structure of *Maurice*." In *Literary Visions of Homosexuality*, edited by Stuart Kellogg, 35–46. New York: Haworth, 1985.

Meyers, Jeffrey. "Vacant Heart and Hand and Eye: The Homosexual Theme in *A Room with a View*." *English Literature in Transition* 13 (1970): 181–92.

Miller, Andrew H. *Novels behind Glass: Commodity Culture and Victorian Narrative*. Cambridge: Cambridge University Press, 1995.

"Mr Kingsley and Dr Newman." *London Quarterly Review* 23 (1864–65): 115–53.

"Mr. Kingsley and Dr. Newman: A Correspondence on the Question 'Whether Dr. Newman Teaches that Truth is No Virtue' " (1864). Reprinted in John Henry Newman, *Apologia pro Vita Sua: Being a History of His Religious Opinions*, edited by Martin J. Svaglic, 339–53. Oxford: Clarendon, 1967.

Morgan, Thais E., ed. *Victorian Sages and Cultural Discourse: Renegotiating Gender and Power*. New Brunswick: Rutgers University Press, 1990.

Mosse, George L. *Nationalism and Sexuality: Respectability and Abnormal Sexuality in Modern Europe*. New York: Howard Fertig, 1985.

Newman, John Henry. *Apologia pro Vita Sua*. Edited by David J. DeLaura. New York: Norton, 1968.

———. *Apologia pro Vita Sua: Being a History of His Religious Opinions*. Edited by Martin J. Svaglic. Oxford: Clarendon, 1967.

———. *Autobiographical Writings*. Edited by Henry Tristram. New York: Sheed and Ward, 1957.

———. *An Essay on the Development of Christian Doctrine*. London, 1845.

———. *The Letters and Diaries of John Henry Newman*. Edited by Charles Stephen Dessain et al. Vol. 21. London: Nelson, 1971.

———. *Loss and Gain: The Story of a Convert*. The World's Classics. Oxford: Oxford University Press, 1986.

Olney, James. "Autobiography and the Cultural Moment: A Thematic, Historical, and Bibliographical Introduction." In *Autobiography: Essays Theoretical and Critical*, edited by Olney, 3–27. Princeton: Princeton University Press, 1980.

Pearson, Hesketh. *The Life of Oscar Wilde*. 1946. Reprint, London: Macdonald and Jane's, 1975.

Peterson, Linda H. *Victorian Autobiography: The Tradition of Self-Interpretation*. New Haven: Yale University Press, 1986.

Pickering, W. S. F. *Anglo-Catholicism: A Study in Religious Ambiguity*. London: Routledge, 1989.

Plummer, Kenneth. *Sexual Stigma: An Interactionist Account*. London: Routledge and Kegan Paul, 1975.

———, ed. *The Making of the Modern Homosexual*. Totowa, N.J.: Barnes and Noble, 1981.

Pope-Hennessy, Una. *Canon Charles Kingsley: A Biography*. London: Chatto and Windus, 1948.

Raby, Peter. "The Making of *The Importance of Being Earnest*: An Unpublished Letter from Oscar Wilde." *Times Literary Supplement*, 20 December 1991, 13.

———. *Oscar Wilde*. Cambridge: Cambridge University Press, 1988.

Reade, Brian, ed. *Sexual Heretics: Male Homosexuality in English Literature from 1850 to 1900*. New York: Coward-McCann, 1971.

"Rev. Charles Kingsley and Dr Newman." *Blackwood's Magazine* 96 (1864): 292–309.

Rowbotham, Sheila, and Jeffrey Weeks. *Socialism and the New Life: The Personal and Sexual Politics of Edward Carpenter and Havelock Ellis*. London: Pluto, 1977.

Sanders, Valerie. *The Private Lives of Victorian Women*. New York: St. Martin's, 1989.

Sedgwick, Eve Kosofsky. *Between Men: English Literature and Male Homosocial Desire*. New York: Columbia University Press, 1985.

———. *Epistemology of the Closet*. Berkeley: University of California Press, 1990.

Seymour-Smith, Martin. *Hardy*. New York: St. Martin's, 1994.

Shaw, Marion. "'To Tell the Truth of Sex': Confession and Abjection in Late Victorian Writing." In *Rewriting the Victorians: Theory, History, and the Politics of Gender*, edited by Linda M. Shires, 87–100. New York: Routledge, 1992.

Sime, A. H. Moncur. *Edward Carpenter: His Ideas and Ideals*. London: Kegan Paul, 1916.

Sinfield, Alan. *The Wilde Century: Effeminacy, Oscar Wilde, and the Queer Moment*. New York: Columbia University Press, 1994.

Smith, F. B. "Labouchère's Amendment to the Criminal Law Amendment Bill." *Historical Studies* 17 (1976): 165–73.

Smith, Sidonie. *A Poetics of Women's Autobiography: Marginality and the Fictions of Self-Representation*. Bloomington: Indiana University Press, 1987.

Stallybrass, Oliver. Introduction to *A Room with a View*, by E. M. Forster, 7–19. Harmondsworth: Penguin, 1978.

Stevenson, Robert Louis. *"The Strange Case of Dr Jekyll and Mr Hyde" and Other Stories*. Harmondsworth: Penguin, 1979.

Sussman, Herbert. *Victorian Masculinities*. Cambridge: Cambridge University Press, 1995.

Svaglic, Martin J. "Editor's Introduction." In *Apologia pro Vita Sua: Being a History of His Religious Opinions*, by John Henry Newman, vii–lx. Oxford: Clarendon, 1967.

Swindells, Julia. *Victorian Writing and Working Women: The Other Side of Silence*. Cambridge, England: Polity, 1985.

{ *Works Cited* }   257

Symonds, John Addington. *Letters of John Addington Symonds.* 3 vols. Edited
by Herbert M. Schueller and Robert L. Peters. Detroit: Wayne State
University Press, 1967–69.

———. *The Memoirs of John Addington Symonds.* Edited by Phyllis
Grosskurth. Chicago: University of Chicago Press, 1984.

———. *A Problem in Greek Ethics.* London: privately printed, 1883.

———. *A Problem in Modern Ethics.* London: privately printed, 1891.

———. *Studies of the Greek Poets.* 3d ed. London: A. C. Black, 1920.

Symonds, John Addington, and Havelock Ellis. *Sexual Inversion.* London,
1897.

Tambling, Jeremy. *Confession: Sexuality, Sin, the Subject.* Manchester:
Manchester University Press, 1990.

Thiele, Beverly. "Coming-of-Age: Edward Carpenter on Sex and
Reproduction." In *Edward Carpenter and Late Victorian Radicalism,*
edited by Tony Brown, 100–125. London: Cass, 1990.

Thompson, E. P. *William Morris, Romantic to Revolutionary.* London:
Lawrence and Wishart, 1955.

Trevor, Meriol. *Newman: Light in Winter.* London: Macmillan, 1962.

Tsuzuki, Chuschuchi. *Edward Carpenter, 1844–1929: Prophet of Human
Fellowship.* Cambridge: Cambridge University Press, 1980.

Tyrwhitt, R. St. John. "The Greek Spirit in Modern Literature."
Contemporary Review 29 (1877): 554–65.

Vance, Norman. *Sinews of the Spirit: The Ideal of Christian Manliness in
Victorian Literature and Religious Thought.* Cambridge: Cambridge
University Press, 1985.

Vincent, David. *Bread, Knowledge, and Freedom: A Study of Nineteenth-
Century Working Class Autobiography.* London: Methuen,
1982.

Virgil. *The Aeneid.* Translated by Robert Fitzgerald. New York: Vintage, 1983.

Ward, Wilfrid. *The Life of John Henry Cardinal Newman.* 2 vols. New York:
Longman's, 1912.

Weeks, Jeffrey. *Coming Out: Homosexual Politics in Britain from the
Nineteenth Century to the Present.* Rev. ed. London: Quartet, 1990.

"Whately, Newman, and 'Phenakism.' " *Macmillan's Magazine* 10 (1864): 291.

White, Allon. *The Uses of Obscurity: The Fiction of Early Modernism.*
London: Routledge and Kegan Paul, 1981.

Wilde, Oscar. *The Artist as Critic: Critical Writings of Oscar Wilde.* Edited by
Richard Ellmann. Chicago: University of Chicago Press, 1969.

———. *The Importance of Being Earnest: A Trivial Comedy for Serious People
in Four Acts as Originally Written by Oscar Wilde.* Edited by Sarah
Dickson. 2 vols. New York: New York Public Library, 1956.

———. *"The Importance of Being Earnest" and Other Plays.*
Harmondsworth: Penguin, 1986.

————. *The Letters of Oscar Wilde.* Edited by Rupert Hart-Davis. New York: Harcourt, Brace and World, 1962.

————. *The Picture of Dorian Gray.* Edited by Peter Ackroyd. Harmondsworth: Penguin, 1985.

Wordsworth, William. *The Prelude: A Parallel Text.* Edited by J. C. Maxwell. Harmondsworth: Penguin, 1971.

INDEX

135, 198; Carpenter reveals in texts, 161, 178, 189–90; ideal of in Whitman, 184; and radical politics, 187; idealized view of, 194, 216; and cross-class relations, 202; Forster's conflict over, 206, 208, 209, 210–11, 212, 217; disguised as heterosexuality, 211, 217; three levels of, 222 (n. 8); revealed in Froude's *Remains*, 225 (n. 37). *See also* Perversion

Sanders, Valerie, 83

Saturday Review, 202

Scandal: threat of, 88, 162

Secrecy, 1, 2, 3, 4, 5, 6, 8, 9, 10, 16; textual strategies of, 12, 19, 64, 68, 83–91, 112–13; Wilde's use of in *Picture of Dorian Gray*, 18, 112; and Newman's character, 26, 46; and disclosure, dynamic of, 29, 178, 211, 218; reproduction of in Symonds's *Memoirs*, 98–100; and same-sex desire, 105–6, 134, 173, 179; in *Importance of Being Earnest*, 123, 127; Carpenter's sexual reserve, 161, 164, 166, 199; textual evasion/reticence as, 171, 190, 192, 203, 214; and writings of Forster, 207, 218; and Catholicism, 227 (n. 72). *See also* Mask

Sedgwick, Eve Kosofsky, 14, 15, 26, 29, 41–42, 163, 195, 201, 221 (n. 31)

Self, individual, 2, 10, 19, 21; Victorian view of, 29; constructed as secret, 83, 117, 146, 233 (n. 57); division of, 83–85, 122, 144; as textual construct, 151; representation of in *My Days and Dreams*, 163, 176, 185, 192

Sex-Love (Carpenter), 164

Sexual Inversion (Symonds and Ellis), 61–62, 65–71, 171, 174, 203, 231 (n. 36)

Sexuality. *See* Gender and sexuality

Sexual reconstruction: in Forster, 206–18

Shaw, George Bernard, 138, 190, 192

Shaw, Marion, 146

Shorting, C., 91–95

Sidgwick, Henry, 97, 99–100

Sime, A. H. Moncur, 197

Sinfield, Alan, 7, 17, 37, 42–43

Smith, Sidonie, 12

Smithers, Leonard, 130

Socialism, 6, 26; Carpenter's involvement in, 164, 168, 174, 186–99; Symonds's view of, 174–75; Sheffield Socialists, milieu of, 182, 186, 188–89, 194, 200; Carpenter as prophet of, 192; and same-sex desire, 196, 199

Socialism and Infamy (O'Brien), 194–95

Sodomite: as species, 114, 140; Wilde accused of being, 43, 119–20, 121. *See also* Perversion; Same-sex desire

"Sonnet Written in London, 1802" (Wordsworth), 142

Speaking out: impulse of, 103, 106; Carpenter's desire for, 177

Spectator, 23, 27, 54, 202

Specular structure: in autobiography, 64; in *De Profundis*, 149–60

Stallybrass, Oliver, 208

Stead, William T., 139

Stevenson, Robert Louis, 74–76, 78, 99

Strachey, Lytton, 250 (n. 24)

Strange Case of Dr. Jekyll and Mr. Hyde (Stevenson), 74–76, 99

Straub, Kristina, 40

Street, G. S., 139

Studies of the Greek Poets (Symonds), 62, 63–64, 67, 81, 95

Sussman, Herbert, 15–16